SHAKE HANDS WITH THE DEVIL

All these hitmen, serial killers, and international narco-traffickers I was locked up with were doing a minute, sitting on fortunes salted away in banks, stocks and bonds, then walking out to begin new lives. People who flew airplane loads of drugs into this country and kill-crazy nuts were walking outside, scot-free.

They were the baddest of the bad and they were rewarded for it.

CLUB FED

A TRUE STORY OF LIFE, LIES AND CRIME IN THE FEDERAL WITNESS PROTECTION PROGRAM

GEORGE E. TAYLOR, JR.
with CLIFFORD L. LINEDECKER

AVON BOOKS ◆ NEW YORK

CLUB FED is a memoir based on the recollections of George E. Taylor, Jr. The events, scenes, and dialogue recounted are true to the best of the co-author's and publisher's knowledge.

AVON BOOKS, INC.
1350 Avenue of the Americas
New York, New York 10019

Copyright © 1998 by George E. Taylor, Jr. and Merlin Enterprises, Inc.
Published by arrangement with the authors
Visit our website at **http://www.AvonBooks.com**
Library of Congress Catalog Card Number: 98-92772
ISBN: 0-380-79569-8

First Avon Books Printing: October 1998

AVON TRADEMARK REG. U.S. PAT. OFF. AND IN OTHER COUNTRIES, MARCA REGISTRADA, HECHO EN U.S.A.

Printed in the U.S.A.

WCD   10 9 8 7 6 5 4 3 2 1

To my father,
George Emmett Taylor, Sr.

Acknowledgments

Many people have played a role in the writing and production of this book and are owed thanks from myself and my coauthor. Among the people I wish to thank are my mother, Jane Taylor, and my siblings, Theresa, Karen, and Bob. A deep debt of appreciation is also due to my agent, Adele Leone of the Adele Leone Agency, Inc.; and to my editor, Stephen S. Power at Avon Books for their support and faith in this project. Thanks as well go to Allen Sonnenschien of *Penthouse* magazine for his friendship and timely encouragement. A big thank you is also owed to Denise, whose unswerving loyalty and fortitude have already been severely tested and who continues to provide me with comfort and support through the dark times.

A special note of appreciation is due to the men in the units who shared their personal court documents and confidences with me, sometimes putting themselves at risk in order to do so.

And out of good still to find means of evil.

John Milton, *Paradise Lost*

Contents

All the people in this book are real and there are no composite characters. The events and conversations re-created here are reported as accurately as it is possible to do so.

GEORGE E. TAYLOR, JR.

This is [George's] story, and the story of a seriously flawed government program established with lofty ambitions that has been permitted to veer off course and is dangerously out of control.

CLIFFORD L. LINEDECKER

Introduction

IF IT'S TRUE that the road to Hell is paved with good intentions, then the architects of the little known and incredibly expensive government boondoggle called the federal Witness Security (Protection) Program (WITSEC) must be wiping their brows and wilting from the heat.

The program, which began developing and first moved into the public eye in 1964 when turncoat mobster Joe Valachi confirmed the existence of the criminal syndicate known as La Cosa Nostra, is a mess. The lofty goals established at that time have not only fallen far short of expectations, but they have been so twisted that some of the most bloodthirsty and ruthless criminals of our time have been rewarded with hundreds of millions of dollars in payoffs, radically shortened prison sentences, and new identities and lives.

Mafia hit men, serial killers, and international drug kingpins have been quietly resettled by federal authorities next door to unsuspecting neighbors who previously were never closer to big-time crime bosses and small-time thugs than while watching television reruns of "The Untouchables."

1

The program, supported with massive amounts of tax-payer funding, has nevertheless been operated and administered as one of the most secret and private activities of the federal government. Despite built-in provisions to provide for budgetary oversight by Congress, the program has been permitted to grow to many times it's original size and to expand its purview with almost no supervision from government.

In 1972, almost a decade after the first seeds of the program began to germinate, WITSEC was caring for a handful of carefully selected witnesses with a budget of just $2 million. By 1996, instead of the thirty to forty new witnesses originally expected to have been ushered into the program, almost 6,000 men, women, and children were included on the WITSEC roster. The budget had ballooned to a whopping $53 million and was continuing to rapidly expand.

Secrets are as difficult to pry out of the WITSEC files as they are from administrators of the CIA, perhaps even more so—for the CIA operates under closer supervision and budgetary oversight from Congress. It's true that secrecy is a necessity in order to protect the people brought into WITSEC, but the need for privacy doesn't mean there should be no public accounting whatsoever. Yet throughout the roughly three decades the program has been in force, there have been only three hearings in Washington to monitor and review its operation: two in the early 1980s—one by the U.S. Senate's Permanent Subcommittee on Investigation headed by Senator Sam Nunn of Georgia, the other by a subcommittee of the House Judiciary Committee; and fourteen years later in June 1996 by the full U.S. Senate Judiciary Committee, chaired by Senator Orrin G. Hatch of Utah.

Too often secrecy has been used to shield vicious killers who have been released from prison with new identities, only to run amok and resume their old ways. The program has grown too large, too fast, and has embraced and rewarded numerous criminals who should never have been considered for federal-witness protection. Program administrators have wasted money, wasted human resources, and wasted lives.

One of WITSEC's sharpest detractors is an individual who on the surface might appear to be an unlikely critic. But George Emmett Taylor, Jr., is eminently qualified to discuss the weaknesses, as well as some of the strengths, of the program. Taylor is a retired smash-and-grab thief, stickup man, drug runner, and professional double-crosser and betrayer of friends. His young adult years were lived in a brutal, treacherous world as a professional criminal and convict—and as a police snitch.

He knows about the deep flaws in the program because he has been there. Recruited into the program as a confidential informant (CI) and government witness in the early 1980s, Taylor has watched from up front as conniving supercriminals manipulated WITSEC and law-enforcement professionals into twisting regulations and abusing some of the very laws they are sworn to uphold.

From the moment he moved into protected-witness status in one of the specially constructed units inside several federal prisons across the country, Taylor began making it plain that he was disenchanted with the program. Like many other witnesses, Taylor felt he was betrayed with false promises, and he became determined to make the government keep its collective word to him. He became a whistle-blower and has already paid dearly for refusing to march in lockstep.

George Taylor is a born renegade. He spent most of his adult life living on the edge, inside and out of prison. While we were collaborating on this book, it became common for me to accept late-night phone calls from George with breathless reports of being run off the highway by drivers of mystery cars with murder on their mind; of being hit by a car while crossing a street; or being chased from his heavily fortified redoubt in the Ozark foothills by deadly enemies blasting away with machine guns. At other times, when it was critical that we remain in close touch, he simply vanished for a week or a month at a time, providing no prior notice and no address or phone number where he could be contacted.

The calls continued after initial work on the manuscript was completed and it began moving through the editing process. One morning George rang and advised me that he wouldn't have a telephone number and permanent address for a while. He and his lady were on the run again, following his ambush by a heavily armed platoon of bikers who shot up his pickup truck and killed his guard dogs while he was driving home from work near Branson, Missouri, he told me. George was shot in the right leg but dug the bullet out himself. At the request of his federal witness-security parole coordinator in Jefferson City, he mailed her the slug.

George has more than lived up to his billing since my agent, Adele Leone, telephoned me one morning and told me she knew someone that I absolutely had to meet. She said that if we met even once, she was certain that I would write a book about him. Adele's instincts were dead right. When George and I met in the suburban Chicago law offices of a lawyer acquaintance, he was everything I had been led to expect—and more. Within minutes of meeting him I was listening to riveting stories about his former criminal career and his unique experiences as a protected federal witness. Importantly, George had documentation and other sources to back up the stories.

The first close personal friend he introduced me to was a former stickup artist whom Chicago police have identified as a ruthless hit man responsible for several Mob killings. Most of George's old friends are criminals and ex-cons. His new friends are prosecutors, lawyers, a few cops, and journalists.

Clifford L. Linedecker

Prologue

I'M A RAT, but I'm not a killer.

I did some bad things, in fact I spent much of my adult life robbing people, smuggling and dealing dope, using women, and betraying my friends. I deserved to do some time in the joint, but I didn't deserve the fifteen years I spent locked up with Mafia wiseguys, cocaine cowboys, outlaw bikers, and psychopathic killers. In my whole life, I never even pistol-whipped anybody. Bad, yeah, but nothing violent.

So what happens to me? After putting my neck in a noose to help the feds clean up some of the pond scum infesting this society, my reward is doing twice as much time as I probably would have done if I had refused to rat on my friends and had taken my chances with a judge or jury—and worse, which we'll come to later.

While I was locked up in the special Witness Protection Unit at a series of federal penitentiaries, watching over my shoulder every day to make sure that some psycho didn't whack me with a prison shiv over a perceived insult or just because he hadn't killed anybody for a while, some of the nastiest characters in the program walked out of the joint with more money than I ever dreamed of.

It was exactly 7:30 A.M., April 19, 1995, when everybody on Mesa Unit at the Phoenix Federal Correctional Institute watched Salvatore "Sammy the Bull" Gravano mince his way out of the joint and walk to freedom. We'd been unlocked since 5:30. That was normal at Mesa, the prison-within-a-prison set aside for federal witness-protection inmates at the Phoenix FCI.

The usual early breakfast was set up in the common area by six o'clock. The food was okay, but me and my friends hardly ever ate it unless something really special was on the menu. Most mornings we just wandered over to the salad bar and loaded up on raw vegetables, then took them back to our rooms where we stuck them into our personal blenders to make fresh juice.

The protective unit at Mesa was set up with an oval of two-man cells on the ground floor and the top range, a row of one-man cells. Midway between the two floors of cells, about chest-high if you were standing on the first tier, there was a mezzanine floor that was used as a combination food service and common area. That's where the food line was. It was also outfitted with vending machines from which we could buy soda pop, milk, and breakfast food—anything made by Kelloggs—shoot pool, play chess and checkers, or just hang around scheming and swapping war stories.

An enclosure surrounded by bullet-proof glass sat at the edge of the common area where hacks could see into the tiers and outside into a portion of the yard where the weight pile was located. Hacks inside another glassed-in rotunda closer to the main entrance to the unit could see into the rest of the yard. Both the inside of the unit and the yard were constantly scanned with television cameras.

The yard was an octagon-shaped area set aside for

inmates to exercise in or to just hang around in the fresh air. It was outfitted with weight-lifting equipment, racquetball and basketball courts. A small asphalt-covered track for runners snaked around a grassy area in front of the basketball court. Thirteen trips around the track equal one mile. Inmate golfers used the grassy area to practice their chip shots, and other guys got up volleyball games.

The weight-lifting equipment was set up nice. It is in lots of prisons, not just in witness units. The American correctional system: the biggest health club in the country. Some citizens are beginning to complain that bulking up convicted criminals so they're stronger and tougher when they get on the outside doesn't make sense. Rodney King, for example, had been inside. He was bulked up from lifting prison weights when he tangled with the Los Angeles cops—and they claimed they were afraid of him. Many corrections professionals, however, say weight lifting makes sense. It helps control the inmates because it's a privilege that can be taken away for bad behavior.

Surprise! I agree with the professionals. Pumping iron doesn't make better bank robbers any more than jogging teaches purse snatchers to run faster. The public flap over weight-lifting equipment wasn't something that we concerned ourselves with. The equipment was there, and we used it.

Most of us who wanted to work out began our personal exercise programs in the dark, an hour or a half hour before daylight. The FCI was in the middle of the desert, and anything that needed to be done outside had to be taken care of before the sun began baking everything. It was that or wait until sundown when the temperatures dropped again. In the summer during the heat of the day, it was common for the temperature to reach

120 degrees, and nobody ventured outside without a damned good reason.

On the Wednesday morning Sammy left the unit for the last time, a SWAT team put together with guys we'd never seen before stormed inside. They were dressed totally in black with stocking masks over their faces. We never did learn exactly who they were, but they weren't any of the hacks from the unit or from the main prison down the road. They were some elite team working for the Justice Department, and they were dressed like Japanese ninjas—except they weren't armed with daggers and throwing stars. They carried automatic weapons in their hands, and sidearms were strapped to their legs with Velcro strips. They could have stepped out of some schlock movie, and they provided a perfect supporting cast for Sammy the Bull.

You gotta see Sammy and hear him talk to believe him. I never seen a troll, but if I ever see one I'm sure he's gonna look a lot like Sammy, except he'll be better-looking and a lot smarter. Sammy was about five foot four, or five four and a half, just about big enough to work as a freak in a sideshow somewhere if he didn't already have a job as a superstar snitch.

Sammy became a marquee idol by ratting on his boss, the so-called "Teflon Don" John Gotti, and helped to put him and at least thirty-six other Mafia big-shots from New York to Sicily in prison for life. Gotti was head of the Gambinos, the most powerful La Cosa Nostra family in New York and in the country. He earned his title as the Teflon Don because all the tinhorn cops and pin-striped prosecutors in New York and in Washington, D.C., couldn't take him down. State prosecutors couldn't do it and federal prosecutors couldn't do it, despite spending thousands of man-hours on undercover operations, millions of dollars in investigation and court costs, and two high-profile trials.

When Gotti walked outside the federal courthouse in Manhattan with his high-priced legal team after beating a list of charges that was as long as your arm, he was smirking for the cameras. All the king's horses and all the king's men couldn't convict the snappy-dressing Mafia chief of anything. Not of involvment in an ongoing criminal enterprise. Not even loitering.

Eastern District U.S. Attorney Andrew Maloney and several of his top lieutenants, including Laura Ward, were obsessed with nailing the showoff Mafia chief. Maloney publicly vowed to send Gotti to prison for life. But everything they tried, including RICO (the Racketeer-Influenced and Corrupt Organization Act) indictments, wiretaps, nothing did any good until 1992. That was when the Gambino-crime-family underboss, Sammy Gravano, flipped. Sammy's testimony nailed him. Gotti wasn't helped by the fact that the feds managed to get his top lawyer scratched off his defense team through some slick maneuvering, using tapes recorded after tapping the Don's phones in the Ravenite Social Club and an upstairs apartment in Manhattan's Little Italy.

Sammy's testimony against his old friend and boss also made him a superstar snitch. He doesn't look like a superstar anything. He's short and so bulked up that he looked like a fat duck when he waddled away, surrounded by his cadre of government bodyguards on the Wednesday morning he left Mesa Unit. He was wearing a bullet-proof vest that hung almost to his knees and made him look even more like an ape than he normally did. Looking at him, you expected his knuckles to drag on the floor.

Sammy couldn't have had any idea of how moronic he looked. Safely inside the protective circle of leather and guns, he was all smiles. When I first met him, his hair was thick and black, but when he left the unit, it was thinning and receding from his forehead. He was also screwing around with an auburn dye, getting ready for his release and his new identity. The hair dye was Just For Men. Sammy knew a bit about that kind of thing. When he was a young guy just out of the army, he took a course back home in New York with a bunch of girls learning the barbering and beautician business. The hair dye was another of his perks. Nobody else in the unit was permitted to have anything like that.

Sammy was used to sleeping until ten or eleven o'clock in the morning, when another inmate who served as his gopher woke him up with coffee in bed and took his breakfast order. But his release date was a special occasion and he got up early. He was roused out of his bunk by the hacks at four A.M., and led downstairs, where he took a shower, had some coffee, then got dressed. He had a busy day ahead of him.

By the time the other inmates got a look at him, he was duded up in a perfectly tailored $3,000-sharkskin suit, with a color-coordinated shirt, silk tie, and spitshined shoes made of the finest Italian leather. The escorts carried his matching powder-blue luggage set—five or six suitcases all designed to fit each inside the other when they weren't in use. Sammy liked nice things, and since becoming a federal witness he was used to traveling first class.

While his escort prepared to move him outside, he stopped at the door in front of the unit manager's office that separated him from the eighty or ninety men who were temporarily restricted to the common area next to food service on lockdown. He stuck his face up to the window and said goodbye to his cronies. He had on a big shit-eating grin, like that happy face people stick on envelopes and stuff. One of the storm troopers stood about a foot behind him, glaring through the window like he was daring anyone to make a suspicious move.

The SWAT team was there for security—because Sammy couldn't keep his big mouth closed. A few days before the early morning show of force, he strutted up to the line of cons waiting outside the commissary window to buy personal items—things like tins of smoked oysters, peanuts, cigarettes, and toothpaste. He was feeling good, and his hips were swishing under his little tight shorts like he was some New York model mincing down a runway to show off the new fall collection. It was the day after his sentencing, and as usual his mouth was flapping. He was bragging about the sweetheart deal he just cut with Janet Reno's U.S. Justice Department.

Sammy moved into a place near the head of the line that was held for him by a snitch and contract killer from New York. The button man was a big, tough, ugly Irishman—and I'd think twice about fighting somebody like that. He was Sammy's bodyguard; a member of his prison gang.

While Sammy eased into line and his crony moved out, the little guy made sure that anybody who might not already know was loudly informed that he just got back to Mesa Unit the day before from Washington. The former Mafia enforcer and underboss who confessed to sharing responsibility for nineteen bodies,[1] but boasted of killing more, got the cushiest imaginable payoff.

Sammy developed some street smarts while he was working his way up in the Gambino-Castellano-Gotti Mafia family, but otherwise he was stupid. He didn't seem to know how much he was pissing off everybody else in the unit with his constant boasting. Most of the guys in line were ruthless killers, and some of them were already doing "all day," meaning life without parole.

[1]In prison, killings weren't described as murders or hits. They were "bodies," as in, "I got nineteen bodies out there," or "they got me for a couple of bodies."

In the eyes of the feds, Sammy might be an exalted figure who was "king of the snitches," but to most of the other cons waiting in line, he was a pain in the ass who was rapidly wearing away their patience.

Sergey Walton, renegade biker, and I were in line, squatting down with our backs against the wall, listening to his shit. But not for long. Sergey motioned at Sammy like he was backhanding or bitch-slapping someone and gave him a hard look. I snarled and muttered, "What a piece of shit."

Being called a piece of shit was about the worst thing that could be said about somebody in that setting. Everybody in the protected unit was a "mouth," and was used to being called a "snitch," a "rat" or a "turncoat." But that's exactly what Sammy is. He's a guy with no conscience, a piece of shit who bragged all the time in the units about how many people he whacked. Standing in line, he told us about testifying one time when a defense lawyer was working him over on the witness stand. Sammy had admitted to nineteen bodies, but the lawyer said he was able to place him in another four or five killings.

"How the fuck did he expect me to remember everybody I killed?" Sammy asked, making sure he was talking loud enough for everybody in line to hear. "You try to remember if you killed nineteen people, and when you did it, or if it was nineteen or twenty-three. Who gives a fuck? After nineteen, four more, that's nothing.

"I shoulda killed another motherfucker, and the judge woulda give me time served instead of another forty-two months," he boasted. Then he looked around, waiting for approving smiles. The only smile he got was from his hit-man shadow.

He finally realized that his big talk was pissing everybody off, and the nasty mood in the commissary line could quickly become dangerous. Lots of guys, including Sergey, couldn't stand the sight of him. Sergey was born during the early days of World War II but he was in great shape and was built like an engine block. He was a vegetarian who worked out at least six hours every day while molding a thirty-inch waist with a fifty-four-inch chest, and he had arms like a pro wrestler. He was tattooed down, and had a number 5 on his ribcage just below his right armpit. That stood for the number of federal agents he whacked. At least that was the story, and nobody was stupid enough to try to facedown Sergey and play the role of fact checker. He was one bad dude to cross, and nobody messed with him.

Once Sergey bitch-slapped Sammy. None of the little mob turncoat's bodyguards had been around, and he curled up like a baby. Tears streamed down his cheeks. Sergey turned away disgusted and stalked off. Sammy's sniveling was typical of the Italian cons. They were tough guys on the street if they had a trigger to squeeze. Inside the joint, where they had to fight their battles without a gun, it was a different story. They got real meek. Or they paid somebody to take care of them.

So when Sammy cut into the line and Sergey showed him the back of his hand, the obnoxious little man got the message. The pompous dwarf sensed the mood in the line and quit blabbering about the millions of dollars in federal bounties he collected for ratting, and how government auditors and financial brains handled his investment portfolio for him while he was inside. He moved to the back of the queue, but he couldn't resist one last remark about some of the details surrounding the soft deal he cut for himself. Originally he was sentenced to twenty years, but after Laura Ward went before the judge to talk for him, he was given a Rule 35—which is jailhouse lingo for a time cut. The judge sliced off a big chunk, trimming the sentence all the way to forty-two months. That came out to roughly three months for each body, about the same sentence a shop-lifter could get.

"If you guys had the same U.S. attorneys that I have, you'd be getting the same deals," he spouted off.

Sammy boasted that he was gonna walk in a few weeks, on April 19. He even gave the time of day. So everybody knew. Sammy had committed a major security breach, but he was too blown up with how important he was and too much of a moron to realize just how serious a mistake he was making. He said he was going to join his old lady, Deborah, and his kids on the outside in a new location with a new name and new business opportunities.

Everybody was upset over his sentence reduction. It was just the latest deal in a long line of special deals he received, and that afternoon the guys were all on the telephones calling their families or bitching to their lawyers. Everybody wanted a deal for themselves, but they weren't Sammy the Bull. They didn't drive the nails into John Gotti's coffin.

The Wednesday morning Sammy duckwalked out of Mesa Unit, an Armored Personnel Carrier was pulled up at the rear of the building, and his escort loaded him inside with his gear. A couple of the ninjas stood a few feet from the APC with their automatic weapons cocked and at-the-ready, watching for any trouble. A small fleet of official cars with spotlights and the emblem of the U.S. Marshals Service on the doors, were parked all over the place. Government helicopters rattled overhead. Nobody was taking any chances with the superstar snitch. A few minutes later, the armored vehicle clattered out of sight in a cloud of dust heading for a little desert airstrip a couple of miles away.

Pomp and circumstance. No wonder Sammy was swelled up with his own importance. He was the most despised man on the unit, and the feds treated him like a king—or a Central American dictator.

Once Sammy was safely away from the unit, the inmates were allowed outside again. We went into the yard to watch the rest of the show. Everybody who could find room, including me, climbed onto the picnic tables so we could watch over the ten-foot-high wall while Janet Reno's personal Justice Department Lear jet roared into the clear southeastern sky with Sammy inside. He had a period of debriefing to go through. We learned later the feds flew him to New Zealand for that. Sammy got homesick and placed a long-distance call from Auckland, or someplace there, to his friends in the unit. He didn't like New Zealand, and he was doing his usual whining, but he knew it was something he had to put up with. When the debriefing was completed, he would be all ready to begin a sparkling new life of opportunity and anonymity right back home here in America.

Watching as the jet disappeared in the distance, we bet among ourselves about how long it would be before the onetime Mafia executioner would step out of line and kill again. Most of us figured that someday one of his new neighbors, an unsuspecting Ozzie or Harriet, is going to march over to Sammy's house and complain about the kids' stereo or a noisy party. Next thing you know, Ozzie will be found floating in a river somewhere without his head, arms, or legs.

That sort of thing has happened before. It's your government and tax dollars working for you.

1

All in the Family

WHEN I TURNED to crime, I was merely moving into the family business. I was a third-generation crook. Crime and the rackets were an old Taylor and Van Boven tradition.

My grandfather, Harry Taylor, was shot to death with a tommy gun in Chicago during the early 1940s over some kind of run-in with other racket guys. Police counted more than 300 bullet holes in his car. That kind of ambush wasn't unusual in Chicago in those days. You had a beef with somebody, you settled it with tommy guns, or Chicago pianos, which is what a lot of gangsters called them then. The winner was the guy who was the fastest piano player. If you were carrying a Chicago piano, you didn't have to be much of a marksman. You just aimed it in the general direction of your target, and sprayed. Machine-gun justice.

Today's cocaine cowboys in cities like Miami, New York, and Los Angeles do the same thing with their Uzis and street-sweepers: aim and spray. Sometimes citizens get in the way, but that's the chance they take for being out on the street when working people are trying to take care of business.

By the time my grandfather Taylor was killed, he was involved in all kinds of rackets in Chicago and the suburban area. Gambling, prostitution, extortion, stickups, loan-sharking; and during World War II, counterfeiting of ration stamps and all those special rackets tied to shortages created by the fighting in Europe, Africa, and the Pacific.

During Prohibition my other grandfather also made big bucks as a bootlegger. Orville Van Boven smuggled first-class booze, professionally distilled and bottled across the Great Lakes in Canada, and moved moonshine from all over the Midwest into Chicago, Milwaukee, and other cities and towns. My family had a lot to do with keeping the blind pigs in that part of the country supplied with bootleg during the wild and violent days of Prohibition.

It was like the dope-smuggling business today. It was illegal, so everybody wanted it. Beer, whiskey, and bathtub gin; pot, crank, coke, and heroin. It's all the same. When people want something they can't obtain legally, there is always someone willing to take chances and break the law to supply it just so long as the payoff is big enough. My grandfathers made big money during the Prohibition years, and for a while a half century later I raked in the dollars selling dope.

The Van Bovens were restless people with a sense of adventure. They started off in the Netherlands, moved to South Africa, and then found their way to the United States. After awhile some of them moved back to the Netherlands and to England, but my grandfather's branch of the family stayed here and settled in a little town just north of Green Bay, Wisconsin.

Most people don't know there was a time not long ago when Dutch gangsters were big in this country. My granddad was one-hundred percent Dutch, but he grew to adulthood in Wisconsin, and if he was alive today he might be a Packers fan. More likely, however, he would be more interested in how much money he could make off the football team through the gambling racket. He had a knack for turning other people's vices and weaknesses into cash.

Of course, during the Roaring 20s, through the Prohibition era and the Depression, on into the World War II years, there was no place in the Midwest as attractive as Chicago for someone who was in the business of catering to other people's vices. Chicago was where the customers were and where the money was, and my grandfather was still in his early twenties when he left Green Bay and moved south to take advantage of the golden opportunities offered in the Windy City.

Other gangsters called him by his nickname, Bogie, and Bogie Van Boven quickly became a man to reckon with if you were involved in the Chicago rackets. He knew all the characters, including a button man who carried his Chicago piano around in a golf bag. My granddad said if anyone saw the guy approaching with his golf bag, they'd better run—or start shooting.

Both my grandfathers were ruthless and tough, but they weren't stupid. All the hoodlums in Chicago were scrambling for money in those days, and they left a lot of bullet-riddled bodies in the streets. Bogie Van Boven and Harry Taylor knew what celebrity gangsters like Al Capone, George "Bugs" Moran, and the Genna brothers were up to; exactly what rackets and areas they controlled. For a long time, both my grandfathers managed not to stray over the line. Then Harry Taylor stepped on the wrong toes, and suddenly retired from the rackets like a lot of other people before and after him. Maybe it was Sam, the guy with the golf bag. I'll never know. It's possible even my grandfather didn't know.

I don't remember my grandfather Taylor, but I grew up listening to stories about him. The only family picture I've ever seen is an old mug shot taken of him years ago one time when he was booked into the Cook County Jail in Chicago.

As I would one day, my father, George Emmett Taylor, Sr., grew up in the business. It was as natural for one of the Taylor boys to become a gangster as it was for sons in other families to follow their fathers into the steel mills, onto police departments, or into the haircutting, medical or law professions. You learned from your father and your grandfathers. When I was a kid playing cops and robbers, I always wanted to be John Dillinger, Al Capone, or Jesse James. Those were guys who made their living on the underside of the law—with their guns, their brains and their ballsy courage. They were my heroes. They were guys like my old man.

As long as I can remember, hoodlums and gangsters were hanging around our house and the house of my grandfather Van Boven. They were friends of both my grandfathers, then of my father, and finally they were friends and business associates of mine.

They passed the time drinking Bud or smoking dope and talking over some kind of business proposition like hijacking a truck, heisting a liquor store, or cleaning out a bunch of television sets being shipped in railroad cars. They were into everything, and always scheming. Everybody was on the game, looking for angles, setting up a deal of some kind.

They were the kind of guys that people didn't mess with, and I looked up to them. They were tough, smart guys who used guns, knives, fists, or feet as well as their brains to make a point or send a message. They were my heroes. Later, when I got to know prison shrinks and sociologists up close, the word hero had been redefined as "role model." All the same, that's the role I wanted to play.

That was the world I grew up in, where the men were all robbers, dope dealers, or somebody else living on the outside of the law. They were in and out of prisons, and it was no big deal. Other families threw parties for their sons, brothers, and fathers when they came home from the army or navy. My family and our friends threw parties when somebody got out of the slammer.

I knew there was another life out there, a world of "Ozzie and Harriet," "My Three Sons," and "The Andy Griffith Show," with Opie, Aunt Bea, and all those characters. But that was a television world, make-believe, about people living what I considered to be boring dead-end lives. Our world was the real world. People died violently in our world.

All of us kids were all born in the Chicago area. My parents were living in Waukegan, along the Lake Michigan shoreline a few miles south of the Wisconsin border, when I showed up on August 16, 1953. Right from the beginning, nobody in the family called me George—and thank God nobody called me Junior. They called me Bud, and the nickname has stuck with me throughout my life—while I was in crime, while I was in prison, and after I got out.

I'm the oldest of my siblings. My sister, Theresa, is eleven months younger than me; then there's my other sister, Karen; and finally my brother, Bob, the baby of the family. Sometime before I started school, my father moved us to Chicago Heights, where Al Capone hung out during his glory years. Even after Capone, Chicago Heights continued to be a stronghold for Outfit guys and for assorted other racketeers and gangsters like the Van Boven/Taylor clan.

When I was growing up there, the Heights was a wide-open town of about 40,000 people, most of them composed of families headed by steelworkers and other men with jobs in the ugly scatter of factories that hugged the southern tip of the lake. Many of the residents traced their ethnic background to southern Italy and Sicily.

When Capone and his fellow mobsters were battling for control of the town's rackets and carrying out bloody ambushes and street-corner shoot-outs during the Prohibition years, it seemed that every other family cooked alky for the bootleggers. Almost every neighborhood had speakeasies, cathouses and gambling dens, and politicians were openly on the take. Except for the absence of the alky cookers and speakeasies, it wasn't much different when I was growing up. Bookie parlors, extortion, and prostitution were big-time businesses, and my old man was up to his ears in the rackets.

Chicago Heights is part of the clutter of suburbs due south of the city, a few minutes drive from the Indiana state line and the constant stench and grimy blanket of smog that slumped over the steel mills that dominated the tri-city area of Gary, Hammond, and East Chicago. Calumet City, on the Illinois side of the line, was a neighboring community, and was also pretty much run by the Outfit. For decades, the southern suburb had a reputation in the Midwest as a "sin city" where the youngest, most beautiful strippers and whores were always available. A three-block long strip of clubs hugged the Illinois side of the state line. Hammond, Indiana, a hard-working, blue-collar town where steelworkers and their wives and families lived and shopped was on the east side of the line. On the west side of the street, it was hooker heaven, and a lot of the same steelworkers shopped there without their wives and families.

Calumet City continued to hang onto its seedy reputation long after the whores and the strip joints were chased out of town. In the 1970s, fed-up housewives successfully petitioned the state to remove the town's name from local license plates. They were embarrassed because too many other motorists were reaching the wrong conclusions, and honking horns or making passes at them after spotting Cal City plates.

Despite the juicy opportunities in Calumet City, Chicago Heights, and other communities along the southern tip of the lake, my father packed up the family when I was about eight or nine years old, and moved us south to St. Louis. I was too young to know if the move was precipitated by some problem in Chicago, or if it was because of some special business opportunities that opened up in St. Louis. Whatever, he had contacts there, and as soon as we settled into our new home, the same kind of hoodlums I had seen in Chicago were stopping by our home. Organized crime guys, Italians and Irish mobsters, bikers. The games were the same. Only the names were changed.

When I was a kid I was good cover for my old man, and in Chicago and in St. Louis he often took me with him when he had business to take care of. We would be riding along and he would spot a police car, and he'd tell me, "Sit up, Bud." I would straighten up in my seat so the cops could see I was in there with him, and the cops would usually drop back and turn a corner or something. He knew they would figure that he wouldn't take his kid with him if he was up to something. It worked like a charm.

In St. Louis, we lived in German, Irish, and Italian neighborhoods, mostly on the south side, about three blocks up the street from the main headquarters of the Anheuser-Busch brewery. It was fun in those days walking past the brewery and looking at the big stone gargoyles in front of the building. They were really cool, the kind of things little boys like. I went to grade school at Webster Elementary across town on the north side, where Paulie Leisure and most of the big St. Louis–Mob guys went when they were kids.

Our family was firmly middle-class, except that my old man didn't punch a time clock at Anheuser-Busch every morning or dress up in a shirt and tie and slowly turn into a vegetable in some office. Most of the time he reported for work in the back room of a neighborhood saloon. He hung out at different bars, and I ran back and forth getting coffee or beer for him and his cronies. They always tipped me with a handful of change from their pockets. Sometimes when they were feeling good, someone would shove a dollar bill in my hand, or a folded-up five. That was after they had pulled off a good score of some kind. I could always tell.

While my old man sat around in the back with his guys and planned crimes, I spent most of my time up front drinking soda pop, playing Foosball or shooting pool with the bartender or some barfly. My old man and his friends always had their own table, and nobody bothered them. They only hung out in bars that were for mobsters.

My old man was a biker, an official club member of the Saddle Tramps. The club had different names, depending on what time of the year it was and where they were, so they could elude the IRS, the FBI, the St. Louis police, and anyone else who might try to catch up with them. Around St. Louis they were Saddle Tramps, in Texas and the Southeast they were El Pistoleros, and when they rode down to New Orleans from St. Louis, Minneapolis-St. Paul, and those places, they wore Gallopin' Goose patches. They rode up in Minneapolis, all through the central part of the United States, and now they're Hell's Angels.

My old man got me my first bike when I was five years old. Actually it was a minibike with a twelve-horsepower Briggs-and-Stratton motor on it. I loved the

hell out of that thing, and rode it all over the neighborhood. Every chance I got, I parked it with the stripped-
down outlaw choppers my old man's friends rode over
to our place.

Most of the engines were at least 1200cc displace-
ment, and the front ends were altered with extended
forks to make them look better and be more of a chal-
lenge to handle. There were never any Harleys in our
yard that looked the same way they looked when they
came off the assembly line. All the shit was stripped off,
at least a couple of hundred pounds from the big bikes,
and there weren't any Beezers and Boy Scouts, Trum-
pets, or Jap Scrap parked in our yard. Those were the
names my old man's friends used for foreign bikes, the
BSAs, Triumphs, and Yamahas that schoolteachers and
wanna-be bikers rode. One of my father's friends had
an old Indian that he rode over to our place once in
awhile. He was always tinkering with it; and it was so
old he couldn't get parts anymore, so he had to jerry-
rig his own. I liked seeing my little bike sitting out there
with that old Indian and all those classic '74s and '80s.
It made me feel all grown up.

Most of the time when my old man was with his cronies, they talked business, but occasionally he told stories about his exploits while he was in the army fighting
in Korea. I learned later that he won a Bronze Star for
heroism after taking a hill with only two bullets. He
went up against thirty or forty Communist Koreans. He
also fought in Europe during World War II. He did okay
in the military. My old man liked the fighting, but he
said the discipline and regimentation was bullshit. Sometimes when he was in a real good mood, he joked that
the army was still better than serving time. He did some
of that when he was younger. Almost all the men in my
family did.

By the time I got to be a teenager and began getting

ideas about making my own decisions and looking around for moneymaking opportunities, we were having troubles and didn't get along at all. My old man had retired from the gang and from crime by then, and he was holding down a regular job. He was tired of all the bullshit and hassle, and we were living a middle-class life. He was a strong, stern man and told me he didn't want to see me make the same mistakes he made. He cussed a lot and had a violent temper, so he was nobody to mess with. But he never took out his temper on his family; he didn't slap my mom around or beat up on us kids.

He got pissed off at me because I was always bringing pot home or showing up stoned with my eyes all blood-shot and my speech slurred. It was the late 1960s when all the hippies and kids my age were turning on with pot, hash, acid, and experimenting with everything else from morning-glory seeds to banana peels. I was no hippie, but I was right in there with everybody else, trying everything on for size. My old man couldn't afford to have that shit around the house because he was an ex-con, and what was he going to say if the Man kicked down the door and started hauling everything out? ''It's okay officer. It's my son's grass?'' No way!

Nobody listens to good advice, especially kids, and I figured I knew it all. What the hell did he know? So although my old man tried to keep his friends separate from his family, I was curious and hung around them. When I was a little kid, and from as far back as I can remember, I wanted to grow up and be a gangster. I got an early start and was already on my way before I was old enough to realize what a bunch of shitheads and losers I was modeling myself after. I thought my old man's homeys were really cool.

I was young and hungry, and I had too much moxie for a kid my age. I was too much of a wise guy. My old man knew exactly what was going on, and he finally got fed up. When I was fifteen, he kicked me out of the house. I was just beginning my second year at Berkeley High School in South County, St. Louis.

It was my own fault my old man chased me out. I was already six feet tall, 160 pounds or so, and was getting too big for my britches. My younger brother, Bobby, got along okay with my old man. So did my sisters, but they were girls and they were expected to behave themselves. Neither one of the girls ever gave my mom any serious trouble, and she was the one who was in charge of things on the home front.

My mother was a good woman who worked hard and took good care of the kids. But when my old man decided it was time for me to go, that was the end of the story. There was nothing she could do, and I was out on my ass with nothing but my bike (a Harley 1200 I liked to drag race—indoors), the clothes I was wearing, and a couple of extra pairs of blue jeans. I moved around, camping at the homes of friends for a while. I would stay at one place until I wore out my welcome, then move on to another. The only money coming in was from a dead-end job at a car wash, rubbing chamois rags over other people's cars for about a dollar an hour.

A guy named Richie Ewald rescued me. He was my Fagin and showed me the ropes about the drug business. Looking at him through the eyes of a fifteen-year-old, I considered Richie an old fart. He was about forty-five or so, and old enough to know his way around. He died in 1980 in the infirmary at the federal penitentiary in Atlanta of a heart attack after he was stabbed by another inmate, but back in the 1960s when I was a kid, he was a big-time pot smuggler and dealer. He took me under his wing and set me up in the business. I started small, with Richie fronting me a pound at a time. I broke it down into ounces and halves, then peddled it to my friends in school. Made some good money, and also managed to keep enough back to stay high most of the time.

I applied myself, built up a clientele, and graduated from the ounce and half-ounce bullshit in a hurry. By the time I was sixteen, I was already dealing in 500-pound lots. Because I was buying in bulk, Richie gave the grass to me for less than $100 a pound. I broke that up into ten-pound lots and sold those to other kids who took care of the street dealing. The profits were faster. No fuss, no muss. The money was rolling in. While guys I had been sitting in English class with a few weeks earlier were still hitting the books and ruining their eyes, I was living it up with a new Barracuda, a 56 Harley panhead, and more sexy girls than I knew what to do with.

I played hard, but I also worked hard, and Richie began moving me up the ladder in his organization. I didn't bother with school anymore, and after I had worked with Richie awhile I became a driver for him, moving bales of pot from Florida into St. Louis, Atlanta, Chicago, Minneapolis-St. Paul, and other big cities in the South, Midwest, and Texas. If I had anything to prove to my old man, I was doing it. I figured I had moved into the big-time, and the sky was the limit.

That's when the roof fell in. It always does just about the time you begin to think that you're indestructible. But I was too young to see it coming. In 1972, another smuggler snitched me out and I took my first serious bust in Dallas. I was driving a rental car, acting as decoy for another guy who had a U-Haul truck loaded with grass. The narcs caught me with less than a half-ounce in the car. Four fucking grams! I tried telling them it was for personal use, but they wouldn't listen and stuffed me as a dealer.

Those were the days right after the old laws were

changed, and dealing even a little bit of marijuana was classed as a felony. In Texas, they were giving out 100 years for people caught with a couple of seeds. Moms and dads were still watching movies like *Reefer Madness,* and walking out of theatres with their faces all serious. They didn't know what a joke it was.

But I had a clean record, no rap sheet, and I was still a teenager, so I figured I could take whatever came my way. It couldn't be that bad. What a surprise. First thing I knew I was chained up with a bunch of other new fish in a school bus pulling up to the administration building at the Texas State Penitentiary in Huntsville. Huntsville isn't some country club or work camp reserved for kids who are first-timers, it's one of America's toughest prisons where hard-core killers, stickup artists and the worst-of-the-worst are locked up. Texas's death row is at Huntsville, and the Lone Star State has a well-deserved reputation for carrying out the death penalty. It's led all states in executions since 1977.

I kept my mouth shut and served fifteen months. It wasn't kindergarten stuff, but I handled it okay. Most of the time I was outside with a work gang, dressed all in white, dragging a forty-foot sack behind me while I picked cotton. Even for a young guy like me, spending eight hours a day stooped over in a cotton field under a hot south-Texas sun filling that bag over and over was exhausting work. We weren't chained, because we weren't people who were convicted of violent crimes, but the hacks treated us like we were. Inmate trusties mounted on horses and carrying shotguns worked with regular prison guards keeping track of us, and we knew better than to try to run for it. The trusties would shoot you faster than the hacks would. They didn't give a shit.

When I completed my time, I was loaded onto a school bus again and driven back north for processing at the Dallas County jail. The jail was in downtown Dallas, and after the cops were through with me there, they directed me to walk across the street to the parole office and finish up the paperwork. I still had three years parole to do. Screw them. I had enough of Texas and I went to the bus station and bought a ticket on a Greyhound for St. Louis. It was two or three years later before I got in trouble back home and Texas authorities caught up with me. I fought extradition and won, but they made me sign a paper promising that I would never return to Texas for as long as I lived. I could pass through, but they didn't want me hanging around. That was okay with me. I was happy to scribble my George ''Bud'' Taylor on their fucking paper. They can give Texas back to the Mexicans for all I care.

Richie was impressed and appreciative when I got back to St. Louis from Huntsville. After all those days picking cotton in the sun, I was so brown I looked like a campesino, but I had reacted like a standup guy, taken the rap and did my time. He had a surprise waiting for me: my own pot franchise. He assigned me some choice territory in Jefferson County. It was my reward.

True to the Taylor and Van Boven family traditions, I had become a successful professional criminal before I was out of my teens. While boys I went to school with only a couple of years before were joining the army, navy or marines, attending college or beginning straight jobs, I was already well into my chosen career as a gangster. I had runners and low-level dealers working for me who were ten years older than I was. I was a man of responsibilities.

Money was flooding in from all over, and if I decided I wanted something, it was mine. If I saw a new convertible I liked, I bought it. If I saw a bike I liked, I paid cash for it. I had a closet full of blue jeans, boots and leathers. And I took beautiful girls to bed, as many as I wanted and whenever I wanted. No fumbling around in some backseat for three or four hours, then stumbling home disappointed with aching nuts for me. I was like a kid in a candy store. Then I met my first wife.

She was a foxy woman, eight years older than I was. We hung around with the same crowd, and I was impressed. She looked good, she was smart, and in my estimation, she was a sophisticated woman of the world. So we got together and had a kid. He's twenty-one now.

Richie and I were dealing directly with suppliers in Mexico when he flew a 500-pound load of high-grade grass and a smaller batch of Mexican brown heroin into an isolated farm field in rural Jefferson County, south of St. Louis. We unloaded the Cessna and had stored the grass in a barn on the property when the law showed up. Jefferson County sheriff's deputies, Missouri state police, and Drug Enforcement Administration (DEA) agents swarmed all over us at once. They were wearing green camouflage fatigues, baggy black SWAT-team outfits and starched and pleated state-trooper uniforms. Everybody was packing grease guns, shotguns, or .44-magnum hog-legs that could blow holes in someone as big as their head.

We started grabbing up handfuls of loose money and heroin. Then we scrambled out the back door and headed for a stand of woods, along an escape route already set up in case of a raid. Everybody ran except my old lady. She was stubborn and refused to run. The rest of us were taking the heroin and most of the money, and she figured there was no evidence so there was nothing the cops could do to her.

While some of the cops searched the house, others went to the barn and found the marijuana. A few minutes later my wife was led to a police car with a pair of handcuffs around her wrists. The cops drove her to the Jefferson County jail in Hillsboro and locked her up.

I talked to a sharp young lawyer with a reputation for

being able to take care of people with problems involving drugs. While we were talking, we shared a monster spliff I rolled from some of the Panama Red that I was holding on to for personal use. I wound up giving the lawyer $500 and a couple of ounces of boss grass, and he made the charges go away. Not long after that, my old lady and I were divorced.

The pot-smuggling business in Jefferson County was getting too hot, and the law was onto both Richie and me so I went into a new line of business. Pills were big. People were doing everything from amphetamines to downers like Dilaudid and anything with codeine in it. I peddled white crosses, black beauties, quackers, Ts and blues. Whatever fell into my hands went on the market.

Pills fell into my hands because I took them away from people who sold them, the legitimate wholesalers and retailers. I went on the road, ripping off drugstores and warehouses for hundreds of pounds of prescription drugs. My technique was simple and basically non-violent.

When I busted warehouses, my crew and I usually went in through the roof. Just wait for the sun to go down, then cut a hole and drop down inside. One of the guys would be waiting with a pickup truck or a van, and as soon as we opened the warehouse doors, we would fill it up. Then we were out of there. A few times we stole somebody's ID and went in, then made some old man who was supplementing his Social Security check by posing as a guard stand around in a corner while we cleaned the place out. But we didn't cowboy the place by going in with a bunch of guns and getting violent. There wasn't any need for that. All we had to do was scowl and bark at those old farts, and they would tell us to help ourselves, just go ahead and do what we had to do.

The pharmacies were even easier to do, and I liked

them because I didn't need any partners. I'm a big dude; six foot, three inches tall, and I was young, slim, fast, and scrappy. I used my size to good advantage. During the year or so that I was robbing pharmacies, I probably hit every drugstore in South County, St. Louis. I drove around until I spotted a place that looked good, then went inside to scout out the place.

In those days, it was easy to get a doctor's prescription for Percodan, codeine, and that kind of stuff, so I would go inside and give the scrip to the pharmacist. I'd watch and see where the schedule-2 narcotics were kept when he filled the prescription. Then I'd leave for a while.

When I returned, as soon as I walked through the door, I'd begin running. I'd storm down the aisle like a runaway train and vault over the counter. Before the pharmacist knew what was going on, this big, hairy guy with boots and a sack would be all over him. I would push the pharmacist to the floor, yell at him to stay down, pull a big, heavy screwdriver out of my belt, push it under the lock on the narcotics cabinet and pop the door open. Then I'd scoop up all the shit that was inside, dump it into the sack, turn around and run out. Everybody else in the place just cowered against the shelves or hit the floor, if they even knew anything was going on before it was all over. I never touched the cash register. The schedule-2 stuff like Percodan was what I wanted. The narcotics were better than money. I never used that shit myself, but the pill-poppers and dopeheads who did were willing to pay whatever I asked for it.

I always worked alone. That way there was nobody to split the money with, and there was nobody else to screw up on a job, or to get drunk or high and blab to a girlfriend about what was going on. It was a good business, safe, and I could do the job in a few minutes. Then I had the rest of the day to myself.

Most guys, when I pushed them down, they stayed down. I did about fifty pharmacies before I met a guy who didn't follow the rules. By that time, although nobody knew who I was, I had built up quite a reputation for my blitzkreig-style robberies. Newspapers called me the Hit-and-Run Bandit.

One day I hit the wrong pharmacy. When I stormed down the aisle, heading for the schedule-2 drawer, the bald-headed pharmacist picked up a sawed-off shotgun and blazed away just as I was vaulting over the counter. Half a dozen pellets hit me in the calf of my right leg, but none of them struck bone. I knocked the sawed-off out of the guy's hands, pushed him down and cleaned out the cabinet. Then I scrambled back over the counter and limped out of the place with all that lead shot still in my leg and the schedule-2 dope in my bag. Later I dug out the shotgun pellets with a pocket knife that I heated up over a burner on the stove, and took a few days off. Then I went back to the same old routine.

The cops never caught me for the drugstore robberies, but after about a year as a robber-burglar they pinched me with a bunch of military duffle bags loaded with prescription narcotics from one of the warehouse jobs. Some citizen spotted my partner circling the block in the getaway car and called the police. I had another talk with my pot-smoking-lawyer friend, and he got me off with two years probation. I had done a lot of crime by that time, but I still didn't have much of a rap sheet, so the judge went easy on me.

Probation wasn't something that was easy for me to live with. I didn't like all the rules; reporting in to some little girl with a sociology degree, or an uptight bozo in a shiny J. C. Penney seersucker suit and a wife and couple of kids to support on $250 a week. So I jumped parole and split for California. I wasn't Public Enemy Number One, and I knew no one would be coming after me. Besides, I had connections and friends in Oakland. They were good people: Hell's Angels.

2

Heroin and Hookers

THE DAY I shoved the kickstand down on my dusty Harley '74 and eased off the leather saddle in front of the clubhouse in the heart of Oakland's toughest black ghetto, my biker friends fronted me twenty pounds of heroin and I went into business.

As far as the Hell's Angels were concerned, I had the local franchise all to myself. The Angels were disgusted with junkies and didn't like messing around with skag. In those days, during the 1970s, they didn't think much of coke, either. They preferred dealing in methamphetamines, which they referred to by their favorite street name, "crank." They usually cooked it up themselves.

Cooking crank was a tricky business, regardless of whether it was brewed in a mobile kitchen driven into the isolation and solitude of the sprawling forests north and east of the Bay Area, in a motel room, someone's private home, or the even more sophisticated surroundings of a fully-equipped laboratory. The crank, or crystal meth, produced and peddled by my biker friends is based on a chemical called P2P, and it's dangerously volatile, as temperamental as TNT. Self-taught chemists and careless amateurs have been blown to bits while cooking up meth in clandestine laboratories. The California State Attorney General's Office once pointed out that about one in every six crank labs is discovered because it blows up.

A woman in Riverside County was convicted of three counts of second-degree murder for killing her kids in the early nineties after a batch of crank she was cooking on the stove of her trailer blew up. She lost her one-, two-, and three-year-olds, but an older kid survived and testified at her trial. The deputy DA who prosecuted her said what she was doing was like storing dynamite in her kids' bedroom. He was right. I wouldn't do it. Especially if there were any kids around.

But hazardous as the manufacturing process is, the resulting fine white powder is worth its weight in gold. Users shoot it up, snort it, smoke it or swallow it, and the rush makes them feel like Superman—or Wonderwoman. Importantly, the ingredients are cheap and easy to obtain. Overhead costs are minimal.

In the last couple of years, a new form of meth based on ephedrine, which is legally used in some cold medicines to clear sinuses, has been muscling its way into the market. Most of the new meth is smuggled in from Mexico. The raw ingredients are moved into Mexico from China, then either processed there or smuggled across the border to be cooked up by chemists in California, Texas, Arizona, or New Mexico. It's cheap and potent.

Wherever its refined, and whatever its called—crank, speed, ice, or just plain meth—the drug is nasty and dangerous. It causes hallucinations, and tends to make users paranoid and very dangerous to be around. The effects can hang on for a couple of years after someone has stopped using it.

Like crank and heroin, producing refined cocaine also

calls for moving the raw material, or the processed narcotics, across borders. At some stage of its production, smugglers sneak it into the country from Bolivia, Peru, or other Andes nations where the cocoa leaf is grown and harvested. Smuggling cocaine, like cooking crank, is a dangerous profession and the costs are driven up accordingly. Also like crank, however, it has a ready market among users who are willing to pay whatever the costs may be. I had the right connections, experience, and the desire to cash in on the opportunities. I knew all about smuggling and distribution; and I didn't care if the raw material was opium poppies or cocoa leaves. If there was a demand and the reward was great enough, I was ready, willing, and able to supply the dope.

So while my friends manufactured and sold crank, I smuggled and peddled coke and heroin. That way everybody was happy. I didn't step on the wrong toes, and nobody stepped on mine. We all made money.

I never became an official member of the Hell's Angels, although there were plenty of people who would have been willing to sponsor me. But I rode with them and stayed on the good side of the people in the club who were important. I had a good relationship with Ralph Hubert "Sonny" Barger, Jr., with Sergey Walton, and a bunch of other guys. Sonny was head of the Oakland chapter, and presided over the club while it went national, then expanded into other countries. Sergey, whom I would get to know even better in the witness units years later, was another of the founding members of the club, a former president of the club's Oakland chapter, and a member of the Filthy Few.

The Filthy Few was, and is, the enforcement arm of the Hell's Angels. They're the elite; the shock troops that the leadership calls on when somebody gets out of line and has to be hit. Sergey was of average height, about six feet, but he was solidly muscled and a mean dude when he was riled. He was tough, fearless, and absolutely ruthless. He was exactly the kind of dude who fit into the Filthy Few, and nobody would want someone like him for an enemy.

Sergey, or Sir Gay as some of his close friends called him, knew everything you would ever want to know about guns. Armaments were his specialty. He was always strapped. Then again, most of the Angels were, most of the time. They dealt with some mean dudes, Mexican, Colombian, and Cuban drug runners, cocaine cowboys from Miami, street gangs, syndicated-crime groups, and other bikers who were looking for opportunities to move into their territory. The Hell's Angels were known to carry around big stashes of drugs or cash, and they had to have protection. A lot of them wore bullet-proof vests.

If a Hell's Angel was worried about packing a piece because the law was breathing down his neck, he let his old lady carry and she would slip it to him if there was trouble. Almost everybody had a buck knife or a dagger stuck in their boot, or a ball-peen hammer hanging from their belt. Hey, somebody had to take responsibility for keeping the streets safe.

Hell's Angels loved silencers, and they made their own in little machine shops they set up. Most of the guys were pretty good with tools. They worked on their bikes all the time, so putting together a few silencers was no big deal. They maintained armories that could have outfitted an army in one of the banana republics in the days before big-time narco-trafficking changed everything in Central and South America. The Angels liked Israeli-manufactured Uzis for going to war and they made their own pipe bombs, but they stocked a little bit of everything.

Sergey was in San Francisco early in 1981 waiting for marshals to transport him to a federal pen for firearm violations when he busted out. When police caught up a couple of months later, they collared him with a military rifle, a 9-mm pistol, and a couple more handguns converted for automatic fire. He was ready for war.

There probably wasn't anybody in the Hell's Angels who hated coke more than Sergey. Sometimes, while we were working on a six-pack of Budweiser or when we were riding, he would ask me why in the Hell I was dealing that shit. Sergey told me I should forget about "that Goddamn coke," and deal crank like everybody else.

"Bud, selling that cocaine, there's no money in it. That cocaine's shit. It's gonna be the downfall of everything," he said. Looking back, I can appreciate Sergey's foresight. He was right about coke, but I didn't know it at the time, and it probably wouldn't have made any difference if I had known. I wasn't a patriot. I didn't give a shit about anybody else. I cared about Bud.

My heroin and coke business was one of the reasons I didn't push for membership in the Hell's Angels. If I belonged to the club, then they wouldn't tolerate my staying in the business I was in. It was as simple as that. There were other reasons as well. It was important to me to keep my options open. I had business and social ties with other gangs like the Vagabonds. And my connections weren't all with bikers. Back in St. Louis and Illinois, I was connected with the Irish and Italian mobs. I was tied in with Pauly Leisure and people like that, guys who ran things. I also had connections with smugglers in Mexico and South America.

If I became a Hell's Angel, then their enemies would be my enemies. Obligations went along with membership. I also liked to call my own shots. I respected Sonny, Sergey, and other guys in the Angels top echelon, but I didn't want them making my decisions for me. I was too much of a lone wolf for that. As a freelancer,

I could move in any circle, and that was important if I wanted to make a lot of money. And I did want to make a lot of money.

Not being officially connected with the Angels didn't stop me from doing deals or hanging around with them. Hell's Angels in fact were my closest friends all the time I was in California, and I spent most of my time with them—for both business and recreation.

If I had something going down I needed to get together with Sergey about, I would phone him and say: "Hey, bro. This is Bud. I need to talk to you."

"Okay," he would say. "Five o'clock."

End of conversation. Hell's Angels don't like long conversations on telephones, and there was no idle chit-chat about the weather or how somebody might be getting along with their old lady. If there was business to be discussed, it was better to do it man to man, out in the open. You never knew when your telephone might be bugged.

We didn't bother to designate where we were going to meet. We already knew. When we got together it was almost always the same place, People's Park on Telegraph Avenue in Berkeley, just across the Oakland Hills from the Hell's Angels clubhouse. It was right down the street from the University of California, Berkeley, campus, where all the hippies and antiwar loonies gathered in the sixties and seventies. That's why it was such a good place to meet and do business, because all those spoiled little rich kids had the cops so intimidated they were afraid to wipe their asses in People's Park. The cops stayed away from the park and didn't hassle anybody, including bikers.

Hanging around with the Angels taught me a lot. They were celebrity hoodlums and took advantage of the national fascination with renegade bikers to branch out and open chapters across the country. The press, and some

of the cops, was calling them the Motorized Mafia, and
that added to their mystique. Eventually, they established chapters in other countries like Sweden, Denmark,
and the home of my forefathers—the Netherlands. But
Oakland was the brain center. Everything was run from
there. I had a good time riding with them, cruising along
those California highways with 500 pounds of stripped
down bike throbbing and roaring under me. It was a nice
feeling to be on a long run with a noisy rumble of Hell's
Angels cruising along all around you on their chopped
hogs. You knew nobody was going to mess with you.
It was a feeling of power.

After about three years in the Bay Area, hanging
around with the Angels and peddling skag, cocaine,
whatever came my way, things started going bad and I
headed back East again. The police were closing in. The
Angels were warring with other biker gangs who were
trying to muscle in on some of the rackets. And it was
becoming increasingly difficult for me to stay out of the
line of fire. I didn't want to get involved.

Except for another minor gunshot wound, I survived
California unscathed. No serious injuries or run-ins with
the law. Even the shooting was an accident. I was sitting
on an easy chair in the Oakland clubhouse one time and
a Hell's Angel was on the couch cleaning an old German
9-mm pistol. He put a bullet in the cylinder and as soon
as he spun it around, the gun went off. The bullet hit
me in the shin bone and almost broke my leg, but I was
lucky. He loaded his own bullets, and he had a light
load in it.

The slug stayed there for years until it finally worked
its way up between the muscle and the skin while I was
at the FCI in Sandstone, Minnesota. My cellie watched
while a prison doctor lanced it. The doc squeezed it out
like a pimple. He did me and another guy at the same
time. Took all the bullets out of both of us. The FBI

was there and collected the slugs in evidence bags just in case there was a need for them later.

Unfortunately there was a price to pay for returning to Missouri. When I broke probation and skipped to the West Coast, no one went out there to look for me—but Missouri law enforcement was waiting for me when I got home. I wound up doing two years at the Missouri State Penitentiary in Jefferson City for parole violation. When I was caught with the sack full of prescription drugs, I was already in violation of my parole stemming from the Dallas bust. The judge had given me a break by placing me on probation, but like they say: lightning doesn't strike twice in the same place.

Jeff City is probably one of the oldest state prisons in the country. It was constructed along the bluffs of the Missouri River in 1868, just after the Civil War ended. You can see the river from the chapel on the upper yard if you look out the window there and over the wall. Everything is solid rock, including the wall, which is about seventy feet high.

The prison was built in time for Jesse and Frank James to do time there. So did one-time Public Enemy Number One, Charles Arthur "Pretty Boy" Floyd, and a witch's stew of other desperados. Until a few years ago when death row was moved to a new prison at Potosi, Jeff City was the penitentiary where Missouri executed its condemned killers, originally by firing squad in the yard. Potosi represents a big step up for death-row inmates. There they aren't kept locked up in their cells full-time like they were in Jeff City. At Potosi they're allowed to exercise in a big yard. Plus they get to choose between the gas chamber or lethal injection, instead of a bullet.

Jeff City was a grim, nasty place to spend two years of my life, but I made my time there a learning experience. The day I was processed in and they handed me a towel with ''Missouri State Penitentiary'' stenciled on it in big, black block letters, I accepted the fact that I was there to stay for a while and would just have to make the best of a bad situation. Most cons do the same if they're smart.

Jeff City was a real hard-ass prison, like Huntsville, with all the dehumanizing miseries and dangers that go with the territory when hundreds, or thousands, of men are locked up together for long periods of time. It was a world of concrete, tile, and steel everywhere, painted with the same dull battleship gray that was flecking and permanently pockmarked with rust. The acrid odors of strong disinfectant mingled with the sour smell of hundreds of bodies. Most importantly, however, it was a world of predatory men with tattoos and dead eyes who were quick to take advantage of the slightest weakness exhibited by any of their fellow inmates.

Inmates fought, stole from each other, loan-sharked, did drugs together, smuggled, bought and sold contraband, and had sex with prison boy-girls. They also snitched on each other, for any advantage they could get with their fellow inmates or with the prison administration. Sometimes an inmate would crack and begin raging around his cell, screaming, smashing his fist against the concrete walls and throwing his own shit through the bars at anyone who came near.

Bullies, weaklings, killers, gang rapers, black and white racists, religious fanatics, mental cases, jailhouse lawyers; you name it and they were locked up at Jefferson City. The same thing exists outside the walls, but out there everything isn't compressed. And most people aren't carrying around an attitude that they have nothing to lose.

I survived there until October 1979, when I was released just in time for Halloween. But I didn't immediately begin trick-or-treating. I took my time to look around while I studied the opportunities available to an ambitious young man who was broke, hungry, and anxious to find about any kind of work, just so long as it wasn't legit. For a while I played around with prescriptions, getting people I knew to pick up scrip from doctors, then reselling the pills and capsules on the street. The business kept me in cigarettes and six-packs, but I wasn't making any real money, so I continued looking around.

Finally I got together with a partner in St. Louis and we began heisting other drug dealers. We had a few beers in the bars and other places they were known to hang out in, playing it nice and friendly while we gathered intelligence. We kept our ears and eyes open. We played the spook game like we were CIA. Whenever we heard about a big shipment of something coming in, we swung into action. We dressed like DEA agents, then staged phony raids on their safe houses or wherever they were storing the stuff.

We carried two-way radios, and wore black windbreakers I had made up for us with the agency emblem on the front and the letters DEA in big, black block print on the back. I figured all that shit out and put it together so that it really looked good. Of course we had another advantage. When three or four guys suddenly bust into somebody's house waving machine guns, jabbering excitedly on two-way radios and looking like a gang of official desperados from Washington, D. C., the dope dealers aren't likely to ask for ID or check under caps for buzz-cuts. We looked authentic enough to get the job done.

We always took the guns away from everybody and put them in handcuffs, then confiscated their drugs. That was when we made them tell us who their connections were. They really believed we were DEA, and nobody we robbed hesitated to rat out their friends, because we told them if they cooperated we would give them a break. Then the next night or a couple of days later, we would move in on the guys higher up and clean them out. We sold all the drugs to out-of-town dealers.

Eventually I got carried away with the game and we got busted. A guy we broke in on was so scared he was almost shitting his pants, and I told him that I was sorry for him and was going to give him a break. Just turn over the drugs to us and tell us who your supplier is, and we'll be friends, I said. He spilled his guts, but the problem was that the guy he ratted on was out of town for a couple of days so we couldn't hit him right away.

So I explained to the rat that I knew it wasn't his fault his supplier was out of town. "What I'm gonna do is let you work for us as our confidential informant, our CI. When this guy gets back to town, I want you to let us know so we can hit him." I told him we would be in touch.

The famous Scottish poet Robert Burns, wrote: "The best laid schemes o' mice an' men Gang aft a-glay." Translating that into modern-day English, he was saying watch your ass. No matter how careful you work something out, it can fuck up. I should have read Burns' poetry before I cut the deal with the guy we scared so bad.

The dumb ass telephoned the DEA office in St. Louis the next day and told the agents that his supplier was back in town. The DEA guys went through the roof when they figured out what was going on, and that was the beginning of the end. The DEA figured out who the phony agent was and came looking for me. They were embarrassed by the idea of some dude ripping off drug dealers by pretending to be DEA, and they didn't want a bunch of publicity. I pulled five years for that—but didn't actually do any time because my lawyer kept the case bouncing around in court until my situation changed. Eventually I got off with five years probation.

Being a robber and selling drugs wasn't paying off anymore, and it was bringing too much heat. So I went into a new business. Women! There was big money in massage parlors and escort services, so I muscled my way into the racket. I had already learned a lot about the massage parlor and escort service business from Sergey and other Hell's Angels, because they had women who worked for them. Mainly it was their wives, girlfriends, groupies and wanna-be biker broads who hung around and thought it was cool to climb on the back of some chopper and hold on to a big hairy, smelly, greasy Hell's Angel.

Most of the organized girly action in St. Louis and Jefferson counties was already being controlled by two operators. Neither of them was operating the businesses like they should have, and they either didn't realize the potential or just didn't know how to capitalize on it. I understood both.

One of the operators was a woman who was working out of a hole-in-the-wall office in the little town of Fenton in south St. Louis County, a couple of minutes drive from the Jefferson County line. She didn't have any connections, so I walked in and told her I was going to help her out and be her muscle. After four or five months, I had taken over her business and put her to work for me as my manager. She was the girlfriend of a guy I knew, and they were both doing so much heroin, they weren't paying attention to the operation. After I took over, we did a little skag together once in a while. Hers went into her arm; mine went up my nose, or I smoked it. It was just a toy for me. I wasn't into the intravenous shit, but she was a serious user.

She handled most of the day-to-day operational problems, leaving me free to work on expanding the business while I continued to keep my hand in other rackets. I kept a close eye on her because she wasn't trustworthy. She was only making $300 or $400 a night when she was in charge. Within a couple of weeks after I first walked inside the door, I had turned the place into a gold mine making ten or fifteen times what she was pulling in.

By that time I also had other domestic responsibilities. I was married again, this time to a woman who thought my money was coming from an asphalt-paving company. We had a son together, then she learned where my money really came from and she filed for divorce. We had a few other problems. Every married couple does. But it was the escort service and the massage parlors that ruined the marriage. My wife simply couldn't accept the idea that her husband was in the sex business.

The girlie trade may have bad for my marriage, but it was a rousing success as a moneymaker. Some of the girls in my massage parlors were just average, but my escorts were premium grade A. They weren't your fifty-dollar girls. If someone wanted to date one of my ladies, he'd better have at least $200 to $500 in the pockets of his blue jeans to shell out. And that was just for starters.

Quality was important to me, and I built up a client list of some of the most important politicians, criminals, and businessmen in the St. Louis area. My ladies had looks and sophistication, and I had escorts to meet anybody's personal tastes. My girls knew how to wear their clothes and how to behave at a fancy dinner party and in the bedroom. We were very exclusive and had long-legged redheads, cute blondes, sexy brunettes, college girls, secretaries, and moonlighting housewives. Sometimes the husbands knew about their wives' part-time jobs, and sometimes they didn't. Of course some of the girls were full-time hookers. It's a living.

The client list, along with all the rest of my business records, was kept on computer diskettes. Everything was recorded: names, addresses, private phone numbers, driver license numbers, Social Security numbers, credit cards, and sexual preferences. The names of girls they contracted for through the agency were listed, along with the names and addresses of hotels or private residences where the dates occurred.

The massage parlors and the main escort agency, which we called A Touch of Class, were already fully staffed when I came into the business. But there was a big turnover, and the customers were always looking for new faces. That was no problem. So many foxy women wanted work that I couldn't find jobs for all of them. We ran a continuous ad in the Yellow Pages, and girls who were looking for work called the same number that customers used. I split everything with the escorts 50-50, but they kept all the tips.

New girls dealt with my managers. They did the interviews, made sure the girl was of legal age, and took care of the massage parlors and arranged the dates for the escorts. It was the manager's responsibility to make sure the girls had their makeup on, their hair and nails done, and were properly dressed and ready to go on fifteen or twenty minutes notice of getting a call on nights they were on duty. Very businesslike!

If there were any complaints from customers, the managers also handled that, but we didn't have many dissatisfied customers. Our girls knew their jobs, and they knew better than anybody that the work involved more than straight sex. As often as not, a client was looking for a sympathetic ear to lay his problems on. If a girl was a good listener and behaved like she really gave a shit about the John's business problems or troubles with his wife, she could make more on tips than her half-share of the normal fee.

I was either married or had a regular girlfriend then— part-time one, part-time the other. So for the most part,

I stayed away from my employees unless I was delivering them to the house of some big-shot.

One of my clients was a powerful congressman, and a few times he arranged for me to fly girls to Washington for private parties he threw for big campaign contributors or other people he wanted to impress. The girls were usually put up in a hotel in Annapolis, Maryland, and they stayed a day or two. Then one of the big guy's aides drove them to the Washington National Airport (now the Ronald Reagan National Airport) or to Dulles International and they jetted back to St. Louis.

The congressman stayed in the background until the girls showed up, and I was paid in cash by one of his aides. I was charging $1,200 a night, plus expenses, and it cost extra for specialties. They paid more for blowjobs, B&D, all of the fantasy stuff. That was long before the Clintons moved into the White House and the president's chubby little toe-sucker pal began advising him on family values. Toes would have been extra. Everything was, but no one acted like they were worried about what the party cost. The taxpayers probably picked up the bill.

The congressman was a good customer, and a nice guy who also threw business my way when he was campaigning or taking care of other business back home in his district. His personal preferences ran to blondes and redheads with blue eyes or green eyes. Brown-eyed girls simply weren't a turn-on for him, irregardless of how beautiful they might be. My girls told me that his sexual tastes were pretty normal. Nothing kinky. Like it's been said of Clinton, the congressman has a special identifying mark on his body that only somebody who has been up close—real close—would know about unless somebody told them. My girls told me about it. He would keep them around for three or four hours, then send them on their way. I would have been better off if the congressman had never heard of me and I had never heard of him. I had no way of knowing it then, but our business relationship would come back to haunt me.

Another of my clients was Paulie Leisure, one of St. Louis's leading mobsters and a friend of mine. Once while Paulie was on the run from the government, he holed up at the Mayflower Hotel, a top hotel in St. Louis. It was a nice place only about four blocks from the Federal Building, where the Gs that were looking for him worked.

Every few days or so he would telephone me and say, "Bud, I need a woman." So I'd ask him what he wanted, and he would tell me she had to be gorgeous, she had to have such and such hair and eyes, and a great ass and legs. That kind of stuff. Paulie liked good legs on a woman, and that always blew my mind because he didn't have any of his own. He got in a beef with some other gangsters, so they blew him up. He was living at his mansion house, a big, beautiful place on the banks of the Mississippi River when he went down to the parking garage and started his car up. Boom! Goodbye legs, hello wheelchair.

"I don't want you sending anybody down here," he'd tell me. "You bring them over yourself." So I'd take a woman to him and leave her there. I did that three times, and I always told the girls not to bother him about money. I would tell her, "I'll see you later. I'll take care of Paulie." After the job, the girl would let me know what I owed, then I picked up the tab. It was good business, and it only cost me 50 percent anyway. The girls knew better than to try to cheat by adding on a bunch of extra charges for specialties. Hell, Paulie should have been a specialty just for not having any legs.

There was big, fast money in girls, and it wasn't very long before a hillbilly crime family noticed what was going on. They were from the Ozarks; 'Lil Abner, dueling banjos, that kind of thing. They were mean, violent, and inbred like the Kallikaks. They were wannabe bikers who rode a mix of Triumphs, BSAs, a few Harleys, and drove old pickup trucks. Most of their bikes were junk, and they didn't have any connections with the Hell's Angels or other organized outlaw gangs. They were their own outlaws, without the capitol *O*. But they stuck together.

They decided to muscle in on my business. "We want the massage parlors and the escort service, or you keep on running the business and pay us a big piece of the action," they told me. But I wasn't some scared broad whose boyfriend spent all her money on skag and backed down the first time somebody hinted a little violence might be shaping up. They had the wrong patsy.

"Go fuck yourself," I told the chief moron. I was already paying off power guys in local politics, and I wasn't shelling out to a bunch of hillbilly mobsters from the sticks of Jefferson County.

They didn't say much, just narrowed their eyes and did their best to look mean and threatening. Then they climbed back on their bikes and roared away. But they weren't backing off; they just weren't ready at that time for a showdown. They knew, and I knew, they were going to get me. Or they were going to try.

They were stupid, but that made them that much more dangerous. There were twenty-five or thirty guys who rode together, and they were all hungry. Everybody told me to stay away from them, that they were so wild and crazy that eventually every one of them would all wind up "Prisoner Killed." My friends were right, but those assholes were anxious and I didn't have the luxury of waiting for them to self-destruct.

The harassment started that night. They borrowed a couple of my cars from a parking lot at one of the shops. Then they started borrowing the cars of customers and hanging around on their bikes scaring people. My girls were also becoming afraid to come to work. It was bad for business, and I couldn't let it go on.

A good friend of mine had one of those monster trucks that sits up about ten or twelve feet high on big wheels. They build the trucks right there in St. Louis, and my friend used his to send a message to the hillbillies. They were all hanging out in a walk-in, limp-out bar one night with their bikes parked outside. My friend drove his truck over all the bikes. After rolling over them the first time, he backed up and drove over them again. The back wheels and the front wheels on those trucks both turn, and he smashed the bikes up good. Ground 'em right into scrap.

He even gave the front of the bar a couple of shots. It looked for a while like he was going to drive over the building and do a replay of *Porky's*. That was a movie that came out around that time about a bunch of high-school kids who demolished a cathouse and gambling den. The flat bikes slowed the Kallikaks down, but it didn't stop them. Before their bikes were smashed, what we had was a difference of opinion over business. After their bikes were flattened, the disagreement became personal. They were really pissed off.

A few nights later when I walked out of one of my massage parlors, a bunch of them were waiting for me. I would have fought them, but they had guns. You can't fight a bullet. They shoved me into the backseat of a car, then roared out of the parking lot heading for the boondocks. Two guys were in the front seat and another was in the backseat with me. About half a dozen more members of the clan were in a car in front of us, and in a pickup truck trailing along in back. There wasn't a bike in sight.

There was no question in my mind about their plans for me. They had worked out an early retirement scheme. I wasn't coming back. They were taking me out to the Mississippi River to whack me. While I was sitting there with my mind in overdrive wondering what in the hell to do, they were taking loudly to each other about floating me down the river without my head and my hands. A guy like that can be hard to identify, even if somebody manages to fish him out of the water or the body pops to the surface all bloated and white.

My companion in the backseat was a big fellow with a beard, who smelled like year-old axle grease and stale piss. He had a big mouth. "You pulled some bad shit, Bubba," he told me. "You were messing with the wrong people, and now you gonna pay." He was all blown up with his importance and the power they had over me.

We were somewhere in the asshole of the world, in rural south Jefferson County, when a car ahead of us stopped to make a right turn, and the car I was in slowed down. I pushed open the door, vaulted over the mouth, and rolled out. I barely felt the jolt on my left shoulder as it slammed into the gravel beside the road, then I scrambled to my feet and plunged down a ridge.

While I crashed through trees and bushes, running for my life, I could hear yelling and the sound of feet hitting the ground behind me. They were shooting at me as I leaped over a little creek and almost fell down an incline, just before I grabbed hold of a sapling and swung myself around.

That cost me the knuckle on my right thumb but saved my life. A bullet took the knuckle off while I was holding on to the tree. My head was on the other side of the tree, level with my right hand. The would-be assassins didn't even know then that I was hit, and they stopped shooting because it was so dark in the woods they were apparently afraid of popping each other. I was on my home turf, and I slipped away from them. I ripped my

T-shirt off and wrapped it around my hand to soak up the blood while I splashed through creeks and stuff, running for my life. The woods was only about half a mile from a friend's house, and I lost the gang before I roared through his front door. He took one look at me, then turned around and pulled a couple of rifles from a gun rack on the wall. He lifted a box of cartridges out of a cabinet drawer. It was only then, after he was all prepared for a fight, that he patched up my hand. It was just another war injury, and it wouldn't be the last.

But there was no way I could let that shit continue, and I knew something had to be done about it. We had to arrange a sit-down and end this thing or go to war. I laid low at my friend's house for a while until I could get my gang together and take care of business. I rounded up bikers, Italian and Irish mobsters, everybody who was involved in the rackets and had an interest in keeping peace. We managed to work things out with the Kallikaks without any more violence, and I kept my business.

In fact I branched out and opened some new enterprises. I used pirated credit-card numbers in a barrage of flimflams. It still amazes me at how quickly an otherwise intelligent person will hand over their credit-card number and other personal information to a whore or to some other stranger. I gathered thousands of card numbers from our clients at A Touch of Class and the massage parlors, along with birth dates, social security numbers, and addresses—everything I needed to turn the plastic into money.

The secret to making money with stolen credit cards or pirated numbers is to move fast once you start. Buy everything you can before the numbers begin showing up on hot sheets that credit-card companies use to list forged or stolen plastic. Then, when the balance is up there close to the limit, get rid of the old card or numbers and switch to a new one. The other half of the scam called for turning the merchandise into cash. With my connections, that was no problem. Television sets, computers, printers, or boom boxes, jewelry or designer clothes; if it was quality goods, there was a black market for it. If there was a black market for it, there was somebody to fence it.

Credit-card swindles are games of wits, as fascinating and as full of doubledealing, bluffs, and showdowns as a hand of crooked poker. Also like poker, when one game gets old you simply switch to another. It's as simple as changing from seven-card stud to five-card draw.

The credit-card business was good to me, but after awhile the St. Louis police were breathing down my neck. So I moved to another county, bought protection, and made so much money I began investing in legitimate business. I bought dump trucks and spreader boxes and went into the asphalt business in the summer, and the snow- and ice-removal business in the winter. My company subcontracted for the highway department, and my trucks went out with their plows and loads of salt and cinders whenever it snowed. The salt and cinders were stored on my property, so as soon as there was even a trace of snow, I loaded my trucks and got them all ready. Once the trucks were loaded and the drivers were on the job, they sat around waiting to begin clearing streets and roads. The going rate was $65 an hour for each truck, and I always sent at least ten of them out. I paid the guys $6 an hour to work for me, so I made good money.

The action in the massage parlors and escort services was beginning to drop off anyway. Everybody was getting scared over the AIDS epidemic, and my accounts receivable were going to hell. The police were also keeping the pressure on and constantly harassed me. And I probably stepped on some wrong toes while I was fooling around with credit cards. So I got out of vice and moved back into robberies. That's when I stepped in shit.

I stuck up another thief who robbed a drug dealer of ten kilograms of cocaine. That's a lot, and it was easily worth $100,000 at that time. It was the kind of score that could have given me some breathing room to get my business affairs in order and take some time off. The coke thief worked at a gas station and convenience store in Arnold, Missouri, and I walked in there one night while he was alone and stuck the barrel of a big .357-caliber magnum up to his head. I had a nylon stocking pulled over my head and a ski mask pulled on over that.

"Now, I got a choice for you to make," I told him. "You can turn over the shit you stole to me. Or I can pull the trigger on this cannon. It's your call. Which is it going to be?"

He decided to hand over the drugs, which he had stashed in a little safe. He also cleaned out the cash drawer for me. A bunch of checks and credit-card receipts were mixed in with the money, and I burned them in the fireplace at home. Later I got in my Cadillac and drove by the gas station. The cops were still there looking around, trying to figure out who the thief was.

The guy I ripped off kept back some of the money he had, and he inflated the hell out of the amount I actually made off with. People do that, so there were no hard feelings. Overall he made a smart decision, and I figured I had pulled off a pretty safe score. The so-called victim was a thief himself, so what was he going to do: call the cops and tell them I just ripped off ten kilos of coke that he heisted from some other drug dealers? He didn't exactly do that, but he came close.

One of my home boys flapped his mouth about my score while he was hanging around a tittie bar, and the word got out that George Taylor had struck it rich. The thief I robbed responded by getting together with some of his friends, and they filed a police report fingering me for sticking up the gas station. Considering all the trouble I went to with the stocking and the ski mask to hide my face, there's no way I would have ever been recognized by the station attendant. I knew it was my friend's big mouth that got me in trouble, but it was already too late to do anything about it. I wound up facing twin felony charges of first-degree armed robbery and armed criminal action. I was in major trouble.

Maybe I was starting to grow up or something, but while I was locked up, I started doing some serious thinking about getting out of crime and becoming a citizen. All the threats, violence, paying people off, and trying to stay a step ahead of the law were getting to me. I had a classy girlfriend that I was really sweet on, and when my lawyer got me out on bail, she and I moved to Virginia while my case started moving through the court system in Missouri. My oldest sister and a brother-in-law lived in Fairfax County, Virginia, and he helped me get a job with a concrete company driving a cement truck.

My girlfriend was Victoria "Vicki" Hampton, the stepdaughter of a St. Louis cop. She was a fine-boned little filly about five foot, two inches tall, with smooth, silky skin, and glorious red hair that hung down over her shoulders. She worked at a club as an exotic dancer and had a four-year-old girl, Nicole, from a previous relationship. Vicki was a tough broad, and she didn't take any shit from anybody, including me. One night when she heard I was popping one of the escorts who worked for me, I made the mistake of falling asleep. Next thing I knew she jammed a sharp little steak knife a couple of inches into my belly. She said she thought about performing a John Wayne Bobbitt–style circumcision on me or lopping off the family jewels, but decided to save them. Losing anything would have been a waste. (Bobbitt didn't suffer his loss until a few years later, but Vicki spelled the process out.)

Vicki wasn't looking to do any serious damage and merely wanted to send a message. It hurt like hell, but it wasn't all that bad. She was careful to pick a soft spot just under my belly button, and I didn't even go to the hospital. She taped the cut up for me and it healed by itself. Vicki was totally pissed, and said she wanted to leave a mark so I would always remember her. She got what she wanted. I still got the scar, and I know it will never go away. We got things together and I was more careful for a while when I played around. I was a wild thing when I was young.

There was no question I was in serious trouble over the robbery. Each count they filed against me carried maximum penalties of twenty years. It was out of character for me to use a gun on a job, and I didn't have any firearms violations on my record, so I figured the judge wouldn't be too tough. Hardly anybody got the maximum. I knew of course that I was going to have to do some time, and I thought about trying to cut a deal. Vicki and I guessed I would probably draw two or three years at Jefferson City. I'd been there before, and a couple of years wasn't a lifetime, so I was ready to take my lumps. I was all set to go in, do my time, stay out of trouble and work for an early parole. Vicki and I talked things over, and we agreed that I would stick to the straight and narrow when I got out so that we could start building a real life for ourselves.

Then our world began to collapse. I already had two previous felony convictions on my record, and the police were talking about taking a closer look into some earlier drug ripoffs they suspected I was involved in, as well as the credit-card scams I ran while I had the escort service and massage parlors. Prosecutors back in Jefferson County advised my lawyer they were thinking about pressing charges of Continuing Criminal Enterprises against me, and anybody who was in the crime business knew a CCE was no small thing. I was facing some serious misery.

They were branding me as a career criminal, like a John Gotti, who should be permanently removed from society. Nobody seemed to give a shit that the guy I robbed was a robber himself, and the people he heisted were drug dealers. I mean, who did the prosecutors think they were protecting by picking on me? They wanted to lock me up for thirty years, real time, almost exactly as long as I had been around on this earth.

3

Rolling Over

MY PROSPECTS WERE rotten and Vicki and I didn't appear to have much that was good to look forward to when I took a telephone call from Dan Swan, an intelligence officer with the St. Louis Metropolitan Police Department. Swan was assigned to a joint federal and state organized crime task force investigating organized crime, drugs, and political corruption in the St. Louis area, and he was prepared to offer me a deal.

If I would agree to rat on my friends, and didn't lie or try to pull any double-crosses, Swan and his colleagues would do what they could to see that I got a break when it was time for my sentencing.

I wasn't raised to become a snitch. I grew up with criminals, played with them, and worked with them. My criminal friends were my life, and it was a life based on a single precept—snitches were the lowest scum on earth. But if I spent the next thirty years behind bars I wouldn't have a life. Two or three years in Jeff City was something I could live with. Doing a minute. That's convict talk for a short sentence. Life in the slammer was another story.

Vicki and I had already been talking about what we wanted to do with our future. I had had a gutful of crime and living the life of a hoodlum, going from one drug rip-off and credit-card scam to another, always figuring the next deal while looking over my shoulder to see if the cops were closing in. There was even more danger from friends when people were in the crime business. No one could trust the people they worked with or the people they hung out with. They might not rat on you, but they might not hesitate to stab you in the back, either. Everybody was on the make every minute of every day, and I was sick of the life. Settling down was looking more appealing than it ever had before. So I told Swan I was interested and willing to talk about his proposition.

Swan and his pals, who included the IRS, wanted to know everything about the vice business in the St. Louis area. Michael Reap, a deputy U.S. Attorney for the Eastern District of Missouri, was in on the deal with Swan and was supervising his office's activities in the vice investigation.

Eventually various big-shots with the federal government promised Vicki and me everything. We heard all about this fantastic program for rehabilitated gangsters who rolled. We would both get new IDs. Even Vicki's daughter would get a new name and identification so we could start over with new lives on the outside. The new identities would be created with top-of-the-line documentation, and the feds would do all the work. I wouldn't have to bother roaming around some cemetery until I found a tombstone with a birthdate close to my own, then use it to obtain a birth certificate, and follow-up with all the other necessary documentation like Social Security cards, medical and school records, that sort of thing. Everything would be handed to us on a platter.

Instead of prison time we were told we would be relocated, given enough money to buy a used car, and set up with a small business loan if we wanted it. Some witnesses were even awarded bonuses for their work on cases that resulted in convictions of big-time hoodlums. That was the deal for both of us. We were, like, "Wow, this is great. A second chance. We're never going to get a deal like this again."

Vicki wasn't in any trouble, so she basically agreed to roll in order to help me. I was her man, then. She got in a minor fracas with the law one time for dancing on a table, but she had all her clothes on and nothing came of it. She kept her nose clean and never had any felonies. Most of her problems came from the company she kept, hanging around with people like me.

We didn't even think about talking to a lawyer first. After all, except for the cops, most of the people we were tied into were lawyers. Deputy attorney generals and prosecutors. Power dudes! Besides, I was a smart guy. I had made my living all my life dealing with lawyers, cops, and crooks—sometimes they were all the same—and I figured I knew what I was doing. It was just another double con, but an important one. We had something they wanted, and they had something we wanted. We spilled our guts.

I was going to become the guy that prosecutors referred to among themselves as "a dirty witness." I could help them out with certain crook-catching services that only another crook could provide. But my services, like those of any other mouth, wouldn't come without special problems. Nobody on either side of the fence would trust me.

When I testified on the witness stand, I could expect defense attorneys to bring up everything I had ever done, thought of doing, or was repelled by. They would grill me about what I was promised to testify. How much was I paid? Did I steal from blind men, rape old ladies, dismember and eat babies? And they would pepper me with those "Do you still beat your wife?" kind of questions. Defense attorneys are slick and as ruthless about carrying out their work as any serial killer is about his. They know how to make you sound guilty and like the worst kind of liar no matter how you answer.

Police and prosecutors would check out everything I told them, then double- and triple-check the information. They would do their own interviews, surveillance, and other investigations to corroborate everything I told them. I would be hooked up to the lie box so many times that it would become almost as much of an everyday occurrence as wearing a wristwatch.

Police and prosecutors wouldn't trust me, but they would need me. My testimony and other work getting the goods on racketeers or corrupt politicians and businessmen could make the difference between a successful investigation and prosecution or total failure. It would be the defense lawyers' job to destroy my credibility by making me admit in open court that I was a cheater, a liar, and a thief. And it would be the job of police and prosecutors, the people who had always been my traditional enemies, to rebuild my reputation or prop it up sufficiently to impress a jury or a judge that even though all those bad things were true—this time I was telling the truth.

That was the easy part. When it was all over, the only friends I would have left in this world would be people like me: other snitches—cornered mobsters, crooked lawyers, corrupt politicians, con-men, pathological liars, and ruthless killers who would sell out their best friend or their country for a reduced prison sentence or an early parole.

It was the old story that everybody thinks of when they're feeling sorry for themselves: I wish I knew then what I know now. When somebody like me rolls over

and turns on their friends, there is no going halfway or
turning back. Once you start talking to the law, it's like
Brer Rabbit and the tarbaby. You can't get out, and the
more you fight and struggle, the more tangled up you
get in the tar.

Vicki and I didn't know that when we left Virginia
and returned to St. Louis to work with the task force.
They paid all the expenses and had everything waiting
for me at the U.S. Marshals Office in Alexandria, Virginia. I picked up the airplane tickets, money for out-of-
pocket expenses, meals, all that stuff, at the office. I was
feeling good when I climbed aboard the airliner at the
Washington National Airport, like I had cut a real sweetheart deal for myself.

Before I knew it, I was on a first-name basis with
county prosecutors, deputy U. S. attorneys, St. Louis city
police, IRS agents, people with the federal Bureau of
Alcohol, Tobacco and Firearms (BATF) the DEA, and
the FBI. The Secret Service even got in on it. Everybody
wanted a piece of the new boy on the block, and they
were looking for information and help setting up stings.

Tape recorders became as much a part of my life as
eating or sleeping. I was as comfortable talking on tape
as I was with using a telephone. Everything I said was
recorded, then transcribed by secretaries, checked,
double-checked by investigators, and placed in thick ac-
cordion files. Some of the information made its way to
courtrooms, and some didn't. Decisions about what use
should or could be made of data I provided weren't up
to me. I just answered questions, talked—and betrayed
my friends.

Some days I talked for ten or twelve hours straight,
with only a couple of breaks for a Big Mac, some fries
and coffee, or a quick pit-stop in the bathroom. They
came at me in shifts. One guy or a couple of guys would
question me for an hour or two, then they'd be replaced

by two different guys with a totally different set of questions. One of the things they always did was try to break down my stories. They'd look for holes in it—tried to catch me in lies. I didn't like that, but it was a necessary evil. If I was lying, or simply made a mistake, it was better to catch it right away than wait until we were in some courtroom where a defense attorney could make everybody look stupid or dishonest. When that happens, an entire investigation can go down the drain.

It was hard work. Mentally and emotionally exhausting. But eventually, I provided information that helped shut down a couple of my former competitors in the escort service and massage-parlor business, Marsha C. Frederickson and Dennis W. Sonnenschein. Nailing down the people running the vice business in the St. Louis area was just the beginning. But that got me in the most trouble.

Task-force officers and members of the St. Louis Metropolitan Police Department Vice Squad forced me to turn over my client lists and other business records from A Touch of Class and the massage parlors. I watched with a couple of vice cops while one of their pals dug up the metal box with the diskettes from the backyard of my next-door neighbor.

More than 5,000 names were stored on the diskettes, and some of them belonged to important people in law enforcement and government. A couple of days after the cops seized my client list, they had a talk with me in a little interview room in an area of the downtown federal building on Market Street that was set aside for the IRS. I was being questioned by an IRS agent and some vice-squad cops when Reap hurried into the room with a couple of FBI agents trailing behind him.

They were all agitated about something, and I knew I was in for some kind of trouble when they hustled me outside, through the hallway and into another room.

They found a bunch of Washington, D. C. area telephone numbers and other stuff on my diskettes, and they
were acting like they were ready to blast into orbit.

"I don't know what that shit is," I told them. "Hey,
I have a couple thousand phone and credit-card numbers
on those diskettes. How in the hell can I tell you what
you want to know if you don't give me a name to go
with the numbers? It could be anybody."

So they showed me a printout with the congressman's
name and a bunch of other information. I figured that
was what had them upset anyway, but they were going
to have to tell me up front. I don't like playing games,
unless they're my games.

"Yeah, that's the guy's private number," I said.

They were really pissed off and demanded to know
how I got the number, and I told them. "He gave it to
me." I had his credit card numbers, his mother's home
phone number, an office number in Jefferson City, and
other stuff.

The Gs were beside themselves, and I had never seen
them lose their cool like that. They tried to tell me I
made up the stuff about the congressman. I kept my part
of the deal and I was being straight with the task-force
guys and everybody else, and I didn't like being called
a liar. I asked the agents where in the fuck they thought
I got the credit-card information if I was lying to them.
But they had been around the block a few times and
heard all the routines.

"You're full of shit," one of the FBI guys growled,
getting up close and sticking his face in mine so that I
could see the puss-yellow that passed for the whites of
his eyes. He was tired and fed up. His face was flushed,
and he was so agitated that he was wheezing.

"You keep laying this bullshit on us, and you can
count on spending the rest of your life in the slammer.
I'll make it my personal responsibility to see that they

bury you so deep inside, you couldn't dig your way out with your own backhoe.''

What could I do? I demanded to talk to a lawyer.

That wasn't the response they wanted, so they tried something else. They told me they would see to it that I was granted full immunity if I cooperated completely with them. My slate would be wiped clean, and I could start over, as fresh as a newborn baby. Then they made it clear that complete cooperation included a promise that I would never reveal anything to anyone else about the people on my client list. If I broke the promise and talked anyway, the deal was off. I didn't have a choice. I told them we had a deal.

Within a few weeks, more people in the vice business were reeling from a series of police raids. Some of the same asshole cops who were being paid off were suddenly shutting down cathouses and massage parlors, picking up escorts and scaring the hell out of marks all over the St. Louis and southern Illinois area. And the IRS was moving in behind all the cops, with their pinstripe-suited accountants, lawyers, ledgers, and adding machines to make tax cases against the big boys.

One time I had a meeting set up with a boss of the St. Louis Mob at a club called Calico's Span Disco to buy a bunch of diamonds, gold, and that kind of stuff. It was all hot, and I was supposed to be arranging a major buy. The task-force guys fixed me up with a little transmitter built into a Bic lighter. It was a beautiful piece of work, wireless cutting-edge technology with half a mile range, and it was set up to work like any other lighter with a real flame and everything. They asked me not to use it to light cigarettes unless I absolutely had to, however, because it was such sensitive equipment and it cost a small fortune to refill it with butane.

That little spy device was a lifesaver. When I got to

the disco, my friend told me there was going to be a little delay. He had arranged for some of his crew to show up in a motor home so they could check me for wires. I was instructed to go inside, take off every piece of clothing I was wearing and put on an entire new outfit he had waiting for me. So I changed clothes, but I asked them if I could keep my cigarettes and my lighter.

"Sure, go ahead. Keep 'em!" That's what I did, and a little later when I talked with my friend, task-force monitors who were outside in a surveillance van listened to the entire conversation and taped it.

I had already rolled on my associates in the vice business and local mobsters I'd known for years anyway, so it was no big deal when the task-force guys told me they wanted help busting drug smugglers. They knew about my days with Richie, and about the contacts I made while I was hanging out with the Hell's Angels. I agreed to help and began scheming with the DEA to grab some of the Mexicans who were smuggling dope into the country from across the border. Reap also worked on the case, lending supervision from St. Louis and the federal level.

We went all over the country, including Galveston, and down around the south Texas and Mexican border towns of Brownsville and Matamoros. I didn't give a second thought to signing that paper promising to stay out of Texas. I had important people now to back me up. California, Arizona, we hit all the big southwestern states where dope was flowing across the border in every imaginable way. It came across in airplanes; gangs built elaborate air-conditioned tunnels; shipped it hidden inside of furniture; inside dead bodies; and people called mules swallowed it in balloons or condoms, then walked across the border and waited for nature to take its course so they could retrieve it and sell it to some junkie.

Juan Garcia Abrego was a big-time smuggler who

worked the Brownsville-Matamoros border area and started business by floating bales of grass across the Rio Grande. By the time he was finally captured in the mid-1990s by narcs in Mexico, drugged, tossed on a plane and flown across the border, the baby-faced drug lord was on the FBI's most wanted list and was making $2 billion a year smuggling cocaine into the United States. Abrego wound up with eleven life sentences.

You catch one smuggler and another takes his place. There's simply too much money in the business to stamp it out. But the feds kept trying. I worked with the DEA for a while when the big guys decided they wanted Raoul Herrera. Raoul was a big-shot dope smuggler, along with some other members of his family, and for a while he supplied most of the heroin for the Chicago area. He was also an old running mate of mine from the days when I worked for Richie, and he had his own ranch outside of Tucson with a landing strip and the whole nine yards. But he was a smart, cagey criminal who stayed in Mexico most of the time and let subordinates take the risks of dealing with the gringos on this side of the Rio Grande.

The feds flew me to Arizona with instructions to lure Raoul across the border. We set up a deal to make a big buy of Mexican brown heroin, and the DEA guys arranged for me to hole up in a motel in Scottsdale. The room was set up with a hidden camera and a microphone, so the DEA operatives in the next room could listen and watch everything that was going on. Raoul was supposed to be carrying 100 pounds of heroin on him when he met me in my room. As soon as I uttered a code word the DEA had given me, they were in on us like gangbusters. Big guys dressed all in black, wearing flak jackets and carrying machine guns streamed in through the doors and windows. Raoul knew exactly what role I played in the bust, and he would have killed me on the spot if he could. But they were on him too fast.

It was a big operation, and at the same time they were grabbing Raoul other DEA, BATF and customs agents were moving in on Herrera's guys in the parking lot, and busting people all over Phoenix, Tucson, even across the border in Nogales. But the feds messed it up. They were supposed to see that I got some cover, and they didn't follow through. As soon as the busts came down, everybody on both sides of the border who was involved in the business knew who ratted on them. The DEA agents behaved like a bunch of amateurs and almost got me killed.

The Justice Department (We referred to it as "Main Justice" when talking about the big guys at the headquarters in Washington) had provided thousands of dollars to the task force to make a big buy, and there were plans to go into Mexico. The DEA wanted Raoul to take me and a couple of task-force guys I would introduce as big drug dealers in St. Louis into the poppy fields. It was supposed to be a big-time operation, and we worked for a couple of months setting it up.

Then I learned, too late, that all the task-force people really wanted was a bunch of publicity. They didn't give a shit about doing the job the way it was supposed to be carried out. We wound up with a couple of piddling buys, but nothing like the major amounts I had set up with Raoul. Basically the operation was a fucking disaster. The DEA agents behaved like a bunch of bush-league novices. The cop-out on the big buy was suspicious enough, and matters were made worse when the DEA clowns and local narcs rounded up a few low-level flunkies tied to the Herrera caper.

Nevertheless, it was a big roundup, and a lot of people got hurt because of me. They were people who were bad to cross, and I had made some dangerous new enemies.

Raoul pulled some serious time after the bust, and the last I heard of him he was supposed to be in the FCI at Leavenworth, Kansas. His people have long memories, and I knew that the border states were permanently off limits for me after the operation.

The gangs who smuggle dope across the Mexican border are totally ruthless; they're armed to the teeth and don't hesitate to kill anybody who gets in their way. Men, women, kids, Catholic priests, politicians, or DEA agents; it doesn't matter. If they get in the way they're gone. Snitches, in particular, tend to have short lives. The Herrera gang, whose tentacles reached from the Mexican states of Sonora and Chihuahua to St. Louis and Chicago, was as cold-blooded and vicious as any of them. Members of the gang lived by the old maxim of the Wild West: Shoot first and ask questions later. Now it was also finger-pointing time, and fingers were all pointed at me.

My cover was blown for nothing, and I was pissed off big-time over being needlessly exposed to so much danger. But the foul-up and the danger to me was no big deal to the DEA. Their agents simply moved on to other projects while I lost credibility and the trust of some very nasty outlaws who were dangerous to cross. So while the scam was still going down, I pinched a half ounce of the high-grade skag for myself. I had big legal bills and needed the money.

Accompanied by a couple of U. S. marshals, I boarded an airliner and was flown back to St. Louis. I sat in the 707 just like any other citizen, wearing civilian clothes, leafing through the inflight magazine and munching on peanuts. When the stewardess came by with the drink cart, the marshals ordered for me. I had orange juice.

One of the task-force guys served as my mule to get the heroin back to St. Louis for me. He didn't know it, of course, but it was stuffed into a pack of Marlboros I asked him to carry for me. Three or four cigarettes were left inside to make it look good.

Nothing was going the way it was supposed to, though. When the agents checked the heroin and realized the weight was short, they figured out in a hurry where the missing shit went. The heroin was gummy, and when I pinched a sample, I left a pretty good set of my fingerprints on the little plastic baggie it was in. They didn't like being double-crossed, and even before the heroin-pinching incident, they had their noses out of joint because they thought I was covering up for some of my contacts in the biker gangs. They were right. I never ratted on a renegade biker in the St. Louis area, in California, or anywhere else.

The task-force guys were fed up with me, and they pointed out in their uniquely forceful manner that I had violated the terms of my agreement with them by stealing the heroin and protecting a bunch of hoodlum bikers—so they were cutting me loose, and the agreement was down the drain. Basically they were telling me that all my cooperation and everything I did for them, the DEA and every other law-enforcement agency I had helped, was for nothing.

It was looking again like I might be facing the next thirty years of my life locked up in Jefferson City. And my prospects now were even bleaker than they were before I began cooperating with the task force. Stories were already circulating throughout the St. Louis underworld that I couldn't be trusted anymore. And snitches in prison don't last long.

About the only good thing to be said about what was happening to me was that for the time being, the task force had put me up in a nice hotel in St. Louis—the Riverside Holiday Inn. It's on the river, right in front of the famous arch. Task-force investigators always stayed in first-class accommodations. I would be put up in my own room, usually a suite, and a couple of investigators stayed next door. My handlers were so pissed off at me by the time we returned to St. Louis, however, that they literally abandoned me at the hotel. I was on my own, and they didn't even provide me with a plane ticket to fly back to Virginia.

So I figured, what the hell, if they're going to leave me stranded here I'm going to live good. People at the hotel thought I was DEA, and I took advantage of the opportunity to run up an $1,800 bill for room service. I just told the hotel people to put everything on my boss's credit card, while I feasted on fine steaks, drank champagne, tipped big-time, and enjoyed all the amenities for two days before the agents found out what was going on and put a stop to my high living. One of the older agents was all red-faced and acted like he was going to pop a blood vessel. I had dumped his ass and the asses of his pals in a wringer. Uncle Sam picked up the check, but they had to do the explaining.

I was a very unpopular dude, and my court case was all cranked up again just as if I had never helped the St. Louis vice cops, the IRS, DEA, or anybody connected to the law. Some of the task-force guys were even threatening to prosecute me for the drug rip-off, as well as charges of fraud because I lived it up at the Holiday Inn and stuck them with the bill. There wasn't much, if anything, a lawyer I talked to could do for me. It looked like I was facing a long stretch behind bars.

4

Mad Dog

THE TASK-FORCE GUYS didn't like me, but fortunately they still needed me. It was the one thing I had going for me, and it led to an offer of one more chance to redeem myself.

About eight weeks before my scheduled trial date, they contacted me in Fairfax County, Virginia, where I was driving a concrete mixer again, and said they wanted me back in St. Louis. They told me that if I would help out on some important investigations focusing on narcotics, stolen food stamps, credit-card fraud, and political corruption, they would go to bat for me. They promised to shield me from federal prosecution for past offenses, and said if I turned in a good performance on the investigations, they would do everything they could to work out a deal that would allow me to walk or get off with a short sentence on the robbery charges.

It was the only game in town, and I took it. Vicki and her little girl returned to St. Louis, while I gave two week's notice to my boss. My employers were very good to me, and when everything was over in St. Louis, I hoped to be able to return and get my old job back.

This time when I sat down with the government guys in the federal building back home, we put the agreement about immunity from federal prosecution in writing. The rest of the deal was a handshake, because the best the task-force guys could do was promise to do their best for me in the local county courts. It was good enough, and I went back to work.

The next nine months were busy. My trial date was postponed, and I worked twelve-hour days, seven days a week, setting people up for the task force. I made drug buys, put together deals to buy stolen food stamps, and cruised the underbelly of St. Louis criminal society full-time. I wore wires and introduced undercover cops to the bad guys. One of the people the task force asked for help with was a mad-dog drug dealer named Eugene Michael Fleer. Geno Fleer and I had run a few deals together in the past.

Fleer looked real clean cut, but he was a wild beast, a two-time loser and ex-con with important mob connections in St. Louis who snorted coke, ate valiums by the handfuls, guzzled whiskey, and made a precarious living as a drug peddler. He was about five foot, ten inches or so, slim, with a clear, olive complexion. He trimmed his hair short, and dressed neat like a preppie. He was a good example of how deceiving appearances can be.

In one way, we shared some of the same work habits. Neither of us had spent much time working at straight jobs. Fleer did a little roofing now and then when he was seriously short on cash, but for the most part he was like me. He was a professional criminal. The big difference between us was that Geno was a lot more violent.

That's how two innocent kids, a three-year-old boy named Tyler Patrick Winzen and his fifteen-year-old baby-sitter, Stacy Price, ended up dead. Their deaths accounted for two of the more nastier murders in recent

Missouri history, and led to years of complicated trial proceedings that had me involved up to my ears.

Vicki and I lived just down the hill from the apartment in rural Jefferson County when the kids were found dead early on the morning of August 7, 1986. The apartment where Tyler lived with his mother is a couple of minutes south of Fenton. It's out in the sticks, the kind of place where parents figure it's safe to let their kids play outside at night. All that changed when the bodies of Tyler and the teenager who lived across the street from him were found dumped in the bathtub.

Cop cars were all over the place, and yellow crime-scene tape was stretched across the front door when Vicki and I walked up the hill to see what all the commotion was about. Eventually we learned what was going on. Both of the kids were drowned. The girl was also strangled and sodomized. The Jefferson County medical examiner concluded after the autopsy that her face and head were probably battered against the sides of the toilet bowl because of the pattern of the bruises. The killer poured scalding water over the bodies in what police said was an apparent effort to get rid of semen, fingerprints, and various trace evidence. But the lack of burn damage on the inside of their throats indicated the scalding water wasn't used in the drownings.

Anytime two innocent children are murdered, people are outraged. Authorities and citizens in St. Louis were determined to bring the killer to justice for committing the savage, senseless crime. Police, with the backing of an angry, noisy press, put the pressure on. They wanted the killer, and fast.

Homicide investigators quickly figured out there was an organized-crime connection, and the kids were either in the wrong place at the right time, or were murdered for some other reason tied to the drug-trafficking business. It was the kind of murder that no intelligent gangster wants anything to do with, and the big guys in the local mob knew that the heat was going to stay on until police had their killer—or he was permanently taken out of the picture.

After talking with John Foens, a maintenance man who worked at an apartment building across the street, police began focusing their investigation on two men. One of the guys was a tenant in the building where the maintenance man worked, Lester Howlett. The other guy was Geno Fleer. Steve Winzen, Tyler's daddy, was also a key figure in the investigation. He was divorced from Tyler's mother, Mari, shortly before the killings.

Foens told investigators that as soon as he learned of the killings, he went looking for his friend Howlett. According to Foens, Howlett greeted the news with a blank look, like it was no surprise. Then he mumbled something about, "I guess we better tell Steve." Before dealing with the job of telling the bereaved father, however, Howlett shot up a hit of cocaine. Foens said he also snorted a line. Then they telephoned Steve Winzen in Las Vegas to give him the bad news.

The maintenance man said Howlett also asked him to take a lockbox full of cocaine to Fleer's trailer in a mobile home court near the town of Imperial, because the police were expected to come by for a look around.

Fleer became part of the equation when Foens informed police he saw him near Winzen's apartment on the day of the killing. Then police learned that Geno and Howlett were cocaine-dealing partners. Howlett was one of the first people investigators talked with, but they weren't immediately able to book him for anything. So they let him go after telling him to stick around the area in case they wanted to talk with him again.

Two days after the bodies of the children were discovered, Howlett was found dead of an overdose in Geno's trailer. The same medical examiner who reported on the cause of death of the two kids confirmed that an autopsy on Howlett's remains showed massive amounts of unmetabolized cocaine in his lungs and in his piss. The ME didn't use the term, but the word was out on the street that Howlett died of a hot-shot. Someone slipped him cocaine that was so pure that he overdosed while he was shooting up with people he thought he could trust because they were his pals. There was another strange thing about Howlett's overdose; word got around that his body was cut and bruised and had bite marks on it.

With Howlett mysteriously dead of an overdose, detectives were more interested than ever in looking at the activities of his reputed dope-dealing partner. Fleer was especially intriguing to them because Howlett died in his trailer. Fleer was never the most sophisticated criminal, and if he had kept his mouth shut he might have gotten away with the double murders. But he was stupid, in addition to being a brutal psychopath. He talked to a girlfriend, and he talked to me. The murders didn't put him away; his big mouth did.

I've done enough time in prisons to know where scumbags who sexually abuse or murder children rank on the pecking order. They're at the bottom, where they belong. If the suspicions of the homicide boys were on target and Fleer was guilty of the crime, he violated both taboos—sodomizing the girl and murdering her and the little boy.

This was one case where I didn't have a second thought about helping the Man wrap up a case against one of my old associates. I'll put on my white hat and snitch on a scumbag like Geno Fleer anytime. I was almost too helpful because eventually I provided police with so many details about the home and the crime scene that they began to wonder if I may have been personally involved. Vicki and I were never inside the house, but

I identified the color of the towels in the bathroom and gave the DA so much information that was on target that they started giving me funny looks.

Fleer was suspicious of me, but he didn't have many friends and he was hurting. Even he couldn't believe what he did, and he had been on a fierce drunken, drug-fueled binge for days when we got together to talk in Calico's Span Disco. He was slobbering and his eyes were misting with tears when he told me about the killings. He said he went to the apartment looking for Winzen but found the kids alone. The girl panicked and started to scream, so he whacked her. Then he had to do the little boy. He was proud of one thing, though. His eyes sparkled when he told me about boiling the water on the stove so he could pour it on the kids and destroy the evidence of any fingerprints he left on the bodies. Smart!

The bad news was that some local racketeers were fed up with all the heat generated by the stupid killings and put the finger on him for execution, according to Geno. He figured out that the best way to stay alive was to take out two of the mob bosses before he was popped by their hitmen. He explained that he told me about the killings of the two kids because he wanted to make sure I knew how serious the situation was.

I had a tough-guy reputation in Missouri then, as the kind of dude who would do anything for a price. Geno wanted me to do the job and take out two important people in St. Louis—Tommy Drago and Joe Martin. Joe's last name is really Martini, but he dropped the *i* years ago. Martin and Drago were tight, and involved in a lot of things. Very powerful guys in certain circles in St. Louis.

Geno's girlfriend's father was a jeweler, and the worried hoodlum promised to pay me off with diamonds heisted from her old man's store. I'm not a hit man and never wanted to be, but I acted like I was interested. I wanted Geno to keep talking, and he was drugged-up and drunk enough so that he described the murders.

He claimed the boy's father was a coke dealer who ripped off him and his running mate, Howlett, for a couple of kilos of cocaine. Their bosses wanted a message sent. He said he was supposed to beat Winzen up and give him a good stomping to make a statement that it wasn't smart to rip off the wrong people for their cocaine. But when Geno went to the house and found the kids there alone, he got carried away. Coke heads can be like that.

Bad news. Although I wore a wire on Geno while we were discussing some drug deals, I wasn't wired when he told me about the double murder and asked me to take out the contract. The good news was that the prosecutor and local homicide investigators developed other sources of information. The assistant prosecutor assigned to the case was later quoted in the *Post-Dispatch* saying Geno told a girlfriend that Steve Winzen arranged a coke deal that the two dopehead pals, Fleer and Howlett, figured was a rip-off.

Even though I didn't have the murder-for-hire conversation on tape, I was ready to nail the mad dog's ass to the barn door and testify in court about our conversation, when problems again developed with the task force. My handlers began reneging on their promise to get the state charges against me dropped.

Before I even went undercover on Fleer, I signed an "official" witness agreement for the case that carefully outlined my responsibilities and the prosecutors' responsibilities to me. It was witnessed by seven people, including five federal marshals, by Vicki, and by my brother, but somebody up the line decided the agreement wasn't binding on the government. Suddenly I was being told that I was expected to keep my part of the bargain, but the government wasn't. And I was supposed to be the gangster?

When the task-force investigators started picking apart the witness agreement, I began to lose interest in the Fleer case. I was sick of being used by the feds and local cops as a flunky. If they wouldn't keep their promises, I was through doing their dirty work. I was willing to help nail Fleer, but I wanted something in return. As I saw it, there were no other options available to me.

I decided to sit for awhile on the information about the incriminating conversation Geno had with me at the disco, but I wasn't finished with him. Other complications would develop that would keep me tied up with his case for years.

Without the story of my conversation with Fleer at the disco, the prosecutor's entire case was built on circumstantial evidence. And when you were considering a case where there seemed to be a very good chance that the death penalty would be involved, the prosecutor needed more than circumstantial evidence. Juries had demonstrated in the past that they wanted rock-solid evidence of guilt before returning verdicts that would lead to a defendant ending his life in the death chamber with gas or a lethal injection. The condemned in the Show-Me State are given a choice of how to die.

My testimony was an important bargaining chip, and I couldn't afford to squander it. The decision inevitably led to a serious ongoing disagreement with John S. Appelbaum, the assistant–Jefferson County prosecuting attorney who was handling the Fleer case. Of course, Appelbaum was bound and determined that I was going to testify, like it or not. Eventually I wound up filing a lawsuit against him for $50,000, but dropped it. Actually he treated me fairly, and I realized that he was just trying to do his job and put Fleer away for the rest of his life.

The murder investigation slowed, and the story was

gradually replaced on the front pages and on six o'clock newscasts by newer murders and other more recent outrages. Fleer finally pleaded guilty to cocaine possession in return for a four-year sentence.

In the meantime, while the murder investigation dragged on, I continued to rat on my friends. Organized criminal gangs and their associates lead an incestuous existence. Everybody knows at least a little about what other people are doing, and it was inevitable that the word would get around that I had rolled and was working for the other side. Police and prosecutors can sit on sensitive information, like the identities of informants, for only so long before it begins leaking out to criminal defense lawyers, courthouse workers—or through careless or corrupt police officers. You may as well try to carry water in a sieve as to try and keep a criminal from figuring out who is ratting on them.

And I'd been at it for four years at that point. My luck couldn't hold out forever, and it didn't. I was doing too much, too fast.

I had just made a monitored purchase of some coke when one of my few remaining friends tipped me off that I was in trouble. He was in jail and he used the only call he was allowed that day to give me a warning.

"I'm just telling you up front, and one time," he said. "You'd better get moving and get your ass out of town."

My girlfriend, Vicki, was in almost as much trouble as I was. And she was easier to find. She was dancing at a local club. We were both worried about ourselves and about her little girl.

When I talked to the detective who was my control and told him I thought someone was going to try to kill my girlfriend and me, he said I didn't have anything to worry about. Arrangements were already being made to move us into the federal Witness Security Program, WITSEC. Among the press and most of the public who had heard of it, WITSEC was better known as the federal witness-protection program.

5

Disaster

ORGANIZED CRIME TASK Force investigators had one more little job for me to work on before moving me out of St. Louis and firmly into the witness-protection program. They wanted my help getting the goods on some politicians and bureaucrats from rural Jefferson County who were being investigated on suspicions of corruption.

Three of the people they were looking at were my lawyer, a county-court judge, and a big-time bail bondsman named Everett Foster.

My lawyer at that time was D. Clinton Almond, a senior partner in the Jefferson County–based law firm of Almond, Williams & Brady. One of his partners, Marsha Brady (no joke), also did work for me but wasn't under investigation. The firm's office was on Courthouse Square, a couple of minutes walk from the Jefferson County courthouse in the center of Hillsboro.

The jurist was John L. Anderson, who just happened to be the judge who was named to preside over my armed robbery trial.

They also eventually checked out Jefferson County sheriff Walter "Buck" Buerger and some other high-ranking officials in his department. Buerger was one of the most powerful politicians in the St. Louis area and had close political ties to the local golden boy, Congressman Richard "Dick" Gephardt, who was Speaker of the House until he had to turn the gavel over to Newt Gingrich.

If I wasn't already one of the most hated men in the St. Louis area, I was rapidly closing in on the title. But I went along with the new game plan. Vicki, who had her daughter to worry about in addition to sharing many of the problems I was facing, was also roped into the scheme. There wasn't much choice for either of us.

I helped the task force set up wiretaps so they could listen in and tape Foster talking about food-stamp and credit-card scams. Prosecutors like tapes, especially when they're working with someone like me, a confidential informer. During cross-examination, a skillful defense lawyer can be expected to try and convince a jury that I'm such a scumbag I can't even be trusted to tell the truth when I recite my name. It's more difficult to cross-examine and destroy the credibility of a tape.

Carrying a bug on Anderson and Almond was a different story. They were officers of the court and required much more sensitive handling than a mere citizen like the bail bondsman. There was trouble from the beginning. Sergeants Ron Clyier and Salvatore Serra, two St. Louis police department detectives assigned to the task force, tangled with a Secret Service agent over the plan. The local cops insisted that we needed approval from the U.S. Attorney General's Office in Washington before either Vicki or I could carry the bug.

It was a nasty argument, and at six o'clock that afternoon, it was still raging when our handlers called everything off for the day and took Vicki and me back to the Jury Inn Hotel in Arnold where they were hiding us under assumed names. The next morning we were picked up at the hotel and Secret Service agent Terrance Korpal told us to wear the bug or our deal for witness protection was out the window.

We went along with the game. We didn't have an attorney there to advise us about what was in our best interests because, Hell's bells, my lawyer was one of the people the task force was checking out. In that situation, you weigh your chances and your odds. These people tell you there is nothing to worry about. And remember you're not only talking about mere cops, guys who write speeding tickets, break up family fights and chase after street-corner roughnecks or stickup men. An assistant U.S. Attorney is telling you what's going on, and what you should do. They were like God to somebody like me at that time. They had my life on a string, and they could either cut the string or use it to lasso me and pull me out of the soup.

So if all they want in return is a little help with some other case, you help. A trade-off. That was our reasoning.

From the very beginning, when I first started to cooperate, task-force guys assured me that if I did any time at all on the robberies, it would only be a minute. Now some of those guys were asking me to wear a wire on the single individual everyone expected to be making the final decision about my future: the judge.

The task force gave me a baseball cap with a tiny transmitter sewn into the spot where the brim was attached to the crown, and unless somebody was right on top of it, they could hardly see it even if they knew it was there. I was told to wear it in Judge Anderson's courtroom, but I never got the chance. Eventually I took off the cap and gave it to Vicki. She sat in the courtroom with me and held the cap with the bug on her lap. Another time I wanted to wear the bug in the judge's chambers, but he wouldn't talk to me, so the investigators fixed Vicki up with it. She wore the wired cap in the judge's chambers, and she wore it on my lawyer. It was like the transmitter in the lighter. Cops monitored everything it picked up from a surveillance van parked outside. The transmitter could be picked up about half a mile away.

We did what we were told, but it was wasted effort. The whole operation self-destructed, and when the story about the effort to tape the judge got out, a major scandal developed. It was awful, and some of the guys on the task force began to backpedal and lay a major part of the blame for the trouble on me.

It turned out that the task force sent me in on Judge Anderson without getting an okay from the U. S. Justice Department. Even prosecutors and cops don't just go out and eavesdrop on somebody with a wire or a bug. They have to have a court order, or an okay from somebody very high up in the Justice Department. So what we had was a rogue task force. Careers were ruined, and some of the investigators wound up taking early retirement. I heard a few years after everything self-destructed, that a Secret Service agent who was on the task force to investigate counterfeiting of money, food stamps, and credit cards had a nervous breakdown. That's believable to me.

Years later when Mike Reap, the U. S. attorney who headed the task force, was questioned about the affair during a post-conviction hearing for me at the Jefferson County courthouse, he said it was difficult to recall all the details after so long a time, but he believed he "probably" authorized me to wear the wire "under certain restrictions."

Six years after the investigation blew up in everybody's faces, the undercover operation was still an embarrassment to many of the people involved, and old wounds were still festering. Most people felt they would be best left to heal in silence. Reap said at the hearing that I was cautioned about the special legal problems related to wearing a wire on my own attorney, and warned not to discuss my robbery case in Jefferson County.

"I recall that, needless to say, on any undercover situation you want to attempt to control an informant as best you can and give them certain legal advice on entrapment and many other issues," Reap testified. "The fact that Mr. Taylor was represented on a separate case caused us to give additional cautions and advices because of the attorney-client privilege, which Mr. Taylor was advised about by us—that, in effect, what he was doing was, you know, breaching the privilege, and did he want to do it? He said, 'Yes.' "

Reap's rambling run-on sentence was typical courtroom testimony. It's the way people talk under oath, especially when the witnesses doing the testifying are lawyers, who are more aware than most that every word or phrase may be dissected and examined for clunkers and other flaws or slips-of-the-tongue. Real-life courtroom witnesses do not talk in the neat, grammatically correct phraseology of television dramas and other fictional accounts.

Reap also testified that he told me that he and his pals would not ask authorities in Jefferson County to dismiss the armed-robbery charges. All they agreed to do, he said, was to lay the facts on the table so that prosecutors in Jefferson County knew I was cooperating in the other investigations. Then authorities in Jefferson County could make their own decision about whether or not I deserved a break.

The big guys should have listened to Sergeants Serra and Clyier. Everybody involved in the investigation wound up with egg on their faces, and when the local media found out about it, the story became big news for a while. The investigation was in the newspapers, and a local television station broadcast a report about George Taylor wearing a wire on his own attorney. The talking heads broadcast bits and pieces of facts, lots of speculation and innuendo. It was classic television investigative news: full of mistakes and unproven accusations. A lot of it was the type of half-assed reports that don't prove anything but can knock the hell out of reputations.

There was even a hearing into the activities of the Organized Crime Task Force. No charges were ever filed against my lawyer or the judge. The investigation was shut down. It was a big disappointment and led to a lot of tight assholes among task-force investigators. The old pucker factor was working big-time.

However, the troubles the task-force people got into were nothing compared to the problems the affair stirred up for me and Vicki. We were caught smack in the middle of the firestorm, and became the fallguys for much of the shit that came down. The promises of immunity and relocation in the witness-protection program for my girlfriend and me went up in smoke.

Almond wasn't happy with me when he learned that I had worn a wire on him, but he refused to step down as my lawyer. Judge Anderson also refused to recuse himself from the case, and when I at last went to trial on the old robbery charges, there weren't many people left who I could count on as being on my side.

To further complicate matters, Almond was representing Fleer on the twin-murder charges involving the two kids. Later, in post-conviction relief hearings, I accused Almond of failing to interview or put a friend of mine on the witness stand to testify as an alibi witness during the armed-robbery trial. Howard Euell Litel, Jr., lived in a trailer near Fenton and claimed to be a diesel mechanic who fixed boat engines. Howie spent more time shooting dope than working on engines, so you couldn't say he was a big success at his job. Four years after my trial, he died in St. Louis of AIDS. All that intravenous dope shooting with dirty needles finally got him.

I wanted Howie to testify that he was with me at a nightclub called Pops in East St. Louis on April 30, 1985, when the robbery I was charged with actually took place. East St. Louis is an industrial town with big plants, like Montsanto, and the people who live there work hard and play hard. It has a strip of tittie bars—and bookies, connected people and those kind of characters are always hanging around. It was one of my favorite places.

The club and the convenience store were about twenty-five miles from each other. We had the time element worked out so that it would have been impossible for me to have stuck up the dope dealer because I was supposed to be at Pop's when it happened. The story was bullshit, of course, but Howie was ready to say whatever I wanted him to. He was never busted for anything, and he could have been a credible witness. But he didn't get the opportunity to lie for me, so we'll never know if the story would have worked.

Instead the broad I took the escort service and massage parlors away from had testified against me, and said she started doing heroin after meeting me. When the prosecutor asked her why, she said: "It was around. Seemed like the thing to do. . . . It was around a lot when he was around, and I just started doing drugs with him."

That really bothered me. Yeah, I smuggled some skag and I sold it, but I never personally got hung up on that shit. A snort now and then, that was about all. And I didn't hang around with junkies or turn anybody else on to it. I wasn't on trial for possessing heroin and didn't think her testimony about that should have been allowed. But my lawyer didn't even object when the prosecutor was questioning her about it. So in early November 1986, after a two-day trial and four or five weeks after I wore the illegal wires, a Jefferson County Circuit Court jury found me guilty on the robbery charges.

My task-force handlers did speak up for me at my sentencing hearing, and told the judge about the help I provided for local, state, and federal law-enforcement authorities. Reap wrote a three-page letter to the court that was included as part of my pre-sentence report, outlining my work for investigators over the last three or four years. He also addressed the judge in open court just before sentencing.

"I only ask that the court take that into consideration in its decision as to what sentence to impose as far as Mr. Taylor, both the good and the bad and the ugly," Reap said.

U.S. Attorney Thomas E. Dittmeier, who was the Justice Department's top banana in St. Louis, also submitted a letter to the judge pointing out that in his opinion, "that without cooperation from individuals like George Taylor, undercover operations are generally not successful." You better bet your sweet ass they're not. That's my observation, not Dittmeier's.

The statements from Reap and his boss were appreciated, and they may have helped, but they didn't keep me out of prison. Judge Anderson ordered two twenty-year prison sentences. When he read the first sentence, I lurched forward and grabbed the railing in front of me. When he read the second, my legs turned to spaghetti and my knees buckled.

It was a strange, sickly feeling, and my physical reaction was totally different from the other times I had been sentenced to the joint. The judge's voice sounded unreal, like he was speaking through water, or talking through some kind of curious vacuum while he told me that he had planned to sock me with two thirty-year sentences. Because of my cooperation with authorities, he said, he instead decided to trim ten years from each sentence and to order them served concurrently. Big deal!

Even if I stayed out of trouble while I was inside and earned "good time,"—no easy matter, given my new rep amongst my peers—I was looking at eight years. Public defenders later helped me appeal my conviction, and this time Judge Anderson recused himself from the hearing. No matter. We lost, and the sentence stayed the same.

Based on sentencing guidelines, I would be eligible to apply for parole in 1991, but one of the people I had worked with from the task force offered some friendly advice: don't count on an early parole. He pointed out that the congressman whose name was lifted from my computer disks was an ambitious man. He predicted I would stay inside until at least 1996, when my former client expected to run for president. In the meantime, my old client list was locked up tight.

My last night spent in the Jefferson County jail was marked by a solid ass-kicking. I wound up on the floor of the cell with my hands cuffed behind me, trying to get into a fetal position so I could protect the family jewels, my kidneys and head. There's not much else you can do when you can't use your hands and you're being stomped by somebody wearing combat boots. I was semiconscious and a bloody mess by the time my assailants finally had enough. My troubles were just beginning.

6

Jeff City

MY RIDE IN the backseat of a Jefferson County sheriff's department cage car west from Hillsboro to the penitentiary was uneventful. I had too many lumps and hurt too bad to even try to make conversation with the frozen-faced cops up front, and they didn't behave like they were interested in trying to cheer me up even if I had been in the mood for talk.

In addition to the two cops in the front seat, a couple more were trailing behind us in a chase car just in case I tried something. Fat chance. Besides my contusions, I was also wearing a belly chain, handcuffs, and a black box with still more chains extending outside.

Black boxes are little metal bars extending between handcuffs where the short chains are normally placed. The box has a hinge on it with a padlock dangling from the bottom. So it's basically a metal bar between your hands to keep you from trying to pick the lock. You can't move your hands when you're wearing one of them. They're hellishly efficient little devices that have left scars on my wrists, which I'll have for the rest of my life. There wasn't going to be any daredevil break for freedom. I wasn't going anywhere except back to the prison at Jeff City.

After we drove across the Missouri River and the car pulled up to the reception area, the Jeff City hacks took one look at me and the condition I was in and refused to accept custody.

"We're not taking him. You got to take him to a hospital," they said.

The sheriff's deputies weren't impressed. They just shoved the commitment papers at the hacks and told them, "He's yours. You take him to the hospital." Then they were out of there. I spent my first few hours back at Jeff City in the dispensary. I had a broken nose, a couple of missing front teeth. I wasn't a pretty picture. But I survived.

I was moved into H-Hall. That's Receiving and Diagnostic, and every inmate is started off there. You get interviewed there, look at ink blots, and make up stories while prison bureaucrats and social workers figure out just where and how you will fit in best when you're moved into general population. H-Hall was the oldest cell block in the penitentiary and hadn't changed much in more than one hundred years: metal bars, metal floors, and metal ceilings inside a crumbling old brick building.

I didn't expect to fit in at all because I knew the stories that I was a snitch had preceded me. I was really worried because all those cops and prosecutors who used me and Vicki had suddenly washed their hands of us. I had thought since I cooperated with them that I would be sent to some kind of camp, but here I was in the worst penitentiary with the toughest, most ruthless cons in Missouri—and I was going into general population.

After laying around for a month I was fat and out of shape. When I was initially locked up, I was a lean and mean 160 pounds, with a thirty-two-inch waist. Now I looked like a piece of shit, my muscles were flabby and loose. It was rotten timing, and the idea of trying to single-handedly fight off a gang of blood-crazed bikers or St. Louis mobsters with revenge on their minds was a worrisome thing.

The hacks walked me down a long corridor and through some tunnels, then smiled, turned around, and told me: "Well, we'll see y'all. Take care, now." Big joke!

It wasn't as bad as I thought it was going to be, though. When I was led past the control center in C-Hall where the guards sit in a locked room surrounded by bullet-proof glass, I saw a bunch of my homeboys. They were guys from south St. Louis that I knew, and they didn't believe the rumors about me rolling over. They figured I was still a standup guy and they welcomed me with open arms. You can't imagine what it was like walking in there and seeing my friends—and knowing they still were my friends. It was a good feeling.

Whenever some inmate repeated rumors they'd heard that I was a snitch, my friends stood with me and we confronted the big mouth. The talker always backed down. Nobody really knew about me for sure, so I was okay and concentrated on keeping my nose clean and doing my time. I kept busy working with public defenders on motions for post-conviction relief. Vicki hung in there with me for months after I was locked up, pestering the feds to keep their word to us. She sat outside Mike Reap's office for hours at a time, but he never talked to her. She tried contacting different people, and wrote letters to authorities in Jefferson City and Washington, D. C., but eventually she and I drifted apart. She was a good woman, but she had her daughter to think of, and she deserved a life of her own. She had a real rough time of it while I was in prison, and went through hell.

Then my other so-called friends with the law dumped on me again. They wanted me to return to Jefferson County to testify in another case they were going to trial on. I didn't even know until I got to St. Louis that the dude they wanted me to testify against was an old friend of mine, Donald Arnt. They simply called me out at Jeff City and ordered me to shackle up because I was going back home to perform as a star witness in a felony case.

Donny was the president of the St. Louis chapter of the Hell's Angels, and the feds supposedly found an arsenal of weapons at a farm he owned. They were also looking into some other things. Donny was a friend of my old man's, and had known me since I was about two years old. I remember him flipping me quarters and fifty-cent pieces a few times when I was a kid. Like my old man, Donny was originally with the Saddle Tramps and was a Gallopin' Goose. By the time my new associates with the task force became interested in him, he was a Hell's Angel, and had been for a long time.

Donny was an old fart with salt-and-pepper hair and a little belly. He was short and stocky, about five foot seven or five foot eight, but he was a dangerous dude to cross. Size and age didn't matter to him, and he wasn't afraid of anybody. Anyone who came up against him or his cronies was setting themselves up for big-time problems, and I didn't want anything to do with the case. I liked Donny, but mostly I was scared to hell of him. If I ratted on him, every biker in southern Missouri and southern Illinois would be gunning for me.

As far as the feds were concerned, that was my problem. And I already knew they didn't give a shit about my problems. They were only interested in their problems. They also knew how to put the pressure on, and when they go after something or somebody, they have all the power of the government and the courts behind them. They put me under subpoena to testify.

So that's how I found myself back in a Jefferson County circuit courtroom in Hillsboro. As soon as I got there and found out that Donny was involved, I asked to see the defense lawyer and told her not to worry about what was going on. She said Donny had heard I rolled. I hated to hear that.

"Look, you tell Donny I'm not going to do anything to hurt him," I told her. "You give him my best, and you give his wife my best. Okay?" The feds were also hassling his old lady.

A little bit later after I was sworn in as a witness, the prosecutor started things off by asking me to point out the defendant.

I peered around the courtroom, squinting my eyes like I was really looking hard. The old dude the prosecutor was talking about was leaning back in his chair at the defense table beside his lawyer, but he wasn't your usual defendant. He wasn't sitting there clean shaven with a haircut and a three-piece suit trying to look like another lawyer. He was dressed like he always was, in denims, boots, and he was even wearing his leather sleeveless vest to show off his tats. His hair was long and pulled back into a ponytail, and he had a little goatee that was mostly white. When I had enough looking around, I turned back to the prosecutor.

"I don't see him anywhere."

That wasn't the answer the prosecutor wanted to hear, so I had a little talk with him and the judge. The judge pointed out that I could be charged with perjury if I lied on the witness stand. I told him if charging me with perjury was what he and the prosecutor wanted to do, to do their damndest. Being prosecuted for perjury was better than being executed by other inmates the minute I set foot back in Jefferson City. If I testified against

Donny, I wouldn't last a day back at the penitentiary. I knew it, and they knew it. The only difference was that I wanted to go on living. They didn't give a shit. All they wanted was Donny.

Fear had a lot to do with my stubbornness, but it wasn't my only motive for not cooperating. I genuinely liked Donny—and would never have given him up or any of his friends. His vice president, a guy named Jimmy, used to live right next door to me. The BATF and some other cops dug up a case of hand grenades and some machine guns from his yard one time while I was still working close with the task force. They asked me all kinds of questions about that, but I was like the three monkeys. I didn't see nothing, I didn't hear nothing, and I didn't say nothing. Jimmy didn't know anything about the weapons cache, either. It was a big surprise.

Donny and Jimmy weren't into anything important by that time and they weren't hurting anybody. They were putting on some age and were basically retired, so about the most they would do was smoke a little pot and go on a Sunday ride on their Harleys with the younger guys.

When I returned to Jefferson City from St. Louis, I had a brand-new set of enemies. But they weren't bikers. They were with the law. Collapse of the political corruption investigation left bad blood on every side. Public officials in Jefferson County who were targeted in the probe would never forget the part I played in trying to nail them to the wall; I wouldn't forget what I consider to have been a major betrayal by people Vicki and I stuck our necks out for; and law-enforcement big-shots who were stung and embarrassed over the fiasco had an easy patsy in me when they were looking around for someone to blame.

Despite all that, I learned that police and prosecutors have a way of overlooking past differences when they decide they need your help. They got in touch with me again, when they decided I could help them set up one of the leaders of the Mexican Mafia who was running a prison heroin ring inside the walls at Jeff City.

When I was a kid, I played a game with other boys my age where we would hold our clenched fists behind us and give the guy a choice of which hand to pick. One hand, we said, was "sure death." The other was "six months in the hospital." It didn't matter which hand they picked, we punched them on the muscle of their upper arm as hard as we could. Either way, they were a loser, and a lot of kids walked around with big black-and-blue bruises on their arms.

That was the kind of situation I was being put in, except the Hell's Angels were six months in the hospital and the Mexican Mafia was sure death.

Among themselves they usually referred to the gang as La Eme, Spanish for the letter *M*. But it didn't matter what they were called; they were a force to be reckoned with at Jeff City. The Mexican Mafia is involved in everything that represents money and power for prison inmates. Members have their hands in all kinds of smuggling, including drugs and weapons, as well as extortion, beatings, and murder. They are as powerful outside the walls as inside, especially in states where there are big Chicano populations, like California, Arizona, New Mexico, and Texas.

In the mid-nineties, prosecutors accused some La Eme guys of killing a woman who worked as an East Los Angeles gang counselor because she was an advisor on the movie *American Me*, which is about the Mexican Mafia. Members of the Chino gang supposedly considered the movie to be unflattering to their organization. They also reportedly shook down the director, Edward James Olmos, the actor who played the police captain in the TV series "Miami Vice." Rich, powerful, or famous, it didn't matter who you were. If you messed with them, you paid for your mistake one way or another.

If La Eme is a nasty force to deal with on the outside of the joint, they're even more fearsome inside. Everything is magnified inside prison walls, and gangs are as much a part of prison life as bars, cell blocks, and hacks. Most prisoners, if they are acceptable to their fellow cons, align themselves in gangs according to race. Blacks align with one of the Moslim sects or try to get next to the Crips, Bloods, Jamaican Posse or join a gang that's particular to their state or region like the El Rukns in Illinois, the Memphis Mafia in Tennessee, or the Folk Nation in Florida. The Aryan Brotherhood, the ABs, is one of the most influential and feared white gangs.

Mexicans usually wind up with La Eme, The Texas Syndicate, or the Nuestra Familia. The Mexican Mafia gets along well with the ABs. Nuestra is mostly made up of Mexicans from northern California, and we called them farmers. They usually hung with the blacks.

Belonging to a prison gang is one of the best ways for a con to protect himself from shakedowns, gang rape, or becoming the reluctant girlfriend of some old pervert. If someone doesn't qualify for membership in a gang, but fits the racial requirement, he can pay rent for protection against rape, beatings, or murder.

This time, L. Douglas Abram, a St. Louis-based FBI agent, dangled another promise of a spot in the federal Witness Security Program as a reward if I helped them nail La Eme's guy. I was interested, but I had heard the witness-protection story before and this time I wanted something in writing before I stuck my neck in a noose for the Man. That was all right with Abram, and he agreed to become my new handler or federal baby-sitter after I was accepted into the program, so I told him I would go along with the plan.

It called for me to buy some smack through his con-

nection. According to the plan I set up with the La Eme
jefe, one of his relatives would turn the dope over to my
girlfriend in St. Louis. After she sold it to her buyers,
my friend with La Eme and I would split the profit.

The catch was the girlfriend. She wasn't really my
girlfriend. Instead she was a pretty, young FBI agent.
We arranged for a meeting between her and the gang
leader in the visiting room to set up the buy, and when
she showed up, she was wearing a tight dress that fit
like a glove and was cut high on the thigh. She looked
good enough to eat, but she was inexperienced and said
all the wrong things. By the time she minced out of the
visiting room in her high heels, the La Eme chief was
already suspicious—but it got worse. She capped the
performance by climbing into a plain, no-hubcap FBI
car in the parking lot.

Some La Eme guys were watching at the gate and
passed the word back to their boss. For the second time,
the feds had put me in a box, and this time I didn't have
any room to maneuver. I was inside. It didn't take the
gang boss long to make his move.

Another con told me the Mexican Mafia chief was
waiting in the yard and wanted to talk to me. You don't
turn down a summons from somebody like him, but I
was sure that I was marked for death. I went to the
meeting with a foot-long prison-fashioned sword hidden
inside my pants that was so razor sharp and thin I could
have shoved it through a brick—or somebody's gut. If
I was going down, I wasn't going without a fight.

I was right about the FBI girl blowing my cover. The
gang boss told me he knew that I tried to set him up,
and that I was going to pay the price that all prison rats
pay. He was surrounded by his cronies, but they didn't
try to take me out in the yard where the guards were
watching. It was going to be later. A swift, efficient,
private execution. The death sentence had been pro-

nounced. It was only the exact time and method that I wasn't being informed of.

If the usual procedure was followed, I realized that I probably had less than twenty-four hours to live. Then I would be killed with a prison shiv stuck in my ribs, have my skull crushed with an iron pipe, plunge to my death over the railing of one of the upper tiers, or be barbecued alive. Barbecue was a favorite method of prison murder. The killers simply show up in front of the victim's cell and dump gasoline through the bars while he's locked up, then toss a lighted match inside.

Even if I wasn't assassinated right away, I knew it was only a matter of time. Once a snitch has been fingered, he don't last long in general population. And isolating someone in a special security unit, where snitches, child molesters, sissies, and various weaklings are kept to protect them from their fellow inmates isn't very good insurance over the long haul. Those are the first people that get it when there is a prison riot. It's the same story wherever the prison is, in this country or in some foreign country.

In Canada, inmates took over Manitoba's Headingley prison during a bloody riot in April 1996 and headed straight for the protective unit, then began dragging people out. Screaming inmates had fingers slowly chopped off, one at a time, with X-Acto knives; and sex offenders—who Canadian cons call skinners—had their family jewels ripped to pieces with anything that was sharp. Gangs of four or five inmates worked on the skinners and the snitches, slowly torturing, then killing them.

After inmates took over the Sierra Chica prison in Argentina for a week, corrections authorities found a scatter of skulls, thigh bones and other body parts in a big oven. A bunch of special-security prisoners were missing—and they didn't go over the wall.

As soon as the jefe delivered his threat, I approached

the first guard I saw and told him I had to talk with prison officials. At my own request, I was locked in protective custody. Authorities also allowed me to make a phone call to Abram, and I filled him in on the grim outlook for my future if I was forced to remain in Jeff City. My new handler was a righteous dude, one of the few people with federal law-enforcement agencies whose word I could always count on, and he immediately contacted the warden and the head of the Missouri State Department of Corrections, George Lombardi, to tell them about my situation. He said I was going into WITSEC, and he wanted me protected.

That night I gathered up a little bundle of clothes, some shaving gear, and some legal papers. Then four big, burly hacks escorted me out of the prison while my fellow cons jeered and screamed threats at me from behind their cell doors. I was certain that even then somebody was going to skewer me with a spear, or find some other way to kill me. At the very least, they would drench me with their own piss, collected in a can and tossed at me through their cell bars. I was wrong. I spent the rest of that night, and several other nights, locked in a single cell in a nearby county jail.

Then I was moved back to the Missouri Eastern Correctional Center, MECC, on old Highway 66 in Pacific. The prison, which most people simply referred to as Pacific, was in south St. Louis County, my old running grounds. It was a special lockup for sex criminals: rapists, necrophiles, child molesters, run-of-the-mill perverts.

For the first few months after I was processed into Pacific, I was kept in the hole to isolate me from other prisoners. They locked me up just like I was on punishment, with nothing to wear except a pair of boxer shorts, a T-shirt, and some flip-flops. It was a grim place to be, and I wasn't one of the most popular occupants there either.

Isolation cells are set up so that inmates can't see their neighbors, but I could hear them. They yelled all kinds of threats, insults, and other shit at me. The cooks, or someone who handled my chow along the line from the kitchen to delivery, also sprinkled all kinds of crap on my food. One of the nastier tricks food handlers sometimes pull when they're preparing food for the hacks or for some inmate they have a hard-on for, is to jack off in the chow. I watched for that, but I was also convinced they were trying to poison me, because I could see the stuff right on top of my food when it was delivered.

One time I spotted a film of some kind of powdery stuff on top of my chow when the trusty handed the tray to me. The hack who was with him also saw it, and I demanded to see the captain. He said there wasn't any captain, so I should shut up and eat my food or he would take it away.

"Well, Goddamit, I want to see somebody higher than you. Somebody's trying to poison me," I shouted.

"There isn't anybody here for you to see except the associate warden," he said.

"So let me see the associate warden!"

The associate warden was a woman, and about fifteen minutes later she came to my cell and asked what was going on. I told her and she went ballistic. She said she would take care of the problem and left. A few minutes later, she returned carrying two huge trays full of food. Some of the big-shots were having a party up front, so I had a bunch of little sandwiches, canapés, cheese, carrot sticks, and olives. It was good, and I didn't have any more trouble after that with suspicious substances showing up on top of my food.

The administration eased up on me after my talk with the associate warden, and I was issued clothes and given a color TV for my cell. Eventually I was even allowed outside and became a concrete worker for a while. It brought in a few dollars to supplement money my sister in Virginia deposited into my inmate account so that I could buy cigarettes, toothpaste, soap and that sort of thing. I stayed at Pacific almost two years.

In the meantime, federal sentencing laws were being rejiggered to provide prosecutors with more leeway in dealing with snitches. Armed with newly attractive inducements such as substantially reduced sentences in return for cooperation, prosecutors and federal agents escalated their war against organized crime. As the feds stepped up their rate of successful prosecutions, more people like me became protected witnesses.

The changes in the sentencing laws were at last approved about a year before the paperwork was finally processed to admit me into the government's federal Witness Security Program. It took awhile. Most of the grunt work preparing for my admission was carried out by bureaucrats and people I never met, but I also spent a few hours dealing with matters like the witness pre-commitment interview.

The interview was an important part of the process, and at the core of ensuring my safety once I moved into one of the witness units. I was interviewed at Pacific and put on the lie box. I had taken polygraph tests before, and it was no big deal. The operator simply wraps an elastic-bandage-type covering around your arm, then watches a little needle on a graph to see if you're telling whoppers. It's not much different than having your blood pressure taken. I had no reason to lie to him about things like who might or might not be dangerous for me to hang out with in one of the units, and I figure I passed with flying colors. No one bothered to spell out the results of my performance to me, but at that point it was basically a monitoring process.

There wasn't a lot of new information to develop during the interview, because my background had been gone over so many times before. Nevertheless, my inquisitor went over everything again. We talked about my prior convictions and past criminal history; aliases and my nickname; marriages and other women I was seriously involved with in the past. The names and ages of my kids were recorded, and we went into my medical history. I told the guy about various drugs I used in the past, including alcohol, and was asked about any medications I might be taking. There weren't any. I assured him I wasn't dying of AIDS and didn't have any kind of VD. I was healthy as a horse.

One of the things my interviewer stressed was tied to past criminal associations. He wanted to know who I ran with, and especially who my enemies were. There were already people in the program whom I was not on friendly terms with, and if we were locked up together, there would be hell to pay. I told my interviewer who they were, and how I had crossed them or how they had crossed me. He drew on that information later when he dealt with the area of the report tied to "threat assessment," and decisions were made about which protected-witness unit or units would be safest for me. My former friend, Raoul, never rolled, but if he had, he would not have been someone I would like to be locked up on a witness unit with. Protected witnesses are not fraternity brothers.

The inteviewer didn't skip anything. We talked about my education—I completed the eleventh grade—legitimate jobs I had held, and any history of escapes from prison. The only thing I escaped from was the military. I was busy running drugs during the war in Vietnam. He even checked out my tattoos and scars. Most of my tats were prison art, inked into my skin by other inmates who were good with a needle and had a flair for design.

A couple date back to my Oakland days when I was riding with Sergey, his buddy Jim Jim, and other Hell's Angels.

A big, beautiful wizard is inked on my back. My right leg is busy, with a skull looking through prison bars, then there's a genie's head, and above that the letters SWP, which stands for Supreme White Pride. As a coverup tattoo on my right arm, I have a Harley Davidson. There are other tattoos on my chest and on my left leg. I'm not exactly the Illustrated Man, but I have my share. Most guys who have done time have tats. They're part of the life.

I wasn't left with many secrets—and like always, the feds had private information they didn't bother to share with me. I wasn't given a copy of the report, which included the interviewer's summary and an evaluation of my general, physical, and emotional condition. One of the entries I would have liked to see dealt with a listing of promises made to me by investigators, prosecutors, or U.S. marshals. I knew what I was promised, but some of my former task-force pals and other people I worked with apparently had a different reading, or especially rotten memories.

At last, my personal background, assistance in criminal investigations, and the testimony I provided in trials was all studied and carefully analyzed by bureaucrats with the Bureau of Prisons. The BOP is the arm of the U.S. Justice Department that runs federal prisons, and they decided that I qualified to become a protected witness.

On December 1, 1989, I walked into a witness-protection unit for the first time and officially entered the WITSEC program. Abram kept his word, and he saved my life.

7

WITSEC

THE FEDERAL CORRECTIONAL Institution at Sandstone, Minnesota, is about halfway from Minneapolis to the southern tip of Lake Superior at Duluth, a few minutes' drive west of the Wisconsin state line. The prison town is about as big as a snowflake, and in the winters it's every bit as cold.

A squad of U.S. marshals checked me out of Pacific at about one o'clock in the afternoon. They wouldn't take custody until I had a new set of civilian clothes to wear. They asked me for my size, then went to a WalMart and bought me a pair of tennis shoes, some Levis, boxer shorts, an undershirt, and a longer T-shirt to wear on the outside. I walked out of Pacific looking just like a regular street guy. I wasn't handcuffed or anything.

Of all the feds and local cops that I've had dealings with, I probably like the U.S. marshals the best. The marshals I came in contact with were uniformly professional in their behavior, and they always treated me square. I'm not saying we became friends. They were too professional for that, and I had my own friends.

Even though we were sometimes closed up in hotel rooms together while I was testifying, ate together, talked together and traveled together, they knew the dangers of becoming too friendly with people like me. Do a favor once and it leads to another, then pretty soon the poor sap realizes that he's stepped over the line and broken the rules or committed a crime. By then it's too late, and his career is in shambles and his life in a mess. So the marshals weren't into doing me little favors or any big favors, but they didn't hassle me, either. They did their job, and that was good enough for me.

The marshals have a proud history to uphold. The U. S. Marshal's Service goes all the way back to 1789, when George Washington personally appointed the first thirteen men to wear the badge. It was the government's first federal law-enforcement agency and attracted some of history's toughest lawmen, people like Bill Tilghman who helped clean up the old Oklahoma Territory a century ago. Maybe I should have been a U.S. marshal and worked the other side. They're neat dudes.

When we set out from Pacific for Sandstone we traveled in a minicaravan of three cars. I was in the middle car with a couple of the marshals, with another car leading the way and a third car trailing behind. The marshals took me to a Denny's restaurant and told me to order anything I wanted. I was hungry and didn't know when I would get another meal on the outside, so I ordered a Grand Slam breakfast with coffee, milk, juice, and a side order of toast. "Go on, eat till you puke," one of them told me. "Uncle Sam's picking up the check."

At Lambert Air Field in St. Louis, which later became St. Louis International Airport, they parked in a special location set aside for law enforcement and led me onto one of the airliners waiting to take off. We were the first people to board. We sat on the left in the tail section, where the restrooms are and the stewardesses stay.

That's where the marshals always sit, and it's the safest spot on the plane.

During the flight from St. Louis to the Minneapolis-St. Paul International Airport, we ate some peanuts and pretzels while we talked about the weather and inconsequential things. I asked about Sandstone, but the marshals didn't really know much about the prison or about G-Unit. They just delivered and picked people up there.

At Minneapolis-St. Paul the marshals loaded me into a brown Bronco, and we took off again in another minicaravan just like we traveled in when we were in Missouri. The drive north along U.S. 35 from the airport to Sandstone took longer than the flight did. It's only 105 miles, but the weather was already turning nasty. The ground was covered in snow, a stiff wind was whipping it across the highway, and according to a report on the car radio the windchill factor that night was expected to be about 85 below zero. One of the marshals reminded me that it was still three weeks before the beginning of winter.

We stopped at a very good barbeque place minutes from Sandstone, and I really packed it away there, figuring it might be years before I got another decent meal. But I had a surprise coming. When I finally walked into the unit, some of the first guys I saw were a bunch of homeboys from St. Louis. They had the kitchen opened up for me and started work on a big meal while I checked in.

It was late but it was still December 1. I was just in time for Christmas.

Processing took about ninety minutes, and most of that time was spent looking through photographs of everybody in the unit. The idea is to see if anybody is locked up there who might be dangerous to a new inmate; maybe somebody they've ratted on before or somebody with another reason to kill them. The funny thing about picking somebody out of the book and telling the hacks you don't want to be in the same unit with them is that both of you usually wind up in the hole.

The hole in the units isn't anything like it is at Pacific, Jeff City, or even the general population areas of the federal prisons where WITSEC has inmates under special protection. In the units, cells in the hole have color television and VCRs, and inmates locked up there have access to a film library. Most people don't even call it "the hole." It's segregation.

My homeboys had a meal, twice as good as the barbeque I'd just eaten, waiting for me when I finished looking at pictures. While I ate I brought them up to date on what was going on back in the Blues City and what was happening to guys they knew in Jeff City. We polished off the meal with a big gallon jug of Gallo white wine. The marshals had fed me and treated me well, but they hadn't given me any wine. I was impressed. If this was an example of what life was like on the units, I figured I could do my time standing on my head. But I hadn't seen anything yet.

As soon as I arrived at Sandstone, I began soaking up information about the prison, the unit, and the program. According to the data on most up-to-date road maps and atlases, the town of Sandstone is home to almost exactly 1,600 people, depending on how many were dying or being born on a specific day. Apparently the population figures don't include the inmates of the Federal Correction Institution located just south of the town limits. It should, because FCI Sandstone is the single biggest business there. More family breadwinners work at the prison than at any other single job in Pine county.

Today it's one of five medium-security federal correctional centers where special mini prisons-within-prisons were constructed to house and care for protected witnesses. Guards and inmates locked inside the area of FCI Sandstone that's set aside for witnesses call the cell-block G-Unit. General population inmates have their own name for it: the Rat Unit.

Witness-protection units, or Protective Custody Units (PCUs) throughout the federal prison system, including Sandstone, were filled to capacity. At that time there were only about thirty guys in G-Unit, but when I left almost two years later, there were over one hundred. Similarly, when heads were counted nationwide in the units in July, a total of 388 WITSEC inmates were being held in federal custody—but 181 of those were in general population at state and federal prisons. Only about 200 were held in the witness-protection units. Yet only four beds were available among all the units for new prisoners, and forty-one witnesses were either on the waiting list or were potentials. They were rapidly expanding the space at Sandstone, but it was hard to keep up with the demand. WITSEC is like any government program. It never gets smaller. It just keeps growing. It feeds on itself.

Only four PCUs were in operation at that time. The Mesa Unit at the FCI Phoenix wasn't opened until November 1989, about one month before I entered the program at Sandstone. Sandstone had a reputation for being the very best PCU in the system for the quality of life, until the Mesa Unit opened and the Minnesota facility dropped to number two. So despite the crowding, I felt good about being assigned there. It was very nice.

Crowding at Sandstone was responsible for the initiation of double-celling in August 1986, and by the time I arrived carrying my little bag of personal effects, it was firmly established as standard operating procedure. Inmates, even witnesses in the units, didn't carry much with them except a few grooming items, some family pictures, and whatever legal documents that might be important to them at the moment. The PCUs beat general population all to hell, but they weren't suburbia. There weren't any attics, basements or attached garages to store things in.

At Sandstone and in the other units, each inmate had a personal lockbox with a combination lock for storage of legal documents, and anything else containing information that was considered sensitive or could possibly compromise the safety of himself or members of his family if they got into the wrong hands. Inmates who were still uneasy and didn't trust the lockboxes could store their material in a secure room set aside for their use by administrators. I kept my papers in the lockbox in my cell. I wanted them close at hand.

G Unit had seventy-three cells, including four segregation cells and seven special management cells that were set aside for guys who were suicide risks, or who otherwise needed constant surveillance by guards. The sixty-two regular cells ranged in size from 66 to 84 square feet. Each cell contained a bed (two if it was a double), a storage area, television, toilet, and a sink. The additional bunk, and the necessary additional floor space, was the only difference between double and single cells. All the cells in the units had regular toilets with lids and handles they could use to do their own flushing. We had ceramic sinks; normal plumbing. Just like civilians. There was none of the stuff you see in general population, where cells have metal toilets without seats and the guard is supposed to control the flushing mechanism. In most maximum-security prisons, guards even control toilet paper and ration it out. They have to.

Prisoners can always find ways to jerry-rig things and thumb their nose at the rules, including figuring out how to flush their own toilets. So there is always some nut who will use the paper, if its available, to clog the doors and flood the cells by repeatedly flushing the toilets. Its like having their own private swimming pool. Then when a hack opens the door, all that water comes rushing out and the whole tier can be flooded.

Inmate ingenuity is amazing, and in regular prison the cons do all the stuff you see in movies, like using the toilets for telephones. They talk and listen to each other through the drains. When I was in the hole for a while in Jeff City, we sometimes ripped sheets apart, then braided the thread, broke windows, and dropped the newly constructed rope into the yard. Our friends down below tied cigarettes and stuff to the rope so the guy in the hole could pull it back into his cell. Its possible to do some amazing things when you have enough time on your hands and want to scheme.

But a regular cell was not in the cards for me. When I checked into Sandstone, G-Unit had a total of twelve double cells, and they came in different sizes. Two of the cells were 84 square feet, two were 77 square feet, and the other eight varied between 66 and 69 square feet. I moved into one of the smaller double cells on the upper tier with a guy from Chicago, James "Duke" Basile. All the blacks lived downstairs, and it was constant noise with their boom boxes and playing all that rap music and hip-hop shit. I was glad to move in with Duke. He's the guy who watched the prison doctor pop the bullet out of my leg. He was clean and quiet; a good neighbor.

Duke and I were talking and realized we knew some of the same people, and we got along right from the beginning. He's a little fellow, who probably doesn't weigh 100 pounds, but he has a big reputation. He's been described in press accounts as a stickup man, jewel thief, and suspected hitman, but Duke says he never killed anybody. *Chicago* magazine once named him as being among the city's top 200 mobsters, and described him as taking over from another hoodlum the job of "chief enforcer."

Duke was on the inside for a long time, and he knew a lot of secrets, including information about Mob hits. After he rolled, he led police to a Mob graveyard and helped put away some of the heaviest hitters in the Chicago Outfit. The government put him up at the Federal Metropolitan Correctional Center (MCC) in Chicago's Loop while he testified against his old friends and associates about a little bit of everything, ranging from assassinations to a messed-up armed robbery at Balmoral Race Track in suburban Crete.

Duke told me he turned because the Outfit put a hit out on him, and among other activities he wound up wearing a wire on an international jewel thief, hit man and notorious psychopath named Gerald Hector Scarpelli. The FBI picked Scarpelli up leaving a motel in the south Chicago suburbs with a machine gun, an arsenal of other weapons, and a Groucho Marx mask. He was on his way to work. Scarpelli also wound up rolling, and a few weeks later he was found dead in a shower stall at the MCC with a couple of plastic bags tied over his head. The FBI said his death was a suicide. Sure, and Mother Teresa drove a German Tiger Tank during WWII.

Duke did okay for himself by rolling, even though he made some deadly enemies. He was looking at a forty-year sentence, which would have meant the rest of his life, and he plea-bargained a deal that set a maximum of fifteen years. Then they promised that he could trim the max even further if he continued to cooperate. Of course he did. What else could he do?

I wound up double-celling with some interesting characters while I was in G-Unit and later in other PCUs. Basically in my case it was always a matter of seniority. But unit administrators also used double-celling as a tool to maintain order and discipline. The way it worked was simple: if you stepped over the line somehow, the powers that be could take away your seniority and assign you to a double cell. Some pretty serious restrictions were written into the regulations that applied to the unit administration, however, so that inmates weren't entirely at the mercy of the people in charge.

Even if a man's seniority was taken away, double-celling was permitted only if there was a shortage of cells. Prior to any double-celling, regardless of what the reasons were, the BOP investigated the criminal and WITSEC background of both men involved to make sure they were compatible and didn't pose a threat to each other.

About six months after I checked in, some witnesses at Sandstone filed a suit against Attorney General Edwin Meese, Warden John Sullivan, and others, complaining that double-celling violated the Fifth and Eighth Amendments of the Constitution.

According to the suit, double-celling amounted to breach of contract. The inmates, who were not identified in the suit, claimed that double-celling put them in danger of other cell mates, and violated the guarantee of safety extended to them when they entered the program. This violated the due process clause in the Fifth Amendment, they contended.

The prisoner plaintiffs pointed out in the lawsuit that an inmate who was double-celled at Otisville was "forced to commit sexual acts with his cell mate." The guy certainly wasn't the first prison inmate ever forced to give a blowjob or to grab his ankles and spread 'em, but that kind of thing wasn't supposed to be happening on the units. For the most part it didn't. No incidents like that were reported at Sandstone, although that doesn't mean none ever occurred. You gotta remember, these convicts are stickup men, drug smugglers, and kill-

ers who live by a code that rewards strength, personal
fearlessness, and mutual respect. It's the law of the jungle; survival of the fittest.

Weak inmates are always at risk from stronger convicts. Even when supervisors and hacks try their best to
protect inmates from each other—and they don't always
do that—a determined old predator can usually find
some way to get at a weaker man. Taking care of an old
con's sexual needs, or submitting to gang rape by half
a dozen prison tough guys can permanently break a
young inmate's spirit and turn him into a sissy. Pretty
soon he is parading around dressing and posturing like
Dennis Rodman. Shit happens! It just doesn't happen
with the same frequency on the units as it does in general population.

G-Unit and every other unit in the program had some
hard guys locked up, who could be dangerously violent
to just about anybody around them. And of course there
were other inmates it wouldn't be good to double-cell
together because they were connected to somebody a
witness had rolled on, or were carrying grudges either
from the outside or from the inside. Nobody wanted to
find themselves teamed up in a 66-square-foot cell with
somebody they had ratted on.

The Justice Department's Office of Enforcement Operations (OEO) had already taken that into consideration,
and set strict guidelines they referred to when pairing up
inmates in double cells. Any prisoner who was known
to be consistently violent was not supposed to be double-
celled. Personal background and testimony as recorded
in BOP files were also carefully consulted by administrators in determining who would bunk together and who
wouldn't.

The claim of Eighth Amendment violations was also
shaky. That's the amendment that prohibits cruel and
unusual punishment, and the plaintiffs had a hard row

to hoe by trying to show that double-celling fit that definition. Similar complaints had already been settled in favor of prison administrators in cases involving general population inmates, but the G-Unit inmates claimed that those earlier court rulings shouldn't apply to people in WITSEC. Witnesses had special status that should be recognized by the courts, they claimed.

The case was heard in the U.S. District Court, Fifth Division, of Minnesota, and the inmate plaintiffs lost. The court ruled it didn't have jurisdiction over the breach of contract claim; double-celling wasn't cruel and unusual punishment; and use of the seniority system to determine which prisoners were double-celled didn't violate due process.

It was a bullshit suit to begin with. But hey, why not try? Prisoners, especially inmates locked up in witness units, have a lot of time on their hands. Stirring the shit gives them something to do. Keeping the BOP, OEO, the local warden and unit manager on their toes was good exercise for the brain.

Duke was a good neighbor, but after we spent a couple of months together I moved into my own cell. It was one of the doubles and was bigger than his. Nobody else wanted it because a White Supremicist had been living there, and he was a pig.

He belonged to a group of people called the Covenant, Sword and Arm of the Lord, who had a place in Arkansas up in the Ozark mountains, and got himself involved in some kind of a plot to poison the water in Washington, D.C. He wasn't after politicians so much, as he wanted to kill all the blacks. Then, while he was celled in G-Unit, he spent most of his time rewriting the Bible, and also wasted long hours hiding underneath his bed. He never took a shower or cleaned anything. A total kook, and his place was a sty. But it was no big deal to me. It was a good cell and it was big because it was on the corner of the tier. I swept it out, mopped the floor, and repainted. Turned it into a nice place.

Inside G-Unit, everything was the best. Our food was prepared by inmates whose work was overseen by skilled cooks, most of them with professional experience on the outside, and they made sure it was put together right. Menus were carefully planned, and we ate steaks cooked to order, pork chops, lamb, chicken, and turkey. Sometimes we even ate venison and other wild game. There was enough of everything to satisfy an army of hungry lumberjacks. Anyone could have seconds, or thirds if they wished.

Each inmate had his own color television set in his cell, outfitted with cable and Pay-Per-View so that we could watch anything we wanted, from football games and boxing matches to triple-X thrillers like *Deep Throat, Behind The Green Door* and *Debbie Does Dallas.*

We were on our own most of the day and could roam around the common areas, watch television, read, type letters or legal briefs, get snacks from the commissary or vending machines, work out on exercise equipment, or just hang out and swap war stories. It was pretty much up to us how we spent our day until lockdown at about eleven P.M. Then we had to stay in our cells until six the next morning. If someone got sick or there was a hassle between a couple of guys in one of the double cells, a guard was less than two minutes away. Two guards were on duty at the unit every night.

The difference between the witness unit at Sandstone and doing time at Jeff City or Pacific was roughly comparable to moving from a double-wide in the Happy Acres Trailer Park to Donald and Marla Trump's multimillion dollar Mar-a-Largo estate in Palm Beach. And Sandstone wasn't unique among prisons where federally protected witnesses were kept.

Amenities at Sandstone included a regular library and a legal library. I took advantage of both, and with input from some of my fellow inmates who had been around WITSEC longer than I had, began learning everything I could about the program. I started off with Joe Valachi.

Valachi was a low-level soldier in New York's Genovese organized-crime family when he got in trouble and started to sing. He was doing time on a narcotics charge at the federal prison in Atlanta with Vito Genovese, the "boss of bosses" of the crime family he was tied to when the word got around that Valachi was a stool pigeon. Genovese gave him the kiss of death, and somehow Valachi managed to escape three attempts to kill him.

He was terrified, and knew it was only a matter of time until his luck ran out. One day in the exercise yard, he saw a guy he figured had the contract on him stoop down to pick up an iron pipe. Valachi roared across the yard, grabbed the pipe away from the guy, and beat him to death with it. The joke was on Valachi. He had the wrong guy. The inmate he killed was a small-time forger with no organized-crime connections, but Valachi was in deep shit with the law as well as with his former friends in the Mob. If Genovese's hitters didn't get him, he was looking at the death penalty anyway for killing another inmate. The feds indicted him for murder. So he turned stool pigeon.

Valachi emptied his guts and told the government everything he knew, and he knew a lot because by that time, 1962, he had already been involved with the Mafia most of his adult life. He worked for Salvatore Maranzano and Lucky Luciano before Genovese took over the powerful crime family. Since that time, newspaper reporters and other writers have talked a lot about Valachi being a top member of the Mafia. He wasn't. He was always a low-level punk, a soldier who collected tribute from shopkeepers, picked up juice payments for shylocks, pushed drugs, and handled a few contracts on people his bosses wanted hit.

Ironically, Valachi hadn't ratted on anybody when Genovese gave him the kiss of death. But once he opened his mouth, neither Genovese nor anybody who worked for him could shut him up. Valachi was the guy who confirmed for the first time that there really was such a thing as the Syndicate, or La Cosa Nostra. In English, that translates as *our thing,* but it sounded better, more sinister, in Italian and the press jumped on it.

The old mobster told his story to agents with the Bureau of Narcotics and Dangerous Drugs (the predecessor of the DEA), the FBI, U.S. Justice Department, and finally in 1964 to the McClellan subcommittee of the U.S. Senate. The Senate hearings were broadcast live on TV, and it was the O. J. Simpson trial of its day. Everybody tuned in, fascinated by the sinister, secret world that was being laid bare. Valachi detailed how the organization was set up, told who the bosses were, and talked about hits and hitters. He spilled on everybody. Valachi wasn't the first mob-connected hoodlum to turn, however.

About twenty years earlier, the government used another canary to bring down a gang of professional assassins known as Murder Incorporated, who carried out hits for the Syndicate. Abe Reles, a hoodlum who was involved in at least thirty Syndicate hits and whose street name was "Kid Twist," was the guy who flipped. He helped put Louis "Lepke" Buchalter in New York State's electric chair and helped put Murder Incorporated out of business.

A couple of other mobsters whose asses were on the line wriggled off the hook because the New York State government and local cops didn't take very good care of their witness. Kid Twist was under police protection, with a cop stationed just outside the hotel room where he was secretly hiding out between court appearances, when he tried to fly out the window. That's what appeared to have happened, because his body was found on the cement six stories down and twenty yards away from the window of the Coney Island hotel where he was under constant police guard. It was either a flying lesson gone sour, or a couple of guys picked him up, swung him by an arm and a leg, and launched him. Maybe they figured if he could sing like a canary he could fly like a bird.

Anyway, that was the end of Kid Twist, and of his testimony. When Valachi began to sing, the government was determined that there weren't going to be any repeat aerial performances. When he testified before McClellan's panel, he was guarded by 200 U.S. marshals. Valachi was too important as a witness to be allowed to take flying lessons. Reles had died before he had a chance to live up to his full potential as a canary. Valachi would. Although he never climbed as high on the Syndicate ladder as Reles, he went on to become the most notorious stool pigeon in the history of organized crime—a dubious honor not even eclipsed by the efforts of Sammy the Bull.

Valachi eventually wound up at the La Tuna Correctional Center in Texas. Twenty-one miles outside El Paso, La Tuna was known in those days as stool pigeon haven, and later became the home of Mafia mouths, Jimmy "the Weasel" Frattiano, and Vincent Charles "Fat Vinnie" Teresa. Frattiano began his criminal career in Cleveland and worked his way up to acting boss of the Mob in Los Angeles before turning. Fat Vinnie was a ranking member of the mob in New England. For a while after Vinnie checked into La Tuna, old Joe fretted that the new guy was secretly planning to whack him. But the two notorious mob snitches eventually became close friends.

Corrections authorities reported that Valachi died of cancer at La Tuna on April 3, 1971, when he was sixty-eight-years old. The official line the feds put out on the old hoodlum was that he spent his time in solitary confinement for his own protection, and an appreciative government deposited $15 a month in his commissary account.

A lot of people never bought that story, or the official version of his lonely death, and there's still talk today, especially on the witness units, that his death was faked by the feds and Joe was quietly spirited away somewhere so that he could live out the rest of his life in peace and prosperity. It was his reward!

The longer someone spends on the witness-protection units, the more they learn about the strange and uneven system of payoffs to favored informers. One of the problems with WITSEC was the way it developed, haphazardly, without anybody in power like the U.S. Congress or U.S. Senate paying the kind of close attention that was needed. Like Topsy in *Uncle Tom's Cabin,* the program "jist grew."

At the beginning of the 1970s, fewer than fifty protected witnesses were enrolled in the program, and the annual costs were about $1 million. Within roughly ten years after Valachi rolled and testified before the McClellan Committee, the government was spending more than $3 million on the program and had more than 600 people enrolled. The number included witnesses and members of their families who also had to be protected.

By the early eighties, WITSEC's annual budget had soared over $28 million and was heading straight up. In 1995, the Justice Department set aside a whopping $53 million in its budget for the program. Witnesses and family members were streaming into the progam, and there seemed to be no limit.

The feds tried different ways of protecting their witnesses after their initial experiences with Valachi, and after the earlier disaster with Kid Twist. They set up safe houses in the mountains, deserts, or deep woods, anywhere that was isolated and presumably could be adequately guarded by U.S. marshals. They watched over witnesses in hotel rooms, high-security areas of federal prisons, and in out-of-the-way county jails in any little podunk town where the feds figured a strange prisoner or two wouldn't be likely to run into any of his old friends from the street and wouldn't be noticed by the local drunks, wife beaters, and shoplifters who were his new neighbors.

The program was expanding too fast, however, for those kind of makepiece solutions to last forever. In the early 1980s, the OEO, which administers the program, approved construction of five special prison units to be used exclusively for protected witnesses. The new units were located at Sandstone; Otisville, New York; Allenwood, Pennsylvania; Fairton, New Jersey; and at the FCI a few miles outside Phoenix, Arizona.

Eventually, I would learn more than I wanted to know about three of the five units. It would be up-close study, from the inside. One of the first bits of information I picked up reinforced a fact of life that all convicts are aware of. All the crooks involved with prisons aren't on the inside.

The original construction contract for the protection units at Sandstone was supposedly a meager $240,000. The final bill wound up in the $4-million range, even though most of the work was carried out by convict labor. The inmates were paid $7.50 a month for their work. Nevertheless, there were no scandals, no indictments over the mess. Taxpayers simply reached into their pockets and wrote out the check.

In the early days after Valachi's revelations, most of the witnesses were people involved in organized crime, especially the La Cosa Nostra, but that rapidly changed. The old Italian organized-crime gangs still account for a big chunk of the number of federally protected witnesses, but today they're housed alongside people like me, members of biker gangs, vicious prison and street gangs, and big-time dope smugglers. There's all kinds of organized crime going on across America today.

Any racketeers whose operations are highly organized and tightly controlled are tough to get the goods on. That's why official Washington created the CCE and RICO, the Continuing Criminal Enterprise and the Racketeering Influence and Corrupt Organization Acts. President Richard M. Nixon signed RICO into law in 1970, and federal prosecutors have been using it to create havoc among the Mafia and other organized-crime groups ever since. RICO permits the government to come in, sweep up records, and grab corporate assets that could have never been touched under previous laws. Anyone who is convicted under RICO or pulls the big CCE better be prepared for a long stay in the joint.

Rudolph Giuliani used RICO to help make his bones as a federal-crime fighter when he was U.S. attorney for the Southern District of New York and prosecuted members of the city's five Mafia families. RICO has been very demoralizing for the Mob, and it is widely credited by some major crimefighters for breaking the old Mafia code of silence and helping convince racketeers like Gravano to roll and enter the federal witness-protection program. They have no choice if they don't want to spend the rest of their lives in prison.

Law enforcement has to use turncoats and informers to infiltrate their inner workings and gather enough evidence for indictments and convictions. Former members of tough drug gangs from Mexico, Colombia, Peru, and other countries who have their own armies or cadres of *pistoleros*, are already showing up in the program. They were guys with reputations, and nicknames like El Lobo and El Loco. I met and lived with some of them.

Turncoats from tough domestic street gangs like the Bloods and the Crips from Los Angeles, Chicago's El Rukns and Gangster Disciples, and New York's Latin Kings (later the Almighty Latin Kings and Queens Nation) are also showing up on the units in increasing numbers. The quality of WITSEC prisoners is going to hell.

When I entered the program, at least 80 percent of the witnesses were involved in some way with the drug business. It's more than likely the percentage has increased. There's so much money in drugs that it attracts the best and the worst of the underworld. For years the Mustache Petes, the old guys who ran La Cosa Nostra, tried to keep their people out of the drug trade. They wanted to stick with the safe old tried-and-true rackets: extortion, unions, shylocking, prostitution, even bookmaking and other forms of gambling. So what happened? The young turks blew away the Mustache Petes who were keeping them from all that money.

But the ethnic makeup and gang loyalties of witnesses is constantly changing, and before long there's going to be an influx of informers from new ethnic gangs developing in this country. America is going to be seeing newcomers in the units who can trace their background to countries like Vietnam, China, Russia, Yugoslavia, Jamaica, and Nigeria. Well-organized gangs from all those places, and from others, are already moving into the rackets in a big way. They're hungry and fearless. I know what I'm talking about. Been there, done that.

Although it was McClellan's U.S. Senate subcommittee that brought Valachi and his revelations about a national crime syndicate to broad attention throughout the country, it's Congress that has responsibility for overseeing the federal protected-witness program. In my estimation, they haven't been doing a very good job.

When I was escorted through the front door at Sandstone, I was one of approximately 400 people in the federal-witness program. About 3,200 people had been in the program since its beginning, however. More than half of them were family members of witnesses. The rest were people like me, who cut deals with the law for whatever advantage they thought they could get for rolling.

Some of the advantages were considerable: like early paroles, reduced sentences, no sentences at all, huge amounts of money—or like Valachi, protection and revenge. Everyone involved gets something from the deals. But they're deals with the Devil that can go horribly wrong.

One thing about these deals I learned in a hurry. Old Scratch always has a joker hidden someplace in the deck. By the time I was transported to Sandstone, I had already uncovered it: the feds had conned the con man. I wasn't Valachi, and I wasn't looking for revenge. I was a relative nobody.

It frosted my balls from the outset that all these hitmen, serial killers, and international narco-traffickers I was locked up with were doing a minute, sitting on fortunes salted away in banks, stocks, and bonds, then walking out to begin new lives. People who flew airplane loads of drugs into this country and kill-crazy nuts were walking outside, scot free. They were the baddest of the bad and they were rewarded for it.

By contrast, people like me who never murdered anyone but put their ass on the line for the Gs or a police task force somewhere, and were sentenced by state courts instead of the feds, were given twice as much time. And there was no fortune waiting for them when they finally did make it to the outside. It was a bullshit operation.

So, almost from my first day at Sandstone, I began keeping careful notes on everything I saw and heard. Then I started stirring up the shit.

8

The Units

BEING LOCKED UP during some of the most normally productive years of my life was a devastating waste, but I wasn't ready to give up and sink into a pit of self-pity—or to spend every minute of my time fighting with the BOP and the administration. I was determined to salvage what I could from the experience, and I also began making up for the previous neglect of my formal education. I started paying attention to good literature and the arts, and signed up for college courses in psychology, sociology, and law. As you might expect, law was a popular subject among inmates working to get an education on the units.

The college work was carried out through correspondence courses. I never planned to become a college professor or social worker; I liked being outdoors and doing the kind of jobs that keep the muscles firm and work up a good sweat. But I was looking forward to a new life outside the walls some day, and I wanted to be prepared to hold my own with anyone I wound up associating with in the civilian world. It took me almost ten years, but I eventually earned a BA degree in Sociology, with a minor in social work.

Most of my reading, studies, research, and correspondence, however, was tied to my efforts to find a way through the legal system to reduce my sentence.

Every prison has a few intelligent or well educated inmates with a good knowledge of the legal processes, including former lawyers who ran afoul of the law in one way or another. Others are simply bright individuals, with single-minded determination to ferret out that elusive legal loophole that will get them on the outside instead of the inside. Several guys in G-Unit knew their way around the legal system, and they helped me out with tips and information.

At first, I began boning up in the law library on my own, with occasional help from other more knowledgeable inmates. Then, as I got deeper into the intricate world of writs, motions, habeas corpus petitions, and 29: 15s, I began enlisting professional help from outside. There's always a public defender or other taxpayer-funded lawyer available somewhere to help a needy convict. I quickly hooked up with a lawyer working for the Missouri State Public Defender. I also learned that when the going gets really tough, the American Civil Liberties Union, or some of their friends in the law business can almost always be counted on to provide professional legal representation to an inmate with a beef.

Besides the fact the hacks don't go out of their way to hassle you, two of the best things about living in the witness-protection units is that you have a lot of time to yourself, and you have access to law and general-interest libraries that range from adequate to very good.

I took advantage of the legal library to begin churning out a blizzard of motions, petitions, and other legal appeals in efforts to get my sentence reduced or overturned, or to obtain an outright pardon. A couple of typewriters were kept available for inmates doing legal work.

Assistance showed up unexpectedly in 1990 when I met a woman through one of my first cousins, and we began to correspond and talk by telephone. Then she started making the long trip from her home in a bedroom community in upper New York State to Minnesota to visit. Almost before I knew it, she had become my outside advocate. Jean was the single mother of a boy and a girl, but she made time for me and my problems. She worked her tail off, writing to the Justice Department, the OEO, the BOP, telephoning people, and doing everything she could to force WITSEC to keep its promises to me.

Another project of mine that got under the skin of my keepers with the BOP and the OEO was my efforts to talk to the press about what I considered my betrayal, and the abuses I had already witnessed in the program. I mailed letters to reporters for the major newspapers in the St. Louis area, including the *Post-Dispatch, Globe-Democrat,* and the suburban *Journal.*

In other efforts to learn more about the status of my case and about the WITSEC program, I filed the first of what would become a series of requests for data under the Freedom of Information Act. Some of the news reporters I eventually contacted also filed under the act, but none of us had much success. I didn't get any answers, and a couple of the reporters collected a few papers with almost everything but the date and the name of the answering agency inked out.

There was no question that trying to talk with the media was a no-no for people in the program, and I realized there were good reasons for the OEO's caution. The whole concept of WITSEC was based on protecting witnesses, giving them new identities, and hiding their whereabouts. Many witnesses, depending on their status, couldn't even stay in touch with close family members such as parents, or brothers and sisters who were outside the program. It made sense to figure that if the media knew where the Sammy Gravanos, the Sergey Waltons, and the George Taylors were, and what new names and identities they might be using, their enemies wouldn't have much trouble tracking them down.

One of the first things I was required to do when I agreed to move into the witness program was sign a Memorandum of Understanding. Most people refer to it as an MOU, and basically it's a contract between two parties. It's a lot like a plea bargain. The government makes a commitment in the MOU to provide security, usually along with other benefits, in return for certain commitments by the witness. Mutual obligations between the two parties are carefully outlined in the MOUs.

Paraphrased and stripped of some of the tongue-twisting legalese, they include:

1. Agree to provide information in investigations and to testify at legal proceedings.
2. Do not commit any crimes.
3. Take all necessary steps to avoid revealing to others the specifics about measures taken for my protection.
4. Agree to comply with legal obligations and any civil judgments against me.
5. Cooperate with all reasonable requests by government officers and employees who are helping provide my protection.
6. Agree to provide another person to act as agent for the service of process.

7. Make a sworn statement of all outstanding legal obligations, including those involving child custody and visitation.
8. Disclose any probation or parole obligations, and if already on parole or probation by state authorities, to consent to federal supervision.
9. Keep appropriate officials regularly informed about my activities and current address.

In short, I was expected to become a citizen and keep my nose clean for the rest of my life.

The U.S. Marshals Service, which handles the MOU, was telling me that I was going to punch a time clock or run a little legitimate business of my own, and live on a regular paycheck. They wouldn't put up with any sidelines like escort services, occasional dope deals, or credit-card scams. After three generations, the Taylor and Van Boven families were permanently retired from the business of crime. I realized that I could wind up driving a dump truck or operating a backhoe eight or ten hours a day, and still earn less in a month than I could make with one good heist as a robber or by flying half a dozen ladies to Washington to party with a congressman and his friends. By that time, however, the idea was looking pretty good.

Better to be digging ditches than to be whacked and tossed in one.

The MOU was a bitch, nevertheless, and I read over all the bullshit about the feds refusing to create any phony credit or work histories. Earlier, when the task force needed my help, I heard a lot about what the bureaucrats with WITSEC could do for me after all the investigations and the courtroom hassles were over, and it was time for me to become a new person. Now I was hearing what they couldn't—or wouldn't—do.

Signing the MOU was serious business, and as I later

learned couldn't have been more stringently enforced if I had scribbled my "G. 'Bud' Taylor" in my own blood. One of the stipulations permitted the government to toss everything out and "terminate the protection" if I lied about any of the facts agreed to in the MOU, or did anything else to violate the terms.

Exactly what did, and what didn't, violate the terms of the agreement, eventually became a knotty question that put me in direct conflict with the OEO and the BOP. According to terms of the agreement, my right to talk with the press was severely curtailed but wasn't totally denied. When the program was established and special units were designated for witnesses, certain safeguards were set up so that witnesses who were in custody could correspond and talk with the media.

A short time after I entered the program, the BOP changed the policy, based on instructions from the OEO, and prohibited all media contacts by WITSEC prisoners. That was the story they told when I complained, and when lawyers who were helping me asked, about the policy. They changed the rules on me in the middle of the game and didn't even put the policy in writing.

The Fleer affair also kept me occupied while I was at Sandstone, and I continued to tilt with Appelbaum over his efforts to get me to testify for the prosecution without first providing me with assurances on paper that I wouldn't be forgotten after the state no longer needed my cooperation. I stuck my neck out for the law before and still wound up behind bars. This time I wanted to make sure that I would get a commutation, pardon, or some other arrangements would be made for an early release before I took the witness stand.

Fleer did about two years on the drug charge, but approximately six months after he got back on the street, he was arrested at his home in Colombia, Missouri, on double-murder charges. Guess whose name was on the prosecution's witness list? George Emmett Taylor, Jr! They had my name and the name of another guy who was locked up with Fleer for a while, and said Geno talked to him about killing the two kids.

Fleer was still represented by my former lawyer, Clinton Almond, and by his partner, Marsha Brady. Almond told reporters he would try and keep a couple of guys the press referred to as "two former convicts" from testifying for the prosecution. "They couldn't even get to the jury without these cons," he declared. I wasn't "former," but I was one of the convicts named in the motion the lawyers filed shortly before the trial was scheduled to begin.

They claimed that "numerous offers have been made to George Taylor in exchange for his testimony," and contended the state hadn't provided information about any deals made with me. They observed that I had filed for a new trial, and said they believed that if I was successful with the appeal, I would be given an opportunity to plead guilty to lesser charges.

Appelbaum told the court that the only agreement the state made with me was to write a letter to the parole board acknowledging that I had testified against Fleer. As it turned out, I never testified in the trial anyway. Other events occurred that made the possibility of my testifying in the case a moot point.

Somebody in the Jefferson County sheriff's department messed up the process the first time the murder trial was scheduled to begin. Judge Anderson, the same judge who sentenced me, had to order a postponement because nobody mailed the summonses to members of the jury pool. The judge had already set aside three weeks on his court calendar for the trial.

It was a major screw-up that never happened before in the history of the Jefferson County court system, and Sheriff "Buck" Buerger said a clerk in his office simply forgot to mail out the summonses. He told reporters, "I regret very much that it happened." So did the mothers of the two dead kids, and so did little Tyler's dad.

When Steve Winzen showed up at the courthouse for the beginning of the trial and was told it was postponed, he confronted the sheriff and demanded to know who was responsible. Winzen claimed that Buerger "just went unglued," grabbed him by the shirt and roughed him up. He said three deputies escorted him out of the sheriff's offices. Buerger responded that he didn't rough up anybody, and said when Winzen refused to leave the office, a single deputy escorted him out. There was talk of a $2.5 million lawsuit Winzen reportedly wanted to file, but the flap eventually blew over.

Buerger later denied that the foul-up was the fault of anyone in his office, and said he believed someone either stole the jury summons cards or they fell out of the mail cart. He was quoted in another news story as saying he believed his clerk put the jury notification cards in the outgoing mail, and they were lost somewhere between his office and Jefferson County's postage meter. It was one more Jefferson County mystery.

Fleer finally took care of the problem by copping a guilty plea in exchange for life in prison instead of the death penalty. I like to think that even though I never went into the courtroom against him, information I provided to the state helped put him away for the rest of his life—so he can never kill another kid. Appelbaum and his investigators developed all sorts of independent corroboration of some of the information I supplied to them.

Although Appelbaum and I had our problems, he treated me fairly and kept his word—like Abram. Appelbaum's still around working with his own law firm now. Abram's dead. I felt really bad when I learned that he was shot to death when he stormed up to the house of a suspected bank robber along with six other members of an FBI SWAT team.

A couple of gunmen had hit the South Community Credit Union in Affton for $35,000, and the FBI gathered information leading them to suspect that James E. Price was the mastermind behind the heist. The SWAT team busted into his house with a search warrant, and Price met them with a hail of gunfire from a .38-caliber revolver. Doug, who was wearing a flak jacket, was shot in the forehead and two of his buddies were also hit before Price went down. One of the injured FBI guys was hit in the arm, the other in the leg. Price and Doug were dead.

When I heard who the shooter was, I wasn't surprised that someone got hurt. Jimmy Price was a wild man, an armed robber, doper and ex-con who swore he was never going back to the joint. He was a south St. Louis County operator and our paths crossed a few times, so when Abram went down some of his friends with the bureau somehow came to the flawed conclusion that I had something to do with tipping Jimmy off that they were planning a raid.

It was a coincidence, nothing more, that I was in St. Louis at the time for a debriefing on a case I was involved in with the FBI. I would never have done anything to hurt Doug Abram. No way. Price was a little guy, maybe 150 pounds soaking wet, but he was tough, mean, and always strapped. He was no friend of mine.

According to the press, Abram was the first FBI agent ever killed in St. Louis County. He was dead at forty-seven and left his wife and a couple of kids behind—a boy and a girl. Doug Abram was a straight shooter, who really believed he was protecting people from the bad guys. He was buried in his SWAT uniform. I felt like I had lost a friend—and a handler I could trust with my life.

During the two years I spent at Sandstone, I learned everything I could about the program, fussed with prison officials, and generally stirred up the shit with everybody I could think of who had anything to do with running WITSEC. I was determined to either get my sentence vacated or seriously shortened so I could get out and go on with my life. That made me unpopular with the administration, so I learned more than most people wanted to know about the process for handling alleged violations of prison regulations.

Inmates were protected by a hearing process set up to deal with suspected violations. The process was kicked off with preparation of an incident report outlining the complaint in detail. Then members of the prison staff investigated and determined if formal charges of violating regulations should be filed. Finally, if charges were filed, the warden ordered an initial hearing before a Unit Discipline Committee. Prisoners were provided with copies of incident reports and charges and were entitled to appear at the hearing, make a statement, and present documentary evidence in their favor. It was all set up very proper, but the system could be a bitch.

Eventually the big shots became fed up with the fuss I was kicking up and assigned me to diesel therapy. That's the only name I ever heard it called, by inmates as well as by the people who were running things, and it was a perfect description. A couple of times I wound up riding a bus for six weeks at a time with fifty to sixty other inmates who had gotten on the wrong side of their keepers for one reason or the other. It was a good way to keep a con out of touch for a while with lawyers, reporters, or with other people who might be causing problems—or were expected to. Don't expect me to know anything about the fine print in BOP or OEO regulations dealing with the official reasons used to justify putting an inmate on diesel therapy. I wasn't privy to that kind of information. I just know that it was an effective tool for the BOP to use in dealing with troublemakers. Living on the bus for up to twelve hours a day, and bunking in local county jails or state and federal prisons at night along whatever route we might be taking, was a big comedown from the luxury of life in one of the protected-witness units.

The food was barely subsistence quality. In the mornings we were given a small carton of milk and a honey bun or some kind of muffin. For lunch, served at one or two P.M., we almost always got the same meal—a baloney-and-cheese sandwich served in a paper bag. If we were lucky, we ate our evening meals at a jail or prison.

Security was airtight on the buses. Inmates were belly-chained, wore leg irons, and had blackbox cuffs between their wrists. The only time we were allowed to leave our seats was for pit stops, and when we had to go we were required to say, "CO [Correctional Officer], I got to use the head." The hacks might escort the guy to the john after a few minutes, or they might make him wait a couple of hours. If they had an interesting poker game going on, it was tough luck for the inmate. He had to hold it until the guard was ready.

Two guards were stationed behind heavy meshed wire near the latrines at the rear of the bus. Three others sat up front, and the driver sat behind a gate in a little compartment of his own. All the guards were armed with shotguns, and one time I saw a hack with an M-16. They also had teargas stashed up front in case someone got unruly.

The buses were designed for security, not for comfort. They were about the same size as a Greyhound and didn't carry any markings identifying them with the BOP, but that's where the similarity with civilian transport ended. The windows were heavily tinted on the outside, but on the inside they were blacked out and covered with heavy sheets of steel mesh.

The accommodations stunk, the company was rotten, and there wasn't a damned thing to do all day. We couldn't even look out the windows or slip on a headset and get down with some shit-kickin' music. After I was inside the joint for a while, I began to realize that a lot of C&W was written exactly for folks like me. I especially liked listening to the late Jim Reeves or Faron Young croon "Four Walls," the tune Willie Nelson wrote about the loneliness of prison life, and stuff like Jerry Reed's "You Got the Goldmine and I Got the Shaft." Most convicts could relate to both tunes. I grew up with rock, but there's something about being locked up that makes a man appreciate the plaintive riffs and mournful lyrics of C&W.

Eventually, after my first but not last, stint of diesel therapy, I was transferred to the witness unit in the FCI at Otisville, N. Y. The nearest town is even smaller than Sandstone and has only about 1,000 people. It's hidden in the foothills of the Shawangunk Mountains. The prison was constructed in Orange County about ten miles east of the Pennsylvania state line. It was a depressed area at the edge of the ski country, and that's one of the reasons state corrections officials constructed the prison there, in order to create some jobs and help the local economy. The other reason, of course, was that it was fairly close to the Big Apple, where most of the prisoners in general population come from. Their wives, girlfriends, and kids could get up to Otisville for visits a whole lot easier than if the inmates were locked up somewhere hundreds of miles farther upstate.

Good intentions; bad results. The prison created jobs, but it also led to a lot of the women and kids belonging to the inmates moving out of the city and settling around the prison. That sent the local welfare costs skyrocketing. Of course that situation wasn't unique to Otisville. That's one of the serious problems people in small communities have that depend on prisons for their living.

Economic conditions outside Otisville were a problem for other people. I was concerned with conditions and my situation inside the area of the prison set aside for witnesses that was referred to by guards and convicts alike as Unit One. The reason for the designation was simple: Otisville was the first of the prisons-within-a-prison constructed and specifically set aside for protected witnesses. Maybe because it was the oldest, it was the worst of all the units as far as the accommodations were concerned. Even a cockroach would call it a dump.

9

Mesa

The dull, the proud, the wicked and the mad.

Alexander Pope
"Epistles and Satires of Horace Imitated"

AT MESA UNIT, I met some of WITSEC's most glittering stars.

Big-time hoodlums like Gravano, Carlos Lehder Rivas, and "Crazy Phil" Leonetti. The biggest and best surprise waiting for me, however, was the presence of my old biker friend, Sergey Walton. I had heard that Sergey flipped, but I could hardly believe it until I learned how it happened. Sergey isn't big on chitchat, but eventually he told me the story himself.

Some of his biker pals put a contract out on him, and he wound up rolling, only on some cops. That got him off the street, and he never ratted out any Angels. It seems, or so I was told, that some of his people tried to pull a Joe Valachi after listening to a bunch of bullshit.

Sergey was boxed in just like Valachi, and he took a similar way out.

Sergey and I became running mates, but I also ran into another old friend from Sandstone: Duke! He was starting to lose his hair, when he read, he wore a pair of glasses that kept slipping down on his nose, and he was still soft-spoken and about as meek-looking as he could be. Appearances can be deceiving.

But there was no question who Mesa Unit's super celebrity was when I checked in. If there was a star walk in front of Graumann's Chinese Theatre for federally protected snitches, Sammy Gravano's name would be etched there in big, bold letters. Lehder would probably also get a star, but he wasn't hated by the other witnesses like Sammy was.

Despite his near constant bodyguards, and special protection from the feds, I know of two or three times that he was beat up or otherwise humiliated while living in the unit. Once he was worked over by a big black dude who belonged to the Jamaican Posse, and another time a little Mexican named José, who was with La Eme, stomped him. Jose walked into Sammy's room one night after getting on a roaring drunk and started bitch-slapping him. Sammy curled up in a fetal position blubbering, "Quit! Quit! I don't want any problems wit' you." It was disgusting. But José was wound up and he continued slapping him while yelling, "*Maricon,* be a man."

One of Sammy's bodyguards finally showed up and pulled José off the cowardly little piece of shit. The next day, José was hurried onto a jet and sent off on a one-way trip to Sandstone. He barely had time to pack.

There was no other payback for either attack. That's always a mistake for anybody doing time. It sends a signal of vulnerability, and even if you're a weakling and know the other guy can smear you all over the next

two cell blocks, you have to put up some show of re-
sistance. One more reason no one respected Sammy.

Sergey got in on the fun when he chased Sammy and
his clowns away from the weight pile. Then again, Sergey ran damned near everybody away from the weight
pile. We had it set up with stations so that we could do
our workouts really fast, finishing up one place, then
going on to the next. We worked out every day and
didn't like somebody who only came out every month
or so getting in our way, because then we would have
to stop and wait while they played. If somebody wasn't
an AB or a Hell's Angel, they knew better than to show
their face out there when Sergey was around.

The only time I know of when Sammy stood up for
himself and didn't call on one of his apes to scare off
whoever was bugging him, he kicked the ass of a skinny
dentist who was doing time for drug smuggling. The
dentist was out of shape and didn't know anything about
fighting.

La Cosa Nostra, the Mafia, Syndicate, or whatever
people are calling it nowadays, is losing its mystique.
Some of the wild and crazy new criminals coming up
don't give a shit about anything and they wouldn't be
afraid of Lucifer himself if they wound up in the same
witness-protection units or in the same general population of some prison.

After Gravano helped the feds finally nail his old
friend, Gotti, a black dude at the federal penitentiary in
Atlanta gave the Teflon Don such a solid ass-kicking
that he was hospitalized for a while. Blood and pasta!
Nobody moved a finger to help "Johnny Boy" while he
was being worked over. I don't know what the disagreement was all about, but the beating sent a powerful message. There's a changing of the guard going on.

Even Al Capone had the shit beat out of him a few
times while he was in Alcatraz, so actually Gotti's hu-

miliation was nothing new. Young inmates used Capone to make their bones and impress their fellow cons, and one time he was cut up pretty bad in the shower room with a prison shiv. Al was soft and fat by that time, and syphilis was already eating away his brain so there wasn't much he could do to protect himself.

The Mafia still has power, but its nothing like it used to be. Its lifeblood is bleeding out of it through wounds opened by the betrayal of people like Fat Vinnie, Jimmy the Weasel, Gravano and Phil Leonetti.

Crazy Phil and an old running mate of his, Lawrence "Yogi" Merlino, were also neighbors of mine at different times. I bunked near Phil at Mesa, and Yogi was one of the first people I met when I checked into Sandstone. They were both important members of the Nicodemo "Little Nicky" Scarfo Mafia organization in Philadelphia before they rolled and helped bring the gang down. Phil was Nicky's nephew and his underboss. Yogi was a soldier, but his older brother, Salvatore "Chuckie" Merlino moved higher up the ladder to the position of capo, (captain), until he was demoted in an organizational shakeup shortly before everything came crashing down.

Crazy Phil earned his nickname in Philadelphia where he was a feared hitter before ratting out his uncle, and other members of the Mob. Phil and Yogi rolled a few days after stiff sentences were ordered for seventeen members of the gang following a RICO conviction that included some 200 counts. Both guys were desperate characters, and Crazy Phil was looking at forty-five years in the joint, Yogi a little less, when they turned and bought deals for themselves.

When Crazy Phil cut his deal to become a federally protected witness, he was the highest ranking member of an American Mafia family ever to roll. Sammy the Bull was still hanging tough in New York, but Phil knew many of the secrets of the Big Apple's five major crime families as well as those of the Philly Mob. He was capable of causing a great deal of misery for the underworld in at least three states. He and Yogi ran things for Little Nicky in Atlantic City for a while after the new godfather moved on to Philadelphia to take over the organization and whip remaining rebellious factions into line.

As soon as Phil picked up his get-out-of-jail card from the WITSEC monopoly board, the feds whisked him away to a secret location and put him through his paces. It was the same routine they used with me, ten-and twelve-hour days of questioning, lie boxes, carry-out food and an occasional piss break.

The only difference was that the stakes were higher, and Phil's rewards were greater. For the most part, the feds kept their word to the Mafia hit man, and while they were still squeezing information out of him, he and his family were processed into the witness-protection program. Yogi and his family, along with a couple of other Philly wiseguys—Tommy Del Giorno and Nicholas "Nicky Crow" Caramandi, and their families—were also brought in and treated right.

"Tommy Del" was a hit man who was in on five murders, including the whacking of Salvatore "Brownie" Testa, the son of one of Little Nicky's predecessors as Philadelphia godfather. Italians: everybody's got a nickname. They love 'em.

I knew Tommy and Nicky Crow in the PCUs. Tommy cut a very good deal for himself and made a lot of money when he turned. I didn't see much of Nick because he got scared and was transferred out after his uncle was processed into the unit. After Tommy and I were both out on the street, we had some long conversations over a trial he was expected to testify in back in

Philadelphia, but we didn't hang out together while we were inside.

Phil was movie-star handsome and he knew it, but he was a joke. Me and Sergey and some of the other guys broke up when we saw him strutting around the unit dressed like a yuppie from Philadelphia's hoity-toity Main Line. He always dressed like he was going to a wedding, or to a funeral. He wore $2,000 or $3,000 silk suits, fine imported leather shoes that would have made O. J. Simpson's Bruno Maglis look like flip-flops by comparison, and freshly laundered shirts. Everything matched and looked new. He was a clothes horse.

A lot of the inmates I knew on the units liked to dress up, and they weren't all Mafia types. A guy who killed a parole officer in New York City changed into three different silk suits one Easter Sunday, and there wasn't one of them that cost less than $3,000. His complete outfits, including shirts, shoes, socks, and handkerchiefs must have cost at least $5,000, and that didn't include jewelry. Here was a guy surrounded by thieves, and he's strutting around in expensive suits and wearing $40,000 or $50,000 worth of jewelry. Some people have their brains in their ass.

Leonetti wasn't like that. He was never going to be a rocket engineer or a brain surgeon, but it was obvious he knew his business, and his record when he was on the street speaks for itself. Even though he walked around like he thought he was Al Pacino or Robert DiNiro, he wasn't some Hollywood actor playing at being a Mafia wiseguy. He was the real thing; one formidable dude. Crazy Phil was a man of power, whose authority and reputation came from his uncle's position, his own performance, and his reputation as a killer.

He specialized in rubbing out his uncle's enemies, and Scarfo had plenty. They died in car bombings and street-corner shootings, and bodies were dumped along isolated country roads. Accidents were always occuring among the South Philadelphia mobsters while Crazy Phil, Little Nicky, and their cronies were taking care of business. For a while it seemed like more bombs were exploding in Philly than in World War II Dresden.

Sammy the Bull even got in on the festivities when some of Scarfo's people went to the Gambino family in New York for outside hitters to take care of one of Little Nicky's chief rivals, a capo named John Simone. Almost nobody outside Simone's family called him by his real name. People used his gang name, Johnny Keys.

Sammy headed up the crew that kidnapped and executed Simone. The Philadelphia capo's body was dumped on Staten Island, and the hit was one of the nineteen that Sammy later admitted to. The job on Johnny Keys was an exception. For the most part the Philly gangsters did their own dirty work while they were sorting out the pecking order.

They were brazen about their work, and Phil and his wise-guy cronies were known for kicking up the waves around Atlantic City in a boat named *The Usual Suspects.* It shouldn't be surprising that Crazy Phil and his goons would eventually be taken down by the feds after flaunting that kind of twisted humor. The feds don't like those kinds of in-your-face taunts from hoodlums.

Crazy Phil and Sammy the Bull both understood the necessity for occasional Mob hits. It was the way the Mafia conducted business. And when the two former enforcers found themselves thrown together inside Mesa Unit, they became good friends. They had much in common. They were both former Mafia underbosses, were both former button men, and they were both turncoats who ratted out their bosses and their friends. They spent hours with their heads together, swapping war stories, talking old business, and fantasizing about the new opportunities that were waiting on the outside. And neither showed any remorse for what they had done.

One of the greatest strengths of the witness program—giving breaks to high-ranking members of a criminal organization for helping round up the people on the bottom—is also one of its most glaring weaknesses. On the surface, it sounds like the feds have everything backward. Not necessarily.

The big fish are the people with the knowledge of what's going on. They know the secrets, and when they roll, everyone is in trouble from top to bottom. A boss, or a number two man like Leonetti and Gravano can provide enough information to rip a crime family apart. Furthermore, when someone like that rolls, other defections usually occur down the line. The whole organization begins to shatter and break up.

Nick and Tommy rolled ahead of Crazy Phil and Yogi, and their cooperation with the law had a lot to do with the trouble members of the Philly Mob found themselves in. Before long, everybody was looking for a way to save their own asses. It was every man for himself. Fuck the women and children—and fuck Little Nicky.

Generally your average crime-family soldier can't create the kind of turbulence and chaos that a godfather, an underboss, or some other senior member can kick up. He simply doesn't have the information to trade that the people upstairs are in possession of. It's like the old saying, "A fish rots from the head down."

When feds want to move on a close-knit and closed enterprise like one of the La Cosa Nostra–organized-crime families, the only way to infiltrate it is to use someone who is already on the inside. That's why the witness-protection program is so important to law enforcement, and that's why it works so well in the investigative phase. They have to work through someone who knows what's going on, and they have to be able to wheel and deal. The government needs something to offer—like reduced sentences, no sentences at all, cash bounties, and of course the most important inducement of all—protection.

Just because it works, however, doesn't mean it's right. A system that rewards big-time criminals like Gravano, Lehder and Leonetti can stick in the craw of defense lawyers for the people who are being ratted out, and horrify criminal-justice purists. Defense lawyers have been known to describe the system in terms like "perverted" and "rotten to the core." It's especially repulsive when its being supported and paid for by officials working for the public with taxpayer dollars.

Government prosecutors have a different way of looking at the process. It's simply a matter of cooperation and necessary trade-offs, they say. Most of the time, they claim the end justifies the means. The object of most investigations in which federally protected witnesses are brought into the picture is to destroy a particular criminal organization. It can be something highly organized like the Gotti and Scarfo crime families, or it can be a loose-knit gang of corrupt politicians. Whatever!

Not surprisingly, I tend to side more now with the defense attorneys. It's a corrupt system that is providing big-time rewards to the wrong people, and too often results in shafting the little guy. Too many government handlers behave like vampires, sucking all the blood out of witnesses. Then when all the arteries and veins have collapsed and there's no more juice inside, they dump the dry husk and move on to a fresh victim.

Coddling criminals in order to catch a criminal is eventually going to backfire on the government in a big way. It's stupid to count on people like Bobby Del, Crazy Phil, or Sammy the Bull to change overnight.

So far, Sammy has apparently been keeping his nose clean, but don't put your money on the guy behaving like your typical suburban lawn-mowing, golf-playing husband and father forever. He was a vicious serial executioner for the Mafia—before he became the Justice Department's fair-haired boy.

Sammy was basically illiterate, and after he returned from meeting Janet Reno's hired hands in Washington, he asked me to read through his plea agreement and explain it to him.

The very carefully worded plea was the most bizarre government document I ever read, and I've read a lot of them. In sheer size alone, it was an impressive piece of work; it was at least six inches thick. But the contents, the deal that was agreed to was hard to believe. There it was however, laid out in front of me in black and white, everything stamped and properly signed by Justice Department flunkies or other suits.

Sammy admitted in the plea deal that he was either the hit man or played some other major role in a whole series of mob rubouts. In typical fashion, he played the bereaved friend or employer after he had people whacked, and attended most of the funerals, ordering flowers and telling families how bad he felt about their loved one's untimely death. Sometimes he gave the widows, kids, or parents a few hundred bucks. What an asshole! One of the guys he helped whack was his own brother-in-law.

So how was Sammy punished for the killings? The feds saw to it that his twenty-year sentence was cut to five. He had already served almost four years, about half of it testifying in courtrooms against his former hoodlum pals during the day and living in nice hotels at night. When I looked over his plea agreement, he had less than one year to serve.

A dummy like Gravano had wrung out an amazing deal for himself. Not only was he getting an early release, but he would be collecting $10 million in federal bounties for his good works. Mother Teresa should be treated so generously!

10

Carlos Enrique Lehder Rivas

SAMMY THE BULL spent hours with another glittering star of the witness-protection program, calling on all the resources of a junior-high-school education while straining his brain to understand the complexities of the elaborate schemes and facile mind of Carlos Enrique Lehder Rivas.

Lehder was a fascinating man and a master criminal who stuck to himself most of the time while I knew him at Mesa Unit; but physically he was a pip-squeak, and if you judged him by the way he looked, you might think he was a hopeless wimp. Sure, and a deadly coral snake looks like a harmless king snake if you simply switch the red, yellow, and black stripes around. Coral snakes kill by injecting poison through their fangs. Lehder's poison was cocaine, and he smuggled it into the country by the ton.

He was a good-looking guy for a little fellow who packed somewhere between 130 to 140 pounds on a wiry five foot, six inch frame. He kept his body in shape working out with weights and doing calisthenics; and he kept his mind sharp by reading books about philosophy, politics, and economics. Heavy material.

Lehder, whose friends and a lot of his enemies called him by the nickname ''Joe,'' welcomed the protection of me and some of my friends. Like the Italians, he was tough if he had a gun in his hand, but he wasn't a dude who would be much good in a rib-cracking, eye-gouging fight or an old-fashioned gang-stomping.

Sergey chased him off the weight pile one time, and he never showed his face again while we were working out. Joe was too little for hand-to-hand, and he knew other ways to control and intimidate people. Money and power.

I'm no ninety-eight-pound weakling now, and no one has ever kicked sand in my face, but when I was inside the units I was bulked up from my weight-lifting regimen and other exercise. That was all supplemented with the special diet that Sergey and I followed, and with regular sleep. At Mesa I was bench-pressing 265 pounds and had my eye on joining the 300-pound club. We did knee bends, squats, push-ups, the whole nine yards. I built myself up from 165 pounds to a sturdy 220 pounds of solid bone and muscle. I looked good, and felt good, and nobody messed with me. Not even the toughest guys in the joint.

Then there was my crowd, the homeboys I hung out with. Of course Sergey was my number one man. But I had other friends and cronies, as well, a toxic mix of bikers, ABs, drug smugglers, vicious killers, and other assorted toughs. Everybody was in great shape, and almost everybody worked out.

Physical size is important on the inside, but it's not the only factor that makes a particular convict stand out from his peers. Joe had brains, lots of them, and a devious criminal mind that was always in gear and scheming new projects. He was also totally ruthless.

He boasted that one time in the mountains of Colombia, he and his bodyguards wiped out an entire village because he thought the cocaine produced at a mountain laboratory for his gang was short. At least that's the way he recounted the event to me while we were sitting in his cell bullshitting and smoking a huge spliff wrapped in rice paper he tore out of a Bible. Pot was easy to get on the inside, but for some reason I've never figured out, we were always short on rolling papers so we resorted to the Good Book.

Joe was an old marijuana smuggler, and he loved to kick back with some strong weed and allow his mind to wander. He was a guy who knew how to turn his fantasies into reality. Joe didn't hit the big time however until he turned to cocaine, and began using his old marijuana contacts to move the more potent drug from his home country, Colombia, to the United States. He claimed to be proud that he never used snort, and said that people who did were stupid. If they wanted to burn out their brains with crack, and devastate their noses by snorting the poison until the flesh and gristle is eaten away and everything collapses into their face, that was their problem. They were customers, not his friends. There was no way that he would ever smoke coke, snort it, or inject it into his veins, he told me. Despite his current situation as a prisoner and turncoat, he was an ambitious man with big plans. He knew they could never be realized by a cokehead.

"You don't sleep in your own poison," he lectured. That was an old saying in Colombia, according to Joe. Maybe, but I've heard stories from other sources that he did quite a bit of napping there. He used to give radio and television interviews in Colombia when he was on the run, and people who watched the shows said he looked, talked, and behaved like he was seriously coked out.

Joe revelled in his notoriety, and I have to admit I was impressed with the little guy. We were sitting in his cell and working our way through Leviticus when he reminded me that he was once described by the feds as the biggest drug dealer in the world. Then the same government turned around and gave him protected-witness status and a sweetheart deal that's right up there with Gravano's.

Actually one of Joe's old associates in Medellín probably deserved the title as number one. But Joe was right up there with the leaders, and there was no one that was better at moving dope across borders than he was. Transport was his specialty, and he was fascinated by anything to do with moving dope. A prosecutor once compared him to Henry Ford, pointing out that what Ford did with automobiles for the American consumer, Joe did with the mass transportation of cocaine for the American consumer.

Drug smugglers use everything from cadavers to living people and pets to transport drugs, especially the expensive stuff like coke and heroin. They sew drugs up in the bodies of dead people being shipped from one country to another for burial. They package it and make dogs swallow it, or they open their stomachs and stick it all around inside, then bring the animals into the United States or some other country as pets. While I was listening to Joe's stories, a female English sheepdog made the front pages in New York after it was picked up at the John F. Kennedy International Airport with ten coke-filled condoms in its stomach. Drug agents in Rome picked up two more female English sheepdogs carrying twenty-five pounds of pure Colombian cocaine in their stomachs that was surgically implanted in Bogotá before the near 6,000-mile trip.

The smugglers like sheepdogs because they're big, with long hair, and females are preferred because if their bellies sag, some customs guy might just figure they're pregnant.

One of the most common ways to sneak drugs into a country is to use swallowers, men and women who fill up condoms or balloons with coke or heroin, then gulp them down. They train by sticking grape-filled condoms in the back of their throat, then forcing them down. Some swallowers use Chloraseptic to numb the throat. After passing through customs the swallower lets nature take its course. Then they retrieve the good shit from the bad. That's an old convict routine, but it's a dangerous thing to do. Sometimes the rubbers break, leak, or spill open while they're inside someone's stomach, and the swallower dies a nasty death.

Joe called them "body packers" or "internals," but that was all small-time shit to him, and he never bothered with them. It was dangerous. A Colombian body packer choked on his own vomit and died in Miami Beach a few years ago after he was taken to a hospital complaining about fever, chills, and an upset stomach. When he was opened up, thirty-two coke-filled condoms were found inside.

That sort of thing happens to body packers all the time, and there's always some hungry peon out there to take his place. A few months after the guy died in Miami Beach, another young Colombian from a little town near Cali body-packed some heroin into Miami and overdosed after the condom leaked. His contact didn't let the kid's death ruin the deal. He simply slit open the boy's stomach, took out the drugs, then dumped the body in a field. A pathologist figured things out during the autopsy when he found two pellets of dope lodged in the dead kid's throat that the smugglers missed.

A couple of Colombian brothers picked up at the Gateway International Bridge between Brownsville, Texas, and Matamoros, Mexico, a few years ago were luckier. They went to jail instead of to the morgue. They had swallowed a bunch of white Asian heroin. The skag was in little cylinders the Colombians call *pepas,* that were baked hard and molded. Then they were wrapped in two layers of tape, and condoms were pulled over the *pepas* before they were swallowed. One of the brothers had carried 100 *pepas* inside his stomach for a week before he was caught. They both slowed down digestion by taking an antidiarrhea drug.

A few years ago in Miami, an innocent man died after drinking a forty-one-cent bottle of what he thought was pony Malta. It was laced with $5,000 worth of liquid cocaine, and it killed him. Someone messed up and delivered the wrong bottle of Malta to a supermarket, whose owners thought they were buying legitimate soft drinks.

"Shit happens," Joe said. "Hey, people crossing streets get hit by cars all the time." Then he launched into a long sermon about Karma and fate. He loved to think out loud, especially when he had a good listener like me. I didn't mind. I had plenty of time on my hands, and there was always something to learn when Joe was running his mouth.

The new guys were coming up with some brilliant ideas that would have stood my smuggler grandfather on his head. Drug agents in California once confiscated a bunch of fiberglass dog kennels shipped into the country from Colombia. Smugglers had molded cocaine into the kennels along with the fiberglass. You have to remember, they have professional chemists and other people with unusual skills working for them. The DEA and U.S. Customs credits chemists in Bolivia with developing a way to bond coke with polystyrene plastic and fiberglass to form an odorless resin, and they're shipping the dope into the country molded into just about anything from sunglasses frames, camera parts, and toys to suitcases

and bathtubs. Everything is molded with heat and chemicals, then the cocaine is removed by heating the composition and dissolving the plastic bonds. If it's done
right, even drug-sniffing dogs can't pick it up. Brilliant!

Joe thought those capers were funny. Some of the
ideas showed real genius, but most of the deals were
still small-time shit. Joe and other cartel bosses were
big-time smugglers, who used everything from cars,
trucks, and fleets of airplanes and boats to sophisticated
air-conditioned tunnels under national borders. There's
no limit to their imagination, and they bring the shit into
the U.S. ten to twelve tons at a time. Colombian security
forces have captured at least two radar-guided minisub-
marines thought to be part of a fleet of underwater ves-
sels used by dope smugglers. Government spokesmen
said each of the drug-subs had room for three-man crews
and three tons of dope. Actually they're only semisub-
mersible and slip just beneath the water while the crew
breaths through six-foot-long snorkels. But they work.
Some drug smugglers are even believed to have their
own jerry-rigged aircraft carrier.

While Joe boasted about his exploits and the way he
worked the Gs after he was grabbed, he punctuated special points he wanted to make by waving the joint at
me. Then he would take a huge toke and continue speaking in that unique rasp of someone holding smoke in
their lungs until the last possible micro-second.

He loved showing off how smart he was, and how
easy he solved problems. Nothing stopped him. If he
couldn't find a pilot to fly for him, and because of the
big money involved that didn't happen often, he simply
looked for some short-order cook or another flunky who
was down on his luck and sent him to flight school.
When the guy graduated, he already had a good job
waiting for him.

The little shit was a character, but I couldn't figure

how he could be so casual about killing. I've been around and I know some hard people, but sometimes goose pimples popped out on my arms and legs when he talked about the intimidation and mass murder that was such a big part of running a big cocaine operation. To him a human life wasn't worth as much as a single gram of coke—unless it was his own, of course, but that was a different story. In his twisted little mind, Joe was uniquely intelligent, and if a few hundred people had to die for him to achieve his world vision, it was no big deal. I wasn't surprised to hear him laud Hitler as one of the greatest, if not the greatest, leader of all times. Obviously, we disagreed on this point.

When Joe talked about going to college in Connecticut, I had visions of an ivy-covered campus filled with juicy little coeds, fraternity-house beer bashes and pot-smoking parties. It was months before I learned Joe never even finished high school and got kicked out for acting up while he was living in Colombia. In one sense, however, he did go to college in Connecticut. His campus was the Federal Correctional Institution at Danbury. Joe did four years there, locked up with a bunch of hippies, antiwar protesters, and other assorted social and political radicals after he was busted in Miami for possession of more than two hundred pounds of marijuana. It was a cushy place to do time—like the units.

Many of his fellow inmates were people with good connections and big ideas, like his own. Joe told me he used the opportunity to make new friends and plot with another marijuana smuggler how they could use their old connections to move cocaine out of Colombia and into the United States. Coke was less cumbersome, easier to move, and much more valuable. After Joe was released and deported back to Colombia, he quickly went from making a few thousand dollars for a shipment of marijuana to millions of dollars for coke.

When I knew him, he was looking forward to getting out in a year or two and settling in Germany where his old man was from, then moving into the big-time dope business in Russia and other countries that used to be part of the old Soviet Union. He once held passports from three different countries, had twenty-five aliases, and spoke five languages fluently, so he could handle himself just about anywhere he was likely to wind up. He was never satisfied, and even though German was one of the languages he spoke, he continued to brush up his skills with books and tapes while he was inside.

After all the drab, gray years of Communism, people were looking for a high and some thrills, he said. He knew how to provide it, and wanted to set up a pipeline and an organization to move and peddle drugs.

Joe invited me to come along for the ride when he moved his new operation into Europe. The USSR had just broken up, and he called Europe and the old Soviet Republics "the new frontier" of drug dealing. He was already working out the logistics, and spent hours alone in his cell figuring out just how he was going to put together a huge new international narcotics distribution network focusing on the old Soviet republics. He looked at the situation there the same as any American capitalist manufacturer or businessman would. It was a world of opportunity, and he wanted a piece of the action. Joe talked like he was some big-time executive for Coca-Cola or another big multinational company. But there was no cola to go with the coke he was talking about.

The little guy said he expected to get out about the same time that I was released, and wanted me to join him as muscle. I was good with my fists and my feet, and didn't back down from anybody. Joe liked that. He told me he would be working with a bunch of foreigners and needed someone he could trust. Everything was already figured out. As soon as I got out, other people on the outside would be waiting with all the cash I needed and would help me get out of the country. All I had to do was jump parole and agree to go to work for him, and he would do the rest.

"How would $2 million be for starters?" he asked. Joe's people knew how to handle passports and other kinds of ID I would need to move around. They were pros at that kind of thing.

Barnyard loads of bullshit were shoveled around the units every day and every night. It happens in every prison and most of it is just that. Bullshit! With Joe Lehder it was different. I knew he could back up his big talk and deliver the goods.

When Joe talked, names of cities and countries like Minsk, Chechniya, Kazakhstan, and Georgia rolled off his tongue in a steady stream. When he said something about the opportunities in Georgia, I thought he was talking about moving into the drug business in Atlanta. He looked at me like I was crazy.

"Not Georgia—*Georgiiiia,*" he repeated, drawing out the sound. "Georgia that used to be part of the Soviet Union. The Georgia where Stalin came from, and (Eduard) Shevardnadze took over and became president," he told me. I didn't ask who the hell Shevardnadze was. Joe was a smart guy, and I didn't want to sound dumb.

We may have both been crooks, but we came from different worlds. Joe didn't think anything of jumping aboard an airplane and flying to some place like Belize, Berlin, or Bahrain. My travels took me to places like Oakland, Tucson, East St. Louis, and Chicago Heights. Except for a few cusswords in Spanish and some Dutch, I didn't speak any foreign languages, and I wasn't his kind of traveler.

Exploring the "new frontier" with him was an interesting proposition, but I turned him down. I was almost

forty years old and had already spent sixteen years in
the joint, more than half my adult life. I was serious
when I decided that I was fed up with being a criminal
and constantly facing the prospect of spending the rest
of my life behind bars. I was ready to become a civilian,
for real, and I told him so. Joe was disappointed, but he
wished me luck.

I admired Joe's mind and his balls—he had a pair of
cojones that would look like watermelons if their size
had anything to do with his sheer brazeness and big
talk—but he was a real swine, and I mean as far as his
living habits were concerned as well as his political
views and attitude about other people. Some of the guys
I ran with when I was riding with the Hell's Angels and
kicking around St. Louis were less than fastidious about
their personal hygiene. Joe Lehder could put any of them
to shame. He was puke filthy.

His job on the units was mopping the floors on the
tiers and common areas, and he did okay. But his cell
was a pigsty, and I stayed out of it whenever possible.
I preferred getting together in my cell or one of the common areas to talk, because he kept the place so dirty.
Half the time if Joe was sitting in his cell and he got
the urge, he wouldn't go to the trouble of walking four
feet to the john. He just wheeled it out and pissed on
the floor. A little dribble on his pants leg didn't bother
him, either. He wore his clothes until they were stiff with
dirt, piss, and whatever.

Maybe because of all his money and power, he was
used to other people cleaning up after him. I've seen
broads like that, but they just dropped their clothes
around and didn't pick up after themselves. They didn't
let their bodies get pig filthy. Joe always smelled bad,
and he didn't seem to notice, or maybe he didn't care,
when people maneuvered to stand upwind of him. He

wasn't a person you wanted to be double-celled with—or have around when you were eating.

Joe also had a thing about dictators, Lenin as well as Hitler in particular. He didn't seem to care which side of the political spectrum they fit in, just so long as they were stone-cold ruthless. Like him! That all tied in with his talk about starting his own country. The main thing about becoming dictator of his own country, however, was the opportunities that would provide for him to turn it into a hideaway he could use to export drugs all over the world. He had a little place like that in the Bahamas for a while called Norman's Cay.

The little island was only a couple of hundred miles from Miami and forty miles from Nassau. It was four-and-a-half miles long and shaped like a question mark. Importantly, it already had its own concrete airstrip—the perfect way station for shipping cocaine into the United States. After he chased most of the former forty or fifty residents away and took over, he had the island patrolled by armed guards and Doberman pinschers. Walter Cronkite, the TV news guy, was sailing his boat around there one time, and Joe's goons chased him off with guns.

Meanwhile, Joe's pilots flew hundreds of kilos of coke between Colombia and Florida. The flights were as regular as that chocolate laxative all the little kids like. He flooded the United States with it.

Joe was bitter about spending so much of his life locked up, and he hated this country. He said he wanted to destroy it, and the way to do that was to turn all the young people onto drugs—especially cocaine.

Joe's mother, Helena Rivas, was from Colombia. Joe spent most of his childhood in Armenia, Colombia. Coffee country! When he was fifteen, after his parents already divorced, he and his mother moved to the United States and lived for a while in Michigan. It wasn't long

after that when Joe began getting into trouble with the
law because he had a thing for cars that belonged to
other people. That was another thing he had in common
with fellow Colombian narcotics kingpin Pablo Escobar.
Early in his criminal career, Escobar was also a car thief.
That was after he quit swiping tombstones from ceme-
teries, scraping or sandblasting off the names, and reselling them. Brilliant criminal mind! Like Joe.

By the time Joe was in his mid-thirties, he was one
of the four main players in Colombia's Medellín drug
cartel. He was also a billionaire who carried packages
of crisp $100 bills around in suitcases and paid in cash
for new cars, houses, whatever he wanted. He was too
flamboyant for his own good, but he got away with it
for so long because he spent most of his time in some
South American countries where payoffs were a way of
life. Robbers like me stick people up with guns. Politicians don't need guns. They just stick their hands out.

The cartel godfathers got too big for their britches,
and it was inevitable there would be a crackdown. The
cartel chiefs were taken down one by one. Escobar, the
most powerful of them all, and the man most responsible
for a bloody war against his own government that
claimed the lives of three presidential candidates, and
hundreds of cops, judges, journalists, and civilians in
ambush shootings and bombings, was the last to go. He
was even blamed for a bomb that blew up a Colombian
jetliner and killed 107 people. The man called El Padrino
(Godfather) also went down the nastiest. Eventually a
special force of 3,000 Colombian soldiers and cops was
hunting for him, and in 1993 he died with his bodyguard
during a Wild West–style rooftop shootout at a three-
story safe house in Medellín. It was a small army, and
it was backed up by U. S. surveillance planes.

When his bullet-riddled body was picked up off the
red Spanish tiles of the roof, he still had two .9-mm

pistols in his hand. It was the day after his forty-fourth birthday. The troops had been tracking him for eighteen months, after he escaped along with nine of his top guys during a prison transfer the previous year, by promising to grease a few palms. Huge amounts of money, even the promise of it, can perform wonders! Money works both ways. When Escobar was tracked down, he had a $6.2-million bounty on his head. By the time El Padrino was blown away, another bunch of energetic and hungry drug gang leaders from the coastal city of Cali was moving in on the Medellín bunch, anyway. The Medellín operation was breaking up.

Joe told me a bit about prisons in Colombia and how his former running mate, Pablo, was treated like a king while he was in residence at an old jail near Medellín that was especially converted to hold him and more than a dozen of his most important lieutenants. Escobar had his own luxury apartment with a spectacular view of the city. The apartment was fully outfitted with a color TV, stereo equipment, computers, and a sophisticated communications system that included eleven private telephone lines, three radio-telephone systems, cellular phones, beepers—and as a backup for all that technology—carrier pigeons. For quiet moments, he had his own video library, and a private bar, fully stocked with the best booze in the world, set at the end of a comfortable reception room. Crown Royal, all the best rums, fine cognac, and Scotch like Chivas Regal, which was also one of Joe Lehder's favorites. The walls were lined with expensive paintings, family portraits, and Wanted posters of himself. The drug godfather lived so good there that journalists referred to the luxury prison as Hotel Escobar. Others called it "The Cathedral." Sounds a lot like one of the Witness Protection Units.

Even Joe wasn't as safe in South America as he thought he was. By the time Escobar checked out, the little guy had already been behind bars for six years. He watched, from a distance, while Escobar went down, and he wasn't exactly heartbroken when his former running mate placed second in the shootout. Escobar was a rat and he deserved to die, Joe said.

Joe was kidnapped in Peru in 1987 and whisked back to the United States. He blamed some of his old friends with the cartel, including Escobar, for giving him up. They thought it would get them off the hook, as well as eliminate competition. They were wrong about getting off the hook, but that didn't help Joe's case. This time when he returned to the United States, he didn't have to sneak in. He was escorted in handcuffs, and he wasn't looking at a minute or two in some cushy lockup like Danbury FCI. He was an international bogeyman, one of the cocaine princes, a billionaire narco-trafficker who was helping tear America apart, or so the drug fighters said.

After he was put on an airplane in Colombia and flown to Tampa, Joe cooled his heels for a while in the super-maximum-security FCI in Marion, Illinois. Then he was transferred to the federal prison at Talladega, Alabama, so he would be closer to his lawyers. He also stayed at the FCI Atlanta for a while before he was finally transported across the state to Jacksonville and locked up on a military base to await his trial. He was treated to the grand tour.

U. S. Attorney Robert Merkle, one of the Justice Department's best trial lawyers, traveled upstate from Miami to head the prosecution, and over seven months he presented 115 witnesses against Joe. They talked about pay-offs to Bahamian officials, they talked about Norman's Cay, and they talked about thousands of kilos of cocaine being moved into the United States. "Uncle Walter" was one of the witnesses, and told the jury about being chased away from the cay at gunpoint. Some of the most devastating evidence came from Joe's own big mouth, however, in the form of radio and television interviews he starred in while he was hiding out in the Colombian jungle, trashing the U. S. government and blaming America's drug problems on the users.

During pre-sentencing remarks, Lehder talked for twenty-eight minutes and claimed he was kidnapped and flown illegally to the United States. "I feel like an Indian in a white man's court," he complained.

If the judge was impressed, he didn't show it. He ordered the maximum sentence—life without parole plus 135 years. That was for beginners. Totaling everything up, before the courts were through with him he was looking at a total of 475 years behind bars. The court was probably serious about the stiff penalties ordered for the Henry Ford of drug trafficking, but sentencing judges don't always have the last word. Joe was a very bright guy and didn't show any signs of being intimidated by the hundreds of years he was sentenced to serve. He had too much money and too much information to trade for him to meekly settle for spending the rest of his life in prison.

When he was sentenced, there was a big splash in the media about the drug kingpin who was permanently removed from the picture by being ordered to serve two life terms. At last we were winning the drug war. Sounded good, but you can't believe everything you hear. I got a different reading on his future when he showed me his plea agreement. He had worked out a series of sentence reductions that almost certainly would get him out before the year 2000.

Joe's prosecution was just a warm-up for the trial of former Panama dictator Manuel Antonio Noriega, which was held in Miami at the other end of Florida. The little general was the key to getting Joe out of his mess. The feds were so anxious to nail Noriega that they cut more

than 100 years off Joe's sentence just to get him to testify. He also provided prosecutors with important information about other deals and dealmakers in government
throughout Central and South America. Joe knew all
their secrets, the institutional corruption that was so inbred in countries like Colombia, and he laid it all out
for the Gs. He was rewarded with more sentence reductions.

Sammy showed more interest in Joe Lehder's fantastic
schemes than I did. They talked about the possibilities
of working together on international business projects. I
got used to listening to Sammy boast about his big new
partnership plans.

Joe loved playing teacher, and every so often he
crammed three or four guys into his cell, put a slab of
cardboard over the door, then taught a course in remedial
crime. While the class held their noses and tried not to
step in anything they shouldn't, he explained the finer
points of transporting multimillion-dollar cargoes of cocaine or heroin from one country to another.

Some of Joe's talk was confusing for Sammy. Every
so often the little toad would bump my arm and whisper:
"Bud, what the fuck is that crazy spick talking about?"
Sammy was serious. He was doing his best to follow
because he knew Joe was explaining how to make more
money than he had ever dreamed of when he was running the streets of Bensonhurst working for Johnny Boy
Gotti, but some of the words and phrases were beyond
him. Sammy had trouble following the lesson plan when
Joe talked about the intricacies of such important matters
as money laundering, and the necessity to accept an occasional loss in the smuggling business.

One day when Joe was talking about ferrying loads
of dope from a mother ship in the Carribean or the Gulf
of Mexico in those sleek and slender cigarette boats that
smugglers refer to as go-fasts, he pointed out that oc-

casionally you lose a few. A speedy little Chris Craft Stinger or a Blue Thunder can skim over the waves at up to eighty miles an hour and cost as much as $100,000, and that got Sammy's attention.

"A hundred fucking thousand clams I ain't losing," he sputtered. "I'm not spending $100,000 for a boat and then lose it. Fuck that shit." Joe patiently tried to explain that $100,000 was nothing when you were dealing in hundreds of millions of dollars, but Sammy was still thinking like a hoodlum from Brooklyn. He said there was no way he would simply eat a loss of $100,000.

Joe was exasperated. "Sammy, you're so fucking dumb, what'd you do for Johnny Boy," he asked. "Zip his fly?" That brought a laugh from everybody but Sammy. He was still pissed off over the idea of simply writing off a go-fast here and there. "A hundred fucking thousand clams I ain't losing," he muttered. "If I lose a $100,000 boat somebody is gonna get whacked. Fuck that shit!"

Sammy eventually figured things out, though, and pretty soon he was going around talking about the new operation he and Joe were planning to set up to run drugs from the Colombian jungle, through Central America to Mexico where they would finally be shipped across the U.S. border to Douglas, Arizona. No more being an underboss for Sammy. He was going to be the big guy, the godfather.

When Sammy finally split, it was a relief. He didn't look all that much like the same little New York hoodlum, but he had the same rotten, cocky personality. Sammy walked out into his new world with hair plugs, and a new nose and chin that were rejiggered. A plastic surgeon even worked around his eyes and pinned back his ears. Sammy told me all kinds of little secrets about himself, and even confided that his real name was Salvatore. Some confidence to share. Anybody could have figured that one out.

The feds helped him open a bagel shop in Pleasant Valley, an upscale little Phoenix suburb out by Tempe and Scottsdale, a short drive from the Mexican border. As usual, Sammy couldn't keep his mouth shut and told me and other people about that. Everyone knew about his new enterprise anyway, because me and a couple of other inmates made a sign for the business in the machine shop. Some secret!

Sammy made it into phase two of the program along with lots of other guys. I've heard that Joe Lehder is one of those who made it, although the government won't confirm that he's free. I'm convinced that my information is good and Joe is outside. If so, he will simply have joined a small army of big-time narco-traffickers and stone-cold killers who graduated from the units ahead of him and joined the civilians.

11

Phase Two

PROTECTED WITNESSES ARE weaned away from Big Daddy during phase two. Except for marquee names like Gravano and Lehder who have struck independent deals for themselves and are filthy rich, most phase-two witnesses go on the government payroll.

Relocated witnesses are given much more than money when they move into phase two, including complete new identities for themselves and close family members. New names, new Social Security numbers—the works.

Some of them do very well for themselves, and even relatively small-timers, as compared to the superstars, have collected up to $3,000 per month for up to eighteen months. Others, like Max Mermelstein, a former engineer who grew up in Brooklyn, then moved to the Sunshine State in search of his fortune, do much better than that.

Mermelstein is one of the guys who rolled and testified against Noriega. He opened up on everybody.

According to Mermelstein, he was living in a ritzy Fort Lauderdale suburb—just a regular civilian with a roll of baby fat around his tummy, working hard to re-

alize the American dream—when he was seduced into
the drug-smuggling business by a friend of his Colombian wife.

According to investigators, Mermelstein warmed up
for his drug running activities by smuggling aliens into
the United States through the Bahamas. Then he moved
into the big time, hooking up with the cocaine cowboys
who were running roughshod around South Florida in
the early 1980s. Mermelstein was an imaginative dude,
who set up a sophisticated operation to run Medellín
drugs into the country in airplanes and power boats. He
moved piles of drugs, and he made piles of money, but
nothing lasts forever.

By the summer of 1985, he was already in deep shit
with his Colombian pals when a task force of federal
and local drug agents swooped in and grabbed him as
he was driving his sporty new Jaguar a few blocks from
his house. Inside the house, where he lived with his wife
and two kids, investigators rounded up a couple dozen
guns and more than $270,000 from a wall safe and a
bag under his bed. They took another automatic pistol,
a German-manufactured Walther, from the Jag's glove
compartment.

For a dude who was supposedly trapped into becoming a big-time dope smuggler, Mermelstein was making
the best of things and living extremely well. There were
times I did very good when I was on the street, but I
never had hundreds of thousands of dollars just laying
around the house. There was a reason Mermelstein was
doing so good. He was an honest-to-God insider; a major
operator who weaseled his way into the top ranks of the
Colombian drug-smuggling operations. Eventually he
admitted to smuggling thousands of kilos of cocaine into
this country.

Mermelstein knew everything about everybody, and
when he rolled—about a month after he was busted—

he told task-force guys things they hadn't even suspected about the drug cartels. He dropped major secrets, like the location of drug-smuggling routes, how many kilos of coke individual drug bosses were moving each month, and gave up names of big-time drug jefes the DEA had never heard of before. He laid other exotic little tidbits on his handlers as well, like the scheme that Cali cartel kingpins put together to smuggle coke in the nose cones of Eastern Airline jets.

Like me and most other people who roll and rat on their old business associates, Mermelstein didn't have much of a choice at the time. He and one of his Colombian partners were indicted in Los Angeles for smuggling 750 kilos of coke into California, and the feds were accusing him of operating a continuing criminal enterprise. He was facing the big CCE, and that's something nobody wants hanging over their head because a conviction means you can be sent to the joint for life with no parole. That's the real thing; not life and you're outside in five or six years. They lock you inside some place like Marion or the new super-maximum-security FCI in Florence, Arizona, and you stay there until you die.

Mermelstein rolled, and he took all kinds of people down with the information he vomited up. People with the Medellín cartel, with the Cali organization, and freelancers and freebooters from all over the Western hemisphere tumbled. Everything is chain reaction when someone who is that big and knows that much rolls, and other people began ratting down the line. Mermelstein and the task-force guys who were handling him did some serious damage.

One of the proceedings he testified in was the trial in Miami of a couple of Colombians charged with laundering more than $20 million for cartel kingpins. Mermelstein didn't even know the guys, but he testified as an expert witness and they were convicted. In response to questioning from a defense lawyer at another trial, Mermelstein stated at one point that he had taken approximately $300 million in illegal money out of this country.

Mermelstein did okay by turning. He admitted helping smuggle huge amounts of coke into the United States that authorities estimated was worth a whopping $12.5 billion on the street. That's a lot of snort and crack, and a lot of ruined lives. But Main Justice and WITSEC saw to it that he paid for his evil deeds. They let him off with a wrist-slap sentence of two years in one of the units and a new identity for himself and sixteen of his relatives. He was allowed to keep more than $12 million in blood money from the smuggling operations, acccording to scuttlebutt on the units. The good old American taxpayer kicked in another $664,000 for expenses, and that's not scuttlebutt. It's well documented. Not bad, when you have to keep in mind that he wasn't really a criminal. He was a victim.

The way Mermelstein explained it, he was an adult with a good education and a good mind who had the bad luck to fall from grace because he was married to a foreigner. If you believe that story of how he was led to become a multimillionaire drug smuggler, he was a victim of circumstances. Prisons are full of guys just like him. They go for the big dollar and wind up with their ass in a sling, so it becomes somebody else's fault. Social workers still believe bullshit yarns like that, but the cons know what's really going down. Lots of guys marry foreign wives, including women from Colombia and other South or Central American countries, and they don't become drug-smuggling kingpins.

Mermelstein isn't the only cartel-connected drug smuggler who has been arrested, then handsomely rewarded by the feds for rolling. Enough pilots who ferried drugs from Central America and South America into the

United States, in fact, were ushered into the federal witness-protection program to staff a small air force.

Most of the drug pilots who were treated so royally by U.S. narcotics enforcement agencies and the U.S. Justice Department had one thing in common. They ratted on Noriega, who for a while was painted by official Washington and by the American press as an international villain who almost single-handedly devastated the nation's schoolyards and corrupted its youth with hundreds of tons of cocaine, marijuana, and other narcotics.

It was a curious thing about Noriega. For years while he was fulfilling his role serving the interests of the United States by protecting the Panama Canal, he was a golden boy. His many faults were overlooked by his friends to the north, and for a while in the 1980s he was even on the CIA's payroll. Then his reputation as a corrupt politician who sold his country out to the drug cartels caught up with him and he began losing his iron-handed control. Riots broke out in Panama City, strikes occurred, and rival military officers came close to dumping him in a coup d'état—and after awhile he wasn't as useful to the big guys in Washington as he used to be.

Early in 1988, a federal grand jury in Miami returned a twelve-count indictment charging him with crimes tied to international narco-trafficking going back almost six years. Among other offenses, Noriega was accused of providing a haven for the members of the Medellín cartel, allowing them to set up laboratories in Panama and obtain chemicals used in manufacturing cocaine, then helping them smuggle the finished product into the United States.

The feds knew that the bantam-weight general didn't do all that by himself, and more than a dozen codefendants were also named in the indictment, including Pablo Escobar. The Justice Department and others involved in the "get Noriega" task force, offered deals to some of his fellow defendants named in the indictment, as well as to other drug smugglers picked up in related investigations. All they had to do to qualify for special handling and handsome rewards, was roll on Noriega. Lehder was one of those people.

The Panamanian dictator's face is so pitted with scars that only a mud wasp could love it and he wasn't much to look at, but he was the big man in Panama before President Bush sent the U.S. Army after him in 1989. The general holed up in the Vatican Embassy in Panama City for weeks, drawing worldwide attention before he was finally coaxed out.

Noriega's trial in federal court in Miami, along with pretrial maneuvering and appeals, had the American media and much of the world press preoccupied for a couple of years. It seemed that everybody throughout the Western Hemisphere and much of the rest of the world, had their collective ears pressed close to the courtroom doors while the U.S. government's intrepid drug fighters came down on the ugly little dictator.

Noriega pulled a forty-year sentence on the drug and racketeering charges, and he's still rattling around in the Miami Correctional Institution. So here's an international bogeyman that the U.S. government paid some $29 million in your tax dollars to convict, to say nothing of handing out sweetheart deals to twenty-nine convicted or suspected drug runners or informants, and he's not even in a maximum security federal prison. He's in a fucking city jail, spending his days improving his mind and soaking up American culture from the TV. Could he be sitting in Miami only a couple of hundred miles or so from Havana because the feds are hoping he will roll someday and testify against Fidel Castro? Stranger things have happened!

The little dictator ended up as the fall guy for a lot

of people. A witches' brew of smugglers and execution-ers worked out deals for themselves, based on their co-operation with federal prosecutors who wanted a piece of him. At least twenty members of various drug cartels were freed or let off with wrist-slap sentences for help-ing nail the forcibly retired general. What line of work do you suppose all those drug smugglers went into after they finished testifying or did their ''minutes'' in witness-protection programs and other PCUs? Engineer-ing perhaps? The medical profession? Fashion design? Go figure!

Many of Noriega's old friends did very well indeed by ratting on him. People like Floyd Carlton Canceres. Carlton was a pilot and major in the Panamanian Air Force, who admitted smuggling $25 million worth of cocaine into the United States. Then he cut a deal for himself by rolling on Noriega that was on a par with Mermelstein's settlement.

A timid guy who somehow carved a lucrative niche for himself among some of the most ruthless and blood-thirsty criminals in the Western hemisphere, Carlton bought his cushy deal, despite moving one thousand ki-los of cocaine out of Colombia into Panama during the 1980s. He used his own charter air service to fly the drugs between Colombia and Panama. His multimillion-dollar sideline was carried on with the blessing of No-riega.

Carlton was facing a dismal future after his arrest and conviction on a pile of drug charges. He was sentenced to life with no parole, plus 145 years, when he rolled and offered to testify against Noriega, Lehder, and other members of the Medillín cartel. Pablo Escobar and the drug-smuggling Ochoa family were others he promised to rat on.

The former drug runner who was known as ''No-riega's Pilot'' was rewarded handsomely for his treach-

George's grandfather,
Orville "Bogie" Van Boven.

George's father, George E.
Taylor, Sr., getting last-minute
jitters before his baptism.

George's mother, Jane Van
Boven Taylor, on her wed-
ding day, September 3, 1952.

George's Harley-Davidson parked in Cleveland, Ohio, hotel room.

Hell's Angel Jim Jim in Port Richmond, California.

George and Patrick "Squeegie" McCoombs.

Party time in Mesa Unit, celebrating New Year's Eve 1992 with friends and beer. George is in the second row on the left. His lifting pal Sergey Walton is in the back center.

George in his cell on Mesa Unit.

George relaxing in a workshop on Mesa Unit.

George with girlfriend Vicki Hampton and her daughter, Nikki, on a visiting day in April 1989.

George and Vicki's home in suburban St. Louis before it was seized by the IRS.

George with his mother (on left) and wife, Jean.

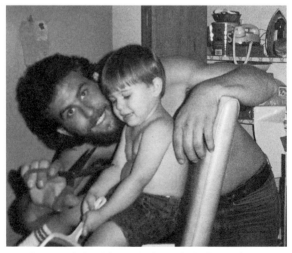

George giving his son Michael his first haircut.

George's guard dogs Bogie (above) and Sergey. Both dogs were killed when George's car was run off the road and he was shot in June 1997.

George in his cell on Mesa Unit, but still going after the government with motions and writs.

ery. While we were locked up together at Sandstone, I had an opportunity to learn just how well he was treated. His English wasn't very good, and he asked me to read his plea agreements and witness-protection promises. I was more than happy to look them over and explain them. For a guy who normally behaved Casper Milquetoast meek, and who didn't have a perfect command of English, he forged a hell of a deal for himself.

In return for his testimony, the former military officer's sentence was slashed to a mere two years with three years probation, and he was moved into phase two of the program with his extended family. I'm referring to the Carlton clan as an extended family because he cut a deal for twenty relatives, in addition to the baby-sitter. They were moved from Panama to the United States as part of the agreement.

Carlton absolutely refused to cooperate unless the feds brought his entire crew into the program. He knew that if he left them behind, they would be slaughtered by the drug cartels as examples of what happens when someone snitches, or for pure revenge. The retired drug pilot delivered for the feds, and they delivered for him.

American taxpayers shelled out a lump-sum bounty of more than $211,000, and an additional generous allowance of thousands of dollars for living expenses that helped keep the black beans and rice on the table for his big family. The deal for expenses included the cost of a car. Uncle Sam also promised not to confiscate any of his property in the United States. Property he owned outside the country was also shielded from seizure.

Carlton provided some of the most devastating testimony of Noriega's trial and played an important role in winning a conviction. He testified that he made four flights from Colombia to remote airstrips in Panama, carrying huge loads of cocaine. Each time he successfully completed one of the flights, he passed cash payments ranging up to $200,000 to Noriega through an aide.

David Rodrigo Ortiz is another Medellín-cartel drug pilot who helped sell Noriega down the river in order to cut a sweetheart deal for himself. Rodrigo was an international drug runner who had piled up sentences in Florida and Texas totaling eighty-five years, and had another fourteen-year sentence with a whopping $90 million fine levied against him in France. When he rolled and testified against Noriega, the Texas charges were dismissed and he served only part of an eight-year sentence as a protected witness. The money and property he amassed during his drug-running days were waiting for him when he moved into phase two.

Eduardo Pardo, a pilot who ran guns to the anti-Communist guerillas in Nicaragua and ferried narcotics back to the United States on return trips, is another convicted drug smuggler who cut a good deal in return for testifying against the little general. Pardo was one of Carlton's employees, and eventualy served nineteen months. He was permitted to keep his money and property, and his friends in the Justice Department even recommended that he be allowed to hang onto his pilots' license.

Jose Cabrera, another of the onetime top bananas in the Medellín cartel, pulled sentences in Florida and New York totaling 133 years. He traded testimony against Noriega for a reduction of the total sentence to fifteen years—and served about one-third of that. The deal he cut included relocation in the program for his family and himself, permission to keep the money and personal property he had amassed, and a free pass from the IRS.

Ricardo Bilonick was also tied to the Washington-directed operation to covertly move arms to the Nicaraguan freedom fighters, and managed to squeeze in a profitable sideline in the drug-smuggling business. The former Panamanian diplomat was tied by prosecutors to the importation into this country of $400 million worth of cocaine before he was convicted and sentenced to a sixty-year prison term. He rolled, was accepted as a protected witness, and actually served a little more than three years in a country-club federal prison for white-collar criminals at the Homestead Air Force Base in South Florida. An appreciative American government allowed him to keep his drug earnings and appealed to the Immigration and Naturalization Service to permit the former big-time narco-trafficker and members of his family to remain in the United States.

Enrique Pretelt was a top Medellín operator who provided key testimony about companies that Noriega secretly owned, and delved deeply into money laundering aspects of the government's case. He was released on parole immediately after his court appearance. Before flipping, Pretalt was serving a thirty-five-year sentence, but that was reduced to ten, and he was freed after being given credit for time served. Pretelt's deal also included a promise from the government not to deport him from the United States, and to allow him to keep almost all the money and property he accumulated during his drug-smuggling days.

Major narco-traffickers who piled on the "get Noriega" bandwagon weren't all fellow Latins from south of the border. Steven Kalish was a pilot and hard-riding Texan who built a multimillion-dollar fortune smuggling tons of marijuana and cocaine into the United States before he was run to the ground and saddled with drug-running convictions in Texas, Florida, and North Carolina. When all his sentences were combined, he was facing life, plus 195 years.

After Kalish told the jury at Noriega's trial that he flew drugs for the former Panama dictator and helped him launder money, he was rewarded with a huge sentence reduction. He eventually served less than eight years behind bars. The deal included protected-witness status and a promise not to prosecute his wife. For a change, the feds required Kalish to forfeit some of his ill-gotten gains, including about $2.8 million in cash, a pile of jewelry, a forty-five-foot yacht, and a red Ferrari. He could afford it. Authorities estimated he pulled in about $20 million during his drug-running days.

Brian Davidow was another gringo who did okay for himself. He pulled a fifty-five-year prison sentence for his drug-running activities, but was rewarded for his testimony in Noriega's trial with a reduction that had him back on the streets after serving less than three years. He was also allowed to keep cash and personal property accumulated while moving a mountain of cocaine the government estimated was worth about $25 million.

It's the old story. It didn't matter how serious your crimes were—if you were willing to lead the feds to a bigger fish, you could earn a pass for yourself, your family, and in cases like Carlton's, for your friends and your baby-sitter. Noriega was probably responsible for springing more criminals from the joint than F. Lee Bailey and John Gotti's mouthpieces combined.

Was nabbing Noriega worth the cost? I'm not so sure. When the Gs so generously reward people like Floyd Carlton Canceres, Jose Cabrera, Steven Kalish, and Carlos Lehder Rivas and turn them back onto the street, the wrong message is being sent. It doesn't matter what you do; if you can't buy freedom with money, you can always get it by naming names.

12

Playing Russian Roulette

THE NEXT TIME your new neighbor's dog takes a shit on your lawn, don't be too anxious to rush next door and raise hell. Your neighbor might be a hoodlum who made headlines littering the streets of the old Hell's Kitchen neighborhood of Manhattan with chopped up bodies, or some brooding psycho you've never heard of who is about to turn stone-cold killer.

Your reclusive new neighbor could be a homicidal maniac like Westie Bob or Mickey Featherstone. Or he might be an Arthur Kane, or a James "Doc" Kristian, Ph.D. If your luck is running really bad, the stranger sitting next to you on the 737 jetliner bound from Washington, D.C. to Chicago could even be a Paul Olson.

I was in the units with Westie Bob and Featherstone. Along with most of the protected witnesses, they were making big plans and looking forward to graduation day. Arthur Kane and Dr. Kristian were already graduates who had moved into phase two of the program and were firmly settled into new lives and new homes next door to citizens who didn't have the slightest inkling of how dangerous their new neighbors were. Olson was a federal witness busy working a drug investigation for the DEA and federal prosecutors.

Westie Bob is Robert Huggard, a wild Irishman who was part of a vicious gang of killers from the old Hell's Kitchen area of Manhattan. Mickey Featherstone was one of his running mates, a Vietnam veteran who came home from Southeast Asia with a seriously twisted brain and a permanently twitchy trigger finger, to join up with the fierce Irish-American street gang that was already terrorizing his old neighborhood. The Westies were a vicious pack of homicidal druggies and booze hounds known for dropping off body parts of victims all over the West Side neighborhood.

While I was in general population at Jeff City I met some mean and ruthless criminals, but on the witness-protection units there were dozens of guys who were meaner, badder, and flat-out more bloodcurdlingly dangerous. Westie Bob was one of the worst; a genuine psycho with more blood on his hands than he had in his veins. He loved to torture and kill.

We weren't close friends and I didn't make a practice of hanging around with him, but there were times when we found ourselves together with a chance to talk. Westie Bob enjoyed talking about the guys he killed, and how the hits went down. He especially liked to tell about taking a chainsaw to his victims and chopping them up while they were still alive and screaming. He always giggled when he described how their eyes bugged out, they pissed their pants or shit themselves—then started to scream.

Huggard was proud of another caper that illustrates exactly how ghoulishly ruthless the Westies were. He boasted about a small-time crook who was butchered and had one of his hands cut off. Westie Bob and his cronies froze the hand and used it to plant fingerprints on a gun in order to confuse police. What kind of sick mind would conceive of a scheme to carry around a dead man's hand so they can use the fingerprints? The kind of booze-soaked minds inside the heads of the Westies, that's who.

Westie Bob hated blacks as much as anyone I met on the units, but the single individual he seemed to despise more than anyone else was Sammy the Bull. He made a point of stalking up to Sammy every day, then looking through him like he was talking to someone else and loudly announcing: "I'm gonna kill that little fucking midget."

Huggard's hatred for the little hoodlum apparently went back to the days when the Westies were doing special contract hits for Sammy's mob family, the Gambinos, when their boss "Big Paulie" Castellano needed outside hitters for rubouts that weren't properly sanctioned by the mob. A lot of the Irishmen didn't like the idea of their boss, Jimmy Coonan, cozying up to the Guineas.

It was a tense situation, and Sammy's bodyguards always made sure they were nearby, but nothing violent ever happened. It could have; it was unusual for the OEO to permit two prisoners with a beef like that to occupy the same unit. Westie Bob got away with picking on the star snitch because he was also a major player in the government's drive against organized crime in the Big Apple. He was an important witness.

Mickey Featherstone also did a few killings while he was hanging with the Westies, but he seemed to be almost mystified by the experience. He wasn't especially proud of his work as a hit man, or of the legal killings he carried out while he was fighting in Vietnam.

Mickey was a little guy with a wild look in his eye, who didn't usually make much sense when people talked with him, and I was only around him for a few weeks after checking into Sandstone. He transferred out right after the holidays, and I wasn't sorry to see him go. He was a good person to avoid, because you never know what's going to set someone like that off.

Westie Bob and Mickey have both reportedly moved into phase two and relocated with complete new identities. Mickey's pre-sentence report said he frequently erupted in uncontrollable psychotic rages when he was under the influence of drugs and alcohol. Obviously the lifelong substance abuser was deemed suitable for relocation because he took the pledge. Yeah, right!

Westie Bob's release was delayed for a while because his psychotic tendencies kept surfacing on his prerelease psychological tests. I heard that the government sent someone in to coach him so the records didn't show how dangerous he was. I'm sure he also promised not to cut up any more people while they're alive before he settled down in his new home in Portland, Oregon. Today the two Westies chums could be anybody's neighbors. They might even be living someplace like Kendall, an exclusive suburb at the southwest edge of Miami in Dade county, Florida.

Arthur Kane shelled out $430,000 in cash for a modern six-bedroom house there early in 1979, about a year after settling into an office job with the Social Security Administration filling out benefit forms for the elderly and disabled. Ownership of the home was listed in the name of his wife, Judith, and it was constructed on a full acre of land with a backyard that shared a common border with property owned by the local congressman, Dante Fascell.

Kane appeared to be a perfect example of Mr. Suburbia. Bespectacled, chunky, with a rapidly receding hairline, and a secure office job, he gave the impression to neighbors that he was devoted to his wife and three daughters. He was a good neighbor, who left home in the morning carrying a briefcase and returned at night in time for dinner like any good husband was expected to do. His wife worked for a while for a travel agency, and she often traveled, while Kane stayed home to take care of business.

For a minor government bureaucrat with a $29,000-a-year job, the new South Florida resident also seemed to have plenty of money, and he quietly opened a $500,000 account with Merrill Lynch, Pierce, Fenner & Smith stockbrokers. He was good with numbers and played the market like a high-stakes Vegas gambler who couldn't lose. Kane was a high-risk speculator who played the margins with borrowed money, and his daring paid huge dividends. In less than ten years, the value of his portfolio skyrocketed to a whopping $7 million.

Kane was a specialist in so-called "takeover stocks," shares of companies earmarked for acquisition by other firms. He made his own decisions and rarely, if ever, asked for advice from his broker. But he played heavy with their money, and about half of his $7 million was purchased on margin.

Nothing lasts forever. In 1987, the stock market crashed, plunging a dizzying 500 points. Along with thousands of other high-stake speculators, Kane lost his ass. For approximately a week, he fretted and bit his nails while watching his fortune rapidly melt away. The value of his multimillion-dollar portfolio dwindled to about $600,000, and Merrill Lynch was calling in his margins. It was time to pay.

A few minutes after eleven o'clock on a Monday morning the frazzled speculator stalked into the South Dade branch office of Merrill Lynch, pulled a .357-magnum from a new briefcase and started shooting.

When the shooting stopped moments later, Office Manager Jose Argilagos was fatally injured. Stockbroker Lloyd Kolokoff was lying on the floor with a bullet in his spine that paralyzed him from the waist down. Kane was dead, from a self-inflicted gunshot to the head. He was a family man to the very last. Three hours before putting the gun to his head, he telephoned his supervisor at the Social Security office and asked if his government life insurance policy paid off in the event of a suicide. His boss said ''no.''

Arthur Kane seemed to be an unlikely shooter, until police began digging up information about his previous life in south Kansas City, Missouri. When the big-time speculator lived there, he was known by his birth name, Arthur Howard Katz, and he had a sinister history as a crooked lawyer who was immersed up to his ears in insurance fraud and shady stock manipulations. The fifty-three-year-old was also an ex-convict with a history of white-collar crime—and had been given a new name, a government job, and resettled in Florida as part of the federal witness-protection program.

Before getting into trouble with the law, Katz made a good living for himself and his family as a lawyer and a stockmarket speculator, but he was pestered by an insatiable greed for money. He was a poor loser, and one time in 1969 after dropping $1,500 in the market, his secretary walked into his office and found him sitting at his desk with the barrel of a little black revolver in his mouth. She screamed and he put the pistol down.

Katz wasn't an individual who had a firm lock on good emotional health. People who knew him during those days in Kansas City later remembered him as a man who was dogged by depression, self-doubts, and feelings of inadequacy. He was a twisted neurotic who exploded into temper tantrums, constantly running off at the mouth, and openly cried in front of fellow workers. He worried that he wasn't living up to the expectations of his father-in-law, Myer Shapiro, who was big in real estate around Kansas City and had a reputation for success playing the market.

The father-in-law had more money than he did, and Katz was convinced that amassing a fortune was the only way he could prove himself. Money and the stock and commodities markets were his obsessions.

In the mid-1970s, Katz, a law partner, and some medical doctors and chiropractors were swept up in a huge insurance-fraud scheme that focused on the filing of inflated or false claims after auto accidents. Some of the crashes were staged. Government prosecutors accused Katz of collecting a minimum of $110,000 during an approximate three-year period while the scam was carried out. His law partner later told reporters the amount Katz actually hauled in was closer to $1 million.

As the investigation progressed, police began to get a look at a different side of Katz: the professional. Rodney Alsop, a chiropractor who was a witness in the case, claimed he was taken for a harrowing two-hour ride by the lawyer, and said he was afraid he could be killed. Alsop fled the area after he was subpoened—but he was eventually found hiding in a big box buried in the backyard of a Boise, Idaho, home.

In serious trouble, Katz flipped and began cooperating with a government strike force and became a federal witness. Among those he testified against in the insurance-fraud scheme was his law partner. The law partner was convicted, but the conviction was later reversed.

Katz began informing on other high-rollers, as strike force investigations around the country probed stock-market swindles and other white-collar scams reaching into some of the highest levels of organized crime. One of the big cases for which he provided a helping hand involved a major swindle tied to stock in a New Jersey company that produces felt-tip pens, Magic Marker. He was one of the front men in the scheme that was carried out three years before he got in trouble over the insurance-fraud caper.

The people who figured out the scam bought inside information that allowed them to cash in when the stock skyrocketed 480 percent in ten months. The stock was dumped by the fast-money con men before it plummeted from thirty-one dollars per share to thirty-seven cents, and many honest investors lost their shirts. Eventually an organized-crime strike force, headed by the U.S. Justice Department and based in Philadelphia, convicted twenty people, including some players who were reputedly mob-connected. Although Katz wasn't a witness at the trial, he testified before a Philadelphia grand jury and provided other information to the investigators. He had hidden ownership of 4,000 shares in the stock that he bought on margin.

One of the primary targets of the probe was Yiddy Bloom, named in a 1980 Philadelphia Crime Commission report as a former associate of Meyer Lansky. Lansky was notorious as the chief architect of the national crime syndicate and Mob financier before his death in Florida in 1983. Bloom was convicted of participating in the swindle and was sentenced to a year in prison and fined $10,000. He was a south Florida resident—and agreed to donate $15,000 to the University of Miami Scholarship fund.

Katz ultimately pleaded guilty to conspiracy to commit mail fraud and was rewarded for his cooperation with the strike-force investigators with an order to serve six months of a two-year sentence. He served his time at a federal halfway house and paid a $5,000 fine. Five thousand dollars may have been serious money to the average American back in the 1970s, but to Katz it was chump change.

His former law partner later told reporters that Katz continued to practice law after being accepted into the witness-protection program, and collected fees and insurance settlements from some of the same cases that were under government investigation. The government held off the indictment for a year while Katz continued to pocket money from the insurance cases, his former law partner said.

When reporters asked a Justice Department spokesman about the statement, he replied that it was none of the government's business how Katz made his money. The feds couldn't prohibit him from continuing to practice, he added. Katz quit working as a lawyer early in 1979 after he was disbarred in the State of Missouri.

Soon after that, he and his family were relocated to South Florida after he reported to his Justice Department handlers that threats were made against him and his family. The Justice Department offered him $1,500 a month in walking around money and promised to kick in the cost of insurance and utilities payments. "It's not much money," a Justice Department spokesman later told the *Miami Herald.* "He was always cooperative."

Katz, who was now beginning life under his new name, Arthur Kane, apparently wasn't much impressed with the offer. He turned the free money down. Except for the help with a new identity and a new job, he was prepared to make it on his own. The people at WITSEC acted like they were glad to be rid of him.

But by dismissing Kane, the WTISEC people were, in effect, also dismissing everyone he would come in contact with in Florida. His neighbors, his fellow workers, and the stockbrokers in the two-story office building at the South Dade office of Merrill Lynch knew absolutely nothing about his background or true character. And by the time they learned of both, it was too late to prevent the tragedy.

As they are wont, journalists lost interest in the case as new, more pressing stories developed on the state, national, and international scene. But many questions related to the saga of the sicko con man have never been adequately answered.

For instance, how did Katz just happen to be relocated to south Florida where so many big players in the Magic Marker scam lived and operated? Several people involved in the scam operated a boiler-room operation out of Miami Beach. And Yiddy Bloom lived only about fifteen miles from Katz's new home. The Justice Department spokesman said simply that south Florida was picked because it was a safe place. Sure, and so was Alaska a safe place. But Yiddy Bloom didn't live in Alaska, and apparently none of the boiler-room boys were roughing it in the forty-ninth state, either.

Another question that went unanswered is tied to the fragile state of Kane-Katz's mental health. He was a high-strung, emotional mess, whose irrational, unstable behavior could hardly have been misunderstood by some of the highly educated, veteran law-enforcement professionals he worked with as a CI and protected witness. There's no evidence I know of that he was ever asked to submit to psychiatric treatment before he moved into phase two of the program. And there is no indication anyone connected with WITSEC did any follow up to determine if his troubles with depression and temper tantrums were getting him into deep water.

Evidently no one in authority was sufficiently concerned about dumping someone like that on unsuspecting neighbors, coworkers, or other new associates. There was no apparent effort to monitor his mental health, his personal or professional behavior and activities. We will never know for sure, of course, because of the official veil of secrecy that shields the witness-protection program.

Seven years after Katz retired permanently from playing the futures market, about thirty or thirty-five miles

north along the Atlantic coastline and up Florida State
Road A1A, another weirdo living a secret life was moving into the final countdown before launching a fatal
shootout with the cops.

James Dyson Kristian was one of those strange characters who sometimes move in next door to normal people.

He worked as a private detective and kept a small
arsenal of weapons and ammunition in his tenth-floor
Hollywood oceanside condominium. Kristian called
himself James Bond, sometimes attached a Ph.D to the
end of his name, and spent about as much time playing
with his guns as he did working at the private-eye trade.
Over a short period of time, he collected an AR-15 semi-
automatic rifle, a shotgun, four revolvers—including a
couple of .357-magnums, two .22-caliber pistols, and
more than 1,000 rounds of ammunition. When he, or his
seventy-nine-year-old wife, Marie, answered the telephone at their apartment, it was always with one word:
"Operations!"

The solidly built, 250-pound, six foot, two inch PI
was a curiously entertaining neighbor, when he wasn't
downright frightening, and he spun fantastic yarns. He
boasted of being a Vietnam veteran, a psychologist, an
ex-cop, and a bounty hunter. The job seemed to depend
on who he was talking to, when he was talking, and the
mood he was in. He seemed to especially like spinning
his bullshit yarns at his favorite hangout, Nick's Bar, on
Hollywood beach. One night he passed out silver dollars
to the bartenders. It was a pre-Christmas tradition.

Most of the time however, neighbors did their best to
avoid him. He was scary and walked around with his
eyes hidden behind a pair of dark shades, dressed in
black and wearing a flak jacket. Almost every day someone spotted him walking to or from his van lugging an
armload of rifles, pistols, and shotguns.

On Tuesday night, December 8, 1994, the fifty-four-year-old mystery man was in a killing mood, and the talk he was doing was sprinkled with curses. Neighbors in the eleven-story Cambridge Tower Apartments heard him yelling at Marie, his wife of two years. A few minutes after ten P.M., she dialed 911 and reported that her husband had locked himself in the bathroom and was threatening to commit suicide.

Hollywood cops hurried to the apartment, accompanied by an ambulance and three paramedics. When the door of an elevator carrying a couple of cops opened on the tenth floor, Kristian was in the hallway fighting with his wife. When the door of a second elevator next to them popped open and Kristian saw two more cops inside, he triggered off a blast with his shotgun. Sergeant Richie Allen had time to get off a single shot with his service revolver in response before the door of the elevator closed. No one was hit in the exchange, and Kristian darted back into his apartment. He was wearing a pair of shorts and a bullet-proof vest.

While the cops were grabbing Mrs. Kristian and sending her downstairs to the first floor, her husband was lugging a big chunk of his personal arsenal outside onto the balcony. Then he started shooting, spraying buildings, cars, and everything in sight with a lethal hail of bullets. Cops dived out of police cars as windows shattered and bullets ripped through metal. One squad car was struck thirty-four times.

For twenty minutes, Kristian kept up the assault, scuttling back inside his apartment for a few moments, then returning to the balcony where he continued to keep the cops pinned down and the neighbors scared to death. Miraculously, no one was injured by the fusillade.

By 11:30 P.M., police snipers had taken up positions in a couple of nearby buildings. A few minutes later, as he took pot shots at a couple of cops below, one of the marksmen who was crouched on the tenth floor of a building next door squeezed off a single shot. It passed through the flak jacket and struck the mad shooter in the chest.

It was dark and police weren't sure he was dead, so they waited two hours before finally entering the apartment early Thursday morning. There they found his body and made an unbelievable discovery. Although he fired off 150 rounds during the standoff, he still had more than 1,000 bullets stored in four military cartridge boxes. The cache also included phony hand grenades, firecrackers, and literature detailing how to make bombs.

After the smoke cleared and police had an opportunity to begin reconstructing the life of the menacing man-in-black, they learned that his birth name was Walter Billings, and he had a long and troubled history as a psychiatric patient. His neighbors didn't know about that, because when he moved to Florida twelve years earlier, his background and early life had been officially blanked out by handlers with the U.S. Justice Department. He was a federally protected witness.

The new name and identity made it possible for him to start over and obtain a private detective's license. It was an achievement that would have been impossible if he used his former name. The new identification also made it easier to put together the arsenal of weapons he collected in his home.

When Hollywood Police Chief Richard Witt talked to people at the Justice Department about the dead sniper the forthcoming information was predictably spotty. Witt quoted Justice as saying the shooter might be someone they had contact with. "It was part of an official investigation involving allegations against a federal agent," the chief told the *Miami Herald.* Billings was believed to have connections to the Boston area.

Kristian-Billings told so many wild stories, and police

had so many different names to check, that it was difficult to get a handle on who he really was and what he
was up to in his earlier life. Available records indicated
he didn't even obtain a Social Security card until he was
thirty-three years old, and that was the kind of information that might hint he had spent some time in his
early youth as a convict. Prison inmates usually don't
need Social Security cards.

Florida appears to be a major dumping ground for
protected witnesses, and it may have something to do
with its location so near to South and Central America
and the Caribbean where drug-smuggling has become an
art form. Emilio Garcia was a native Cuban who came
to Florida straight from one of Castro's jails, and he fit
right into the mold, even though when he got into trouble and turned, he was selling heroin in New York. The
cops caught him with one and a half kilos, which is a
lot more than someone would carry around for personal
use. Garcia was fed up with jails, so he agreed to work
for the cops as a CI.

He became one of the best, and helped the DEA and
multiagency task forces nab some major drug dealers.
Government authorities credited him with helping them
make hundreds of arrests, and confiscate enormous
stores of cocaine and heroin in Miami, New York, California, and Mexico. He was an Errol Flynn or Duncan
Renaldo type, a real-life swashbuckler who once teamed
up with an accomplice to rip off a couple of hard characters who had $11,500 to spend on drugs. There was a
shootout, and Garcia and his pal's Cadillac was riddled
with bullet holes. Nobody was hurt, but when he looked
at the newspaper headlines the next day, he was surprised to read that the intended victims were a couple
of undercover narcotics agents.

As a CI, Garcia once told the feds about a plot by
some Cuban exiles to kidnap President Richard M.

Nixon's wealthy pal, C. G. "Bebe" Rebozo and hold him for a $5 million ransom. The plot was abandoned because too many people heard about it, but Garcia passed on the information to the feds anyway.

Eventually he and his family were moved into the witness-protection program and began moving around the country. They settled at different times during their travels in Orlando, San Diego, and Rhode Island, while WITSEC kicked in $890 per month for living expenses. Using his WITSEC-provided Social Security number, he took a job for a while in Rhode Island selling vacuum cleaners at Sears. Author and former Miami newspaper reporter Edna Buchanan wrote that he boasted to her about selling a vacuum cleaner to Henry Kissinger's wife, Nancy.

He got in trouble again when he was arrested for impersonating a CIA agent. The family man and appliance salesman who had been known to neighbors as Emilio Martinez was publicly identified as former drug dealer Emilio Garcia.

Garcia was disillusioned with his handlers and with the program by that time, anyway. He complained they hadn't kept their promises and bitched that the only job they found for him was as a dishwasher at $100 per week. And they didn't pay medical and dental expenses, like they had promised.

By 1995, Garcia had lived under a variety of phony names but hadn't done any work as a CI for eight or ten years, and he was back in his personal danger zone in Miami. Friends worried that one of his old enemies would catch up with him and put a bullet through his head. But when the fifty-two-year-old informer was gunned down in a hail of bullets on busy Ocean Drive in South Beach during the middle of a sunny early September afternoon, the murder had nothing to do with his snitching. The accused killer was the jealous boyfriend of a woman he was a close friend with.

Florida doesn't get all the dangerous witnesses who have been relocated. Far from it. It doesn't matter where you live in the United States, chances are good that within a few minutes or a few hours drive, a protected witness who shouldn't be running around without a ball and chain around his ankle is somewhere nearby.

Benjamin Rosado was a lifetime criminal with busts for rape and sodomy who was moved into the program after testifying against a guy who whacked a dope dealer. The upstanding citizen was relocated a few miles outside of St. Louis in St. Charles, Missouri, and settled back into his old ways doing crime.

Local police were suspicious of him and ran his fingerprints through a national database to check for a criminal record. There were no hits. Police weren't aware that there were plenty of prints, but they didn't show up in the data check because records of the suspicious character who had moved into their town were sealed.

St. Charles solved the secret of Rosado's background the hard way, when one of their officers ran into him committing a burglary. Rosado shot officer William Bergmann to death. A federal judge later approved payment of nearly $70,000 to the widow because the government dumped Rosado in St. Charles without taking necessary steps to prevent him from returning to his old criminal ways.

Simply being in close proximity to the wrong person for a couple of hours might even get you killed if the stranger beside you happens to be a protected witness. When an airliner mysteriously crashed in September 1994, authorities quietly investigated the possibility the tragedy might be tied to the presence on the flight of a passenger involved in an important drug case the feds were pursuing in Chicago. Paul Olson was a protected witness who was flying home to the Windy City from Washington, D. C., where he had been interviewed for two days by federal prosecutors when the 737 suddenly rolled and plunged nose-first into a field a few miles outside Pittsburgh. One hundred and thirty-two people were killed instantly in the deadly crash, including the witness and two U.S. marshals.

When USAir released the list of passengers who were aboard the doomed jet, Olson's name was followed by the notation, ''Hometown withheld per family's request.'' There was good reason for the secrecy. Olson was not only involved in a current case but had testified a couple of years earlier in important prosecutions brought by the DEA and the IRS.

F. Lee Bailey, who was known as a criminal defense attorney for such clients as Boston Strangler Albert DeSalvo and accused wife killer Dr. Samuel Sheppard, added to the suspicions that the crash may have been deliberately caused when he told the press he believed a bomb was involved. Bailey, who was talking to families about the possibility of representing them in wrongful-death suits, said two bombs might have exploded in sequence.

So, could more than one hundred people have died because they had the bad luck to be on the same flight with a federally protected witness that someone wanted to kill bad enough to set off a bomb—or bombs—in a packed jetliner?

You make the call: a necessary sacrifice for justice, or the Justice Department and the American government playing Russian roulette with the lives of innocent citizens?

13

Monsters Among Us

OUR OWN GOVERNMENT has long been releasing monsters among us, and the worst part is that they knew how dangerous these killers were and exactly what they were doing. They let them out anyway. I guess the people at OEO figure its no big deal because eventually the monsters will kill again, and then they will either be whacked by the cops or dumped back inside. So a few unsuspecting citizens die first! People die every day.

It's hard to believe that even an agency that's as badly run and corrupt as WITSEC would spawn people at the top who didn't see anything wrong with allowing a homicidal maniac like Marion Albert Pruett to run free. Not only that, but they gave the guy a pass after he conned them by pinning a prison murder he committed on another inmate.

Funny thing about some of the people in corrections and with various other law-enforcement agencies. They'll grill somebody like me for weeks, put me on lie boxes, spend hundreds of man-hours running down collaborating witnesses, and generally bust their balls confirming information I provide on a drug smuggler or hoodlum. Then they swallow some bullshit story from a scumbag like Pruett whole-hog, reward him for the information, and shaft the poor slob he has pinpointed as his fall guy. It's unbelievable. These cops don't belong to some troop of naive little Girl Scouts. They're tough, experienced criminal investigators who have seen it all and should know, if anyone does, how the bad guys act. And how they lie.

Pruett wasn't someone I knew in the units. He was already outside before I showed up, but his story was notorious among the protected witnesses who were still doing time as a prime example of someone who should never, ever move into phase two.

He was doing nine years at the FCI in Atlanta when his cellie, a drug dealer named William Zambino, was stabbed to death with a prison shiv. Pruett rolled and testified against another inmate in the killing, and was paid for his efforts with a place in the WITSEC program.

Pruett is a little guy with dark, wavy hair who usually wore a mustache and beard, and got off on hurting people. He was like a lot of little guys, a Jimmy Cagney–type banty rooster who strutted around talking tough and showing off, trying to make people forget he was a shrimp. He covered himself with prison tattoos: skulls, daggers, broads, that type of thing, in order to demonstrate what a real man he was.

Pruett was a real piece of shit, but that didn't stop the government from relocating him. They gave him a new name, Charles "Sonny" Pearson, and set him and his old lady up with a new home and businesses in a dusty, lickspittle town of about 5,000 people in New Mexico called Rio Rancho. Pruett also used the name Lee Esmond for awhile, but most people in Rio Rancho knew him as Sonny Pearson. It was a quiet place, about a fifteen minute drive north of Albuquerque, surrounded by Indian reservations, national forests, and scrub desert.

Marion and Michelle never bothered to get married, and they moved in together after her husband, a prison teacher, mysteriously disappeared a few weeks after Pruett moved into phase two of the program. No one seemed to be very interested in what happened to Michelle's husband, and the feds set her and Sonny up with her own little cafe in Rio Rancho. They bought him a dump truck so that he could haul stone and gravel. The Pearsons also collected an $800 check from the government every month to put the bacon and the beans on the table until they had dug in their toes and planted their feet solidly in the workaday world of their neighbors.

The Federal Marshals Service does the grunt work involved with relocating witnesses. They provide the witnesses and their families with new names, arrange for jobs, help get the kids in schools, and generally take care of all the bullshit details that have to be dealt with. If a witness has a problem, or some crisis develops that he can't handle or isn't sure about how to deal with, like a wife filing for divorce or someone showing up who knew him from the past, he, or she, goes to the Marshals Service for help.

More often, like Billings and Katz and almost every other relocated witness, they're simply left alone unless they cry out for help. No follow-ups, and no weekly reports to some monitor who's watching over their shoulder. That's the way Sonny Pearson liked it.

The Pearsons didn't appear to be exactly the kind of people who are invited to join the Jaycees, some ladies' sewing circle or auxiliary. They barely moved into the little town before the local constabulary began to wonder if their hard-working new citizen with the dump truck was up to no good. Sonny was back to doing drugs and helping himself to other people's property. Police didn't have a clue that the arrogant little southerner was a stone-cold killer with a history of grisly murder and runaway drug abuse behind him. When witnesses are relocated, no one, especially the local law, is told of the new resident's criminal past. That isn't the way the program works.

Local police in Rio Rancho were still watching and waiting when the local truck driver they had figured for a small-time hoodlum finally reverted to his former violent ways. Two years after the Pearsons settled in, Sonny notified police that Michelle was missing.

From the time Sonny filed the report, the cops figured the missing woman hadn't simply packed a suitcase and caught a Greyhound bus to get out of town. The yarn Sonny spun in his slow North Carolina drawl didn't hang together the way it should. Furthermore, he didn't seem very concerned about his missing wife, and spent more time bragging about the important contacts he had with the federal government than trying to help figure out where Michelle had gone.

There were other hints that something was drastically wrong, as well. Gennaro Ferrara was Sandoval County Sheriff, and he was a former New York City cop, so he had run into characters like Pruett before. The experienced lawman picked up on Sonny's prison lingo, the words and phrases he used that marked him as a long-time con. If there were any doubts he had spent a long time behind bars, his prison tats clinched things. His arms, legs, and chest were covered with them.

Nevertheless, when Sheriff Ferrara ran a check through the Justice Department's huge National Crime Information Center (NCIC), computers in Washington asking for a printout of any criminal records that might be available on the guy, they struck out. Sonny Pearson was clean.

Sheriff's interrogators talked to Sonny for three days while holding him as a material witness, and went around in circles without making any serious progress.

Then they returned his billfold and other personal property, and gave him his walking papers. Sonny strutted out the front door. A judge ruled there was insufficient evidence to hold him as a witness or to charge him with a criminal offense in the case. There was no body, and no evidence that a crime was committed.

Sheriff Ferrara and his pals were frustrated, and despite the strikeout with the NCIC, they were convinced that something rotten was afoot. And whatever it was, it involved Pearson and the FBI, Justice Department, the BOP or some other powerful agency of the federal government. Somebody was holding back information.

The first big break in the case developed when barbecued chunks of Mrs. Pearson began showing up here and there in the desert a few miles outside of town. That was it for Ferrera. He hadn't given up trying to get information from the federal government, and when body parts began showing up, he started seriously kicking up the shit. He wanted to know who Sonny Pearson was and what was going on.

The Federal Marshals Service finally let the sheriff in on the big secret. Sonny the gravel-truck driver was really Pruett, the ex-con, a man who coined his own nickname, "Mad Dog," from the street name for M.D. (Mogan David) 20-20, a highly fortified grape wine that's a favorite among down-and-out alcoholics because of its potency.

Now that Ferraro had a better idea of what was going on and what he was up against, he went looking for Pruett to bring him in, but it was too late. Pruett had fled the coop. Although the gravel-truck driver skipped, the sheriff picked up one of his friends, and the guy spilled his guts. He described how Pruett beat Michelle to death with a ballpeen hammer, strangled her with a belt, then chopped her body up, dumped the pieces in the desert, doused them with gasoline, and set them afire.

Pruett was a sociopath, one of those people who doesn't give a shit about anyone but themselves. Whatever they want; whatever pleases them; whatever they need to get off is all that matters. If that means some little girl has to be raped and her body chopped up, or a citizen who happens to be the hardworking father of six or seven kids has to die because the sociopath wants his bowling money to spend on dope—so be it. They don't count. Their lives aren't diddly shit.

Prisons are full of people like that, and I have to admit that a few guys who were my friends have either fit or come close to fitting the definition of sociopath. But despite all the antisocial things I've done and the crimes I've committed, I never hung around with people like Pruett and I never considered his kind of mad-dog killer to be one of my homeboys.

When Pruett cleared out of Rio Rancho, he set off on a cross-country robbery and murder rampage that cost the lives of at least five people. Three of them were convenience store clerks, trying to make a few bucks by working long hours in what has become one of the most dangerous jobs in the United States. They didn't fight back or even give him a hard time. Pruett blew them away for practice. He is the kind of ape who loves to kill. Holding the power of life or death over someone, and choosing death, makes him feel like he's a big man.

James Balderson was a twenty-four-year-old college kid from Alliance, Nebraska, with a knack for computers who was working at a 7-Eleven in Fort Collins, Colorado, when he was shot to death during a robbery. About an hour after killing Balderson, Pruett wasted twenty-one-year-old Anthony Tait. Tait was a student at Colorado State University and was clerking at a store in Loveland when Pruett decided the poor kid's life wasn't worth living.

Bobbie Jean Robertson, another convenience store

clerk, was kidnapped in Fort Smith, Arkansas, and murdered. Peggy Lowe, a bank-loan officer in Mississippi was another victim. While the nasty little druggie was rampaging across five states wasting convenience store clerks, he was also pulling six bank robberies. The woman manager of a bank in Bridgeville, Pennsylvania, was luckier than the others who had the misfortune to cross Pruett's path during his rampage. He dumped her from his car and left her standing, unhurt, at the side of a road.

Pruett, nevertheless, was behaving with the crazy unpredictability of a typical spree killer. Once they get started they can't stop, and they feed off their own violence while the tension and pressure builds. It's like what happens in a huge forest fire or what happened as a result of the fire-bombing of Dresden or Tokyo. The flames begin to feed on themselves until a nearly unstoppable firestorm is created. And WITSEC has yet to learn they can't contain such a force of nature.

All told, Pruett probably netted a few hundred dollars, some sandwiches, wine, and a few six packs of beer from his orgy of robbery and murder. Most of the loot apparently went into his arm, up his nose, or down his gullet. He only had a few bucks on him when he was finally run down and captured without a fight. During a search of his car, police confiscated syringes and other drug works, along with the pistol he used in the killings.

He pulled life sentences for the murders in Colorado, but he was sentenced to death in Mississippi and in Arkansas. Arkansas was given first crack at executing him. Pruett walked into his death row cell a few feet from the execution chamber at the Cummins Prison in 1982, and he's still there. He's had time to grow a thick mountain-man beard, try unsuccessfully to shake down a Mississippi newspaper for $20,000 in return for information about a ring belonging to one of the women he

killed, and offer to lead investigators to the body of a
Florida victim if he was promised a paid spot on "Geraldo." He didn't get the appearance on "Geraldo," but
you can bet he is still figuring out angles and developing
new schemes. That's what he does.

The bureaucrats who run WITSEC were responsible
for Pruett's murder spree. It's not good enough to apol-
ogize that they made a mistake, that no one could have
foreseen that Pruett would explode and go on a rampage.
Try telling that to the parents, the brothers and sisters or
husbands and wives of the people who were blown
away.

The cold, hard fact is, if the Gs had leveled with Ferrara when the sheriff first went to them for help trying
to figure out who Sonny Pearson was and what he was
doing in Rio Rancho, at least five people would probably
still be alive. The sheriff could have held on to the guy,
and he would still have been in custody when his old
lady's body parts started showing up around town.

Pruett should never have even been on the outside in
the first place, or in the witness program. What kind of
information is so vitally important to the Gs or to local
cops that it could justify freeing someone like Mad Dog
Marion Albert Pruett, then relocating him with a new
name and background among unsuspecting neighbors?
WITSEC was cooking up a recipe for violence when
they relocated him, and they should have known better.

It may sound strange, or phony, that I'm coming on
so law-and-order, but I'm a citizen now, just a regular
guy who wants to work at a straight job so that I can
support myself and my woman. Importantly, I also know
what I'm talking about because I've been there to talk-
the-talk and walk-the-walk. I've known a lot of socio-
pathic killers in and out of the units, and I know the
devastation and heartbreak they can cause when they're
allowed to run free. They're especially dangerous when

they have the power and the protection of the federal
government behind them.

I'm not saying there shouldn't be a witness-protection
program, and I never have. But WITSEC needs a major
overhaul, and closer oversight. Years have gone by when
it seems like no one in all of Congress is paying any
attention to the program. That's bad, and it can't be allowed to continue on that way because it's wasting
money, other valuable resources, and most important of
all, it's costing innocent lives. The press can't do the job
by itself; and except for instances like Pruett's rampage
and a few other exceptions, the press hasn't shown very
much interest in what's going on at WITSEC.

When the press does try to dig out information, reporters are met by a wall of silence and bureaucrats who
beg off answering questions by citing security reasons.
The WITSEC bureaucracy is about as firmly entrenched
as it can be, and it has shown it won't give up its secrets
without a fight. The only people with the authority to
really crack open the nut and get to the dirt inside are
the lawmakers in Washington who are members of the
House and the Senate.

For a while after Pruett's capture, the story of his
status as a federally protected witness and the horren-
dous crimes he committed were big news. The shit hit
the fan and the U.S. General Accounting Office, official
Washington's most powerful watchdog agency, conducted one of its rare audits of the program. The findings
reported by the career accountants, lawyers, and other
investigators working for the nonpartisan GAO, which
has responsibility for overseeing the operation of other
government departments and agencies, were brutally
critical and had OEO and BOP bureaucrats and the U.S.
Marshals Service scurrying for cover. It appeared that
WITSEC might even be forced out of existence.

Another audit tracing the program's performance conducted by the U.S. Controller General concluded that the recidivism rate of protected witnesses is about the same as that of other parolees. There was some indication it might have been even a bit less, but that was no solace to the victims of Pruett's mad rampage. Pressure, meanwhile, continued to build as Congress also launched a hearing into the deepening scandal. The congressional probe was one of the rare hearings conducted into the program before and since that time.

The hearings made the front pages of newspapers, and they were a big deal. Impressive! Politicians postured and promised. Newspapers pounded readers with stories about savage killers rewarded and set loose on the streets by the very government agencies that were supposed to be protecting the public. Everyone involved was shocked, remorseful, and tossing around promises of major reforms and tightened oversight.

U.S. Justice Department bureaucrats defended themselves by testifying that Pruett's rampage was little more than a bizarre quirk, an aberration from the norm that wasn't likely to happen again. They promised nevertheless that standards for admission to the program would be tightened in order to prevent similar outrages from occurring in the future.

James Balderson's father, Frank Balderson, testified at the congressional hearing, and called for abolition of the program. Balderson was a lawyer, and he reminded the panel members—most of whom were also lawyers—that the testimony of a witness who is paid is worthless. Balderson said that no convicted felons should be given early release for their testimony.

If the feds followed Frank Balderson's advice, there wouldn't be much left of the program. According to recent government audits, criminals account for more than 97 percent of protected witnesses.

I can sympathize with the grieving parents of the

young man Pruett murdered in Colorado. He didn't deserve to die any more than Pruett's other victims deserved to die, and the nasty little dopehead shouldn't have been running loose, but I don't agree that all the testimony of protected witnesses is worthless. I provided testimony and other help to the task-force cops I worked with that helped put away dozens of criminals ranging from killers and big-time drug smugglers to vice kings (and queens.) I would have helped lock up more people, for longer periods, if all the cops and the prosecutors who worked with me had known what they were doing and behaved like the professionals they were supposed to be.

Frank Balderson had a big burr under his saddle, and he carried out a personal crusade to clean up the mess, which included his testimony before powerful legislators in Washington. He testified before a House subcommittee on Courts, Civil Liberties and the Administration of Justice and before a special hearing of the full U.S. Senate Judiciary Committee. Balderson called for restricting WITSEC protections to innocent people. Criminals who testified against each other shouldn't be shielded or otherwise rewarded by the government, he said. But there's only so much one person like Balderson, or a small group of people, can do. The secrecy surrounding the program is tough to crack, and the people at the top are determined to protect their turf. They don't want serious changes.

Although he was a lawyer, Balderson, like the families of other Pruett victims, couldn't even sue the government that freed the mad-dog killer to carry out his murder rampage. The feds declared sovereign immunity from lawsuits. So much for justice.

Balderson had some allies in his campaign, including a few congressman, but nothing much happened for a couple of years. Finally in 1984, congress gave its stamp of approval to legislation called the Witness Security Reform Act. The new law had four major components, including a requirement for the Justice Department to make it more difficult to be accepted into the program. Other elements of the bill included: a requirement that witnesses pay civil court judgments; tightening of management accountability by the Justice Department; and establishment of a fund to reimburse victims or their families when a protected witness commits another crime or runs amok.

Like they say in Washington, the act was more sound than substance. Like they say in the joint: What a bunch of bullshit!

If Justice and the OEO really intended to pay any attention to the order to trim the number of witnesses inducted into the program by tightening the requirements, why is WITSEC still growing by leaps and bounds? More people are being ushered in than ever before.

Frank Balderson's testimony in Washington was heartbreaking and dramatic, but an ambitious young associate U.S. attorney general, Rudolph Giuliani, was the star of the early 1980s Capital Hill probes into the dangerously flawed WITSEC program. Giuliani was one of the main people running WITSEC, and he was in the early days of a political career that by the mid-1990s would lead him to election as mayor of New York City.

Giuliani promised Congress that WITSEC would be trimmed and restricted to a few new witnesses each year who were necessary to help out in special investigations focusing on organized-criminal enterprises. When Giuliani outlined his bold approach to revising the program, WITSEC was growing at a rate of about 30 percent per year, and had obviously gotten too big for its britches. It was too expensive, and many witnesses were being accepted who never should have been considered for protection.

Giuliani's promises sounded good! With a man like this career federal prosecutor at the helm and firmly in control, it seemed that the program would be cleaned up and streamlined. The abuses would be rooted out, and the scoundrels and incompetents responsible for the poor planning and execution would be sent packing. Congressional leaders didn't foresee, or didn't care, how empty Giuliani's promises would become. A little more than a decade after he made his promise, the program had grown by more than 60 percent. The abuses were worse than ever.

Witnesses I talked to in and out of the units told me that the order calling for payment of civil court judgments is another laugh. A normal creditor could spend half a lifetime trying to dig through the multilayered protective screens that Justice Department bureaucrats have put up around witnesses, and never learn their new name, where they live, or even confirm they're in the program.

The mandate for improved management accountability is also a bunch of bullshit. It includes wording that is supposed to put pressure on the Justice Department to keep the promises made to witnesses by the FBI, DEA, IRS, BATF, and various other law-enforcement suits. As someone who moved into the program a couple of years after the Witness Security Reform Act was adopted, I can honestly say that a whole bunch of people in those agencies apparently never got the word. They lied when they were recruiting witnesses before the act was passed, and they lied when they recruited witnesses after the act was passed.

For survivors of victims of relocated witnesses, establishment of the fund wasn't much of a carrot to offer, but it was better than nothing—and payments are doled out more often than most people would suspect. Pruett is merely one of the worst, most glaring examples of protected witnesses who have been freed, then quickly reverted to their former criminal ways. At least twenty or twenty-five protected witnesses or former witnesses have killed again after graduating from phase one of the program, and I couldn't begin to count the number of other major crimes committed by protected witnesses after moving into phase two. After all, nearly all protected witnesses are people who have spent their lives as professional criminals. Crime is their job; it's what they do.

By 1996, victims' fund payments still topped off at $50,000. The Baldersons collected $25,000 for the death of their son, and the couple probably spent that much or more in their campaign for justice. The $25,000 is an especially piddling amount when compared to the kind of multimillion-dollar bounties and other benefits that star-quality witnesses like Gravano, Lehder, and Mermelstein are paid or permitted to keep from previous criminal enterprises.

Some people probably left the 1980s hearings in Washington believing that Pruett's victims had accomplished something eminently worthwhile with their deaths, and that the witness-protection program would be cleaned up so that no one else would have to die because WITSEC was freeing dangerous felons to prey on innocents. If that was what they thought, they didn't know how government works. They didn't know how deep the flaws were in the program.

Another mad-dog killer was already waiting in the wings to prove just exactly how dangerous a program with such powers and such little oversight could be.

14

A Promise to Be Good

IF PRUETT WAS a monster, James Allen Red Dog was a creature dispatched from the deepest bowels of Hell. Red Dog was as cold-blooded and ruthlessly mean as they come.

As it's easy to figure out from his name, he was an American Indian, a full-blooded Sioux, and he wore his straight black hair shoulder-length, with a part in the middle, Indian style. He also wore a set of square-rimmed glasses, but they didn't make him look bookish. Whenever there was a camera around, he made sure his face was contorted in a cocky smirk, and he looked and acted exactly like the kind of person he was. He was a bloodthirsty killer, who reveled in other people's fear and pain.

Red Dog was a dude who began killing early in his criminal career and couldn't, or didn't want to, stop. He was also a killer who knew how to work the system; he benefitted from one incredible lucky break after another that had him in and out of prisons while he continued his killing ways long after he should have been executed for his crimes.

His first known killing occurred in 1973 when he shot the manager of a pizza shop to death during a stickup on an Indian reservation. He lucked out with a fifteen-year prison term instead of life, or worse, when a judge ruled that he was mistakenly charged with manslaughter instead of first-degree murder.

So he was sentenced for armed robbery and got the max. It was still a good deal, but after seven years on the inside, Red Dog broke out of the FCI at Lompoc, California, with a convict pal. Lompoc is in Santa Barbara county, about one hundred fifty miles northwest of Los Angeles, and even though it was designated as a maximum-security prison, it wasn't the most difficult place in the world to bust out of. For example, Christopher Boyce, a young American who spied for the Soviets and was written about in a couple of books and a movie, *The Falcon and the Snowman,* also escaped from Lompoc.

Almost as soon as they were out, the two prison buddies murdered a couple of poor slobs who met them in a bar and invited them to sack out at their apartment. Red Dog and his friend stabbed the Good Samaritans, both Indians, in their sleep. They also kidnapped another man and stole his car. They kept him hostage for two days while Red Dog's running mate repeatedly raped him. The motorist finally escaped in Las Vegas and notified police.

This time when the law moved in on the murderous Sioux and hauled him in, he got off with a wrist-slap—nine-year concurrent sentences for each of the killings and the kidnapping of the motorist. Then he was returned to Lompoc. If Red Dog really was a demon, Old Scratch was clearly working overtime to protect and reward his busy minion.

He raised so much hell after he was locked up again, that he wound up being shuffled from prison to prison.

Every place he went, he caused trouble. He was a genuine bad-ass, and after joining with the Mexican Mafia to smuggle drugs inside the prisons, he wound up in the Federal Correctional Institution at Marion, Illinois. Marion was constructed to replace Alcatraz because the notorious old federal penitentiary in San Francisco Bay was falling apart. "The Rock" was eventually closed in 1963, and the prisoners there were moved to the imposing granite and steel state-of-the-art facility constructed near the southern tip of Illinois.

The penitentiary was built just outside the town of the same name, a couple of hours drive southeast of my stomping grounds in suburban St. Louis. The new prison was surrounded by a pair of tall steel-mesh fences topped by huge concertinas of razor wire and other piles of wire scattered between them. Eight gun towers, with heavily-tinted glass so the guards inside couldn't be seen, also loom over the perimeter.

The new federal correctional center became the country's only "level six," penitentiary, meaning that at that time it was the most secure prison in the United States. The new super-maximum-security penitentiary was reserved for special inmates, and although it was part of the federal Bureau of Prisons, about one-third of its 350 male inmates were transferred there from state prisons and the District of Columbia.

Marion got the worst of nearly a half million men from state prison systems, and of others doing time in the federal prison system. The Super-Max has held men such as Mafia chief Gotti; serial killer and ex-Nazi Joseph Paul Franklin; career criminal, skyjacker, and escape artist Garrett Brock Trapnell; former CIA agent Edwin P. Wilson, who sold weapons and explosives to Libya for use in training terrorists; Boyce, who was transferred there after he was run down and recaptured following his escape from Lompoc; and prisoners like

Red Dog who posed special disciplinary problems. In fact, almost all the inmates at Marion were sent there because they caused serious problems in other, less secure prisons.

Even in the super-secure and notorious surroundings of Marion, Red Dog found a way to stand out from the crowd. After arranging for the wife he married while he was in prison to smuggle a batch of poison inside, he murdered another inmate for stealing from him. Red Dog passed the powder to the unsuspecting thief, telling him that it was cocaine. The inmate snorted the poison and died. Prison paybacks can be deadly and final.

Then Red Dog pulled off his biggest coup of all. He got in trouble with the Mexican Mafia, and knew he had to do something fast or he would be killed. His solution was ratting out two other inmates who had reputedly joined in the smuggling scheme in return for a place in the witness-protection program. He sweetened the pot for the Gs by snitching on other inmates involved in prison gangs and on people involved with some of the more dangerous elements of the American Indian Movement, AIM. The cunning killer played his trump and it turned out to be a get-out-of-jail-free card. His wife testified about her part in the smuggling-and-murder scheme, and was also moved into the witness program as part of the deal.

It didn't make any difference to the feds that murder charges filed against the two inmates he ratted out were dropped without going to trial. About a year after the murder, on his earliest possible parole date, Red Dog walked out of prison a free man. Neither he nor his wife were charged in the inmate's murder or in the smuggling incident. So I guess the inmate's death was a suicide.

Mrs. Red Dog shared in her husband's reward for rolling over by being relocated through the witness program to a suburb of Wilmington, Delaware, where she settled in with a new name and job. Her husband, legally outside prison bars for the first time in years, fared only a little less well than she did. He flunked the psychological tests witnesses have to take before being moved into phase two, so he was released on his own.

For once the shrinks made a correct decision, and they were proven right: Red Dog pulled a gun on a cop in Montana. Red Dog was tossed back in the joint, but within a year he was out and moved back across the country to join his wife in Delaware. Red Dog used her new identity as cover for himself, and none of the neighbors and none of his wife's new friends had a clue that he was a violent ex-con with a history of murder behind him and a lust for blood.

WITSEC wasn't watching him because he was no longer in the program. Even if he had been, it's doubtful if the Gs would have paid much attention to his behavior or activities. Once a witness moves into phase two with a new identity and job, he or she is virtually forgotten. Most of whatever contacts occur between witnesses and their friends with individual handlers or the OEO are initiated by the ex-cons when they need help with personal problems.

Police in Delaware didn't learn anything about Red Dog's history until he went next door to the house of his wife's best friend and murdered the woman's son. He had spent the earlier part of the chilly day in February 1991 boozing at a local watering hole, and trying to impress a woman by boasting that he was a hit man who was so good at his work that his Mob employers called him The Terminator.

Red Dog's new victim, Hugh Pennington, was hogtied and carried into the basement, where his throat was so viciously slashed with a hunting knife that he was nearly decapitated. Only a thin scrap of flesh held Pennington's head to his neck. Still roaring drunk and with his blood lust fully activated, Red Dog returned to his own home, where his wife and the mother of the victim were visiting. He told the woman her son had been hurt.

Believing Red Dog was going to take her to her son, she left with him and became his final victim. He kidnapped her and held her in an isolated farmhouse, where she was repeatedly raped before escaping two days later. When police hurried to the house, Red Dog escaped into a nearby woods. A couple of days later the cold and bedraggled killer was recaptured without a fight.

Local lawmen had a difficult time figuring out just who the vicious criminal they had in custody really was. It was several weeks before the mystery was solved and they were able to tie him to the witness-protection program. Even then the solution to the puzzle came by accident. Someone with the BOP mistakenly sent documents to Steven Wood, the local prosecutor, indicating that Red Dog was under their protection.

Wood was outraged, and when the story of the crazed killer's true identity and past was revealed, newspapers and the electronic media had a field day. Federal officials indicated they wanted the accused killer returned to their jurisdiction for prosecution, but the angry prosecutor wasn't buying. He saw to it that Red Dog was put on trial in Wilmington on charges of murder, rape, and weapons offenses. On February 14, 1992, Red Dog was handed a grim Valentine's Day present. After pleading no contest to the charges, he was found guilty on all counts. His conviction occurred almost exactly one year after he committed the murder and rapes. On July 12, almost five months after the verdicts were reached, he was sentenced to death.

On Wednesday, March 3, 1993, Red Dog was led into the death chamber at the Delaware State Penitentiary in Smyrna, strapped to a gurney, and executed by lethal injection. Red Dog refused to appeal either his conviction or the death sentence, but he didn't go to his execution without putting on a world-class show that featured a public feud between rival medicine men.

The condemned man announced that he was a warrior, and in the days leading up to his execution, he practiced Sioux spiritual rituals in his cell. Immediately prior to the execution, a Sioux medicine man administered the last rites to him there. Later another Sioux religious leader, Charles Thunderhawk Lone Wolf, denounced the medicine man who attended the execution as a fraud who gave Red Dog bad spiritual advice. Lone Wolf had advised Red Dog to fight for his life and cautioned that anything less would be suicide. "He doesn't die a warrior's death," Lone Wolf declared. "That is a bad misconception."

Members of Red Dog's family said they supported his decision to die. In a prepared statement they declared:

"Our brother will take these last steps to his death with pride and dignity . . . and proud that he's giving in return for what he took—a life."

The family's statement seemed to be sincere, and acknowledged that a balancing of the books was being carried out for committing a dreadful act. There was no similar acknowledgment, or indication of regret and admission of responsibility, from WITSEC administrators for the role the federal program played in the tragedy by freeing, then simply walking away from, an individual who had shown himself so many times before to be dangerously violent.

Maybe they figured it was enough that he finally paid the extreme penalty for his crimes. But when a dose of lethal drugs were fed into the veins of the cold-hearted serial killer, it wasn't any thanks to the people who run WITSEC. It was in spite of them.

After Red Dog's final murderous outburst, U.S. Senator Joseph R. Biden, Jr., sponsored legislation to force

federal officials to notify state law-enforcement authorities whenever a protected witness is moved into their
jurisdiction. Biden was one of Delaware's native sons
and a powerful Democratic Senator who at one time was
considered as a possible candidate for the presidency.
The law was passed without any serious opposition and
signed by the president, but it was way too late to help
Pennington or his mother.

15

Security Lapses

ALL THE VICTIMIZING by protected witnesses doesn't occur outside the walls. Inside the joint there's always somebody bigger and meaner than you—unless you're Ronnie Joe "Jap" Chriswell.

Actually, although Jap is almost six foot tall and a solid 180 to 190 pounds or so, lots of inmates are bigger than he is. None of them are any meaner, and there are none who are more feared. Everyone in the units who knows anything about him and has a lick of sense steers clear of his evil temper.

The ancestry of his Japanese-born mother accounts for his nickname, and despite, or possibly because, of his own mixed race, he hates blacks. I was a good friend of Jap's while we were inside, but even though I was bulked up from my weight lifting and other exercises, he wasn't somebody I would have wanted to cross.

His well-known hatred for blacks didn't mean that he wouldn't strike out at me or any other white, Oriental, Mexican, or American Indian who happened to cross him. If an extraterrestrial happened to have been locked up in the units with him and pissed him off, it would have been, "Goodbye E. T." And the little fellow wouldn't have floated away in a UFO. He would have had his head beaten in, been strangled, had his scraggly little throat slit, dumped over one of the upper tiers, roasted inside his cell, or died in some other violent manner. Jap wasn't particular about the exact manner in which someone who crossed him died; just that they died.

He wound up doing all day in the Georgia state correctional system after going on a hate-crime tear through his native state, wasting blacks. Then he continued the killing spree behind bars and murdered another inmate.

After the prison murder, Jap was sent to the FCI at Leavenworth, Kansas, and as soon as he walked inside, he began hanging out with local white supremicists. Jap was with John Greshner, a white-supremacy leader, when Greshner chopped up another AB with a prison shiv. The guy was killed right in front of a guard, but everything happened so fast it was all over before the hack knew what was coming down.

Jap was then transferred to the control unit at Marion. He was in Super-Max and had reached the end of the line. There was no place worse to be, and no way out. Or so it seemed. By that time, Jap had so many black and white enemies and so many other inmates who wanted to kill him that he flipped in return for protection. He became the eyes and ears for the warden's boys, and when word of his double-crosses got around, he was more unpopular than ever. Jap was a marked man and so many threats were made against his life that he was moved to the witness units for protection.

I first met him in Unit One at Otisville, and he was one of a handful of inmates there who knew he would never move into phase two. Jap had so many years to do, he couldn't even be considered for a parole hearing until well into the next millenium. The only way he would ever go back to his boyhood home in Conyers, Georgia, was in a pine box or in a bottle of ashes for his momma to set up on the mantel.

It didn't take Jap long to get into serious trouble after being moved into Otisville. He tangled with Westie Bob and took the New York hoodlum hostage. It was the most entertaining day at Unit One in the whole month of April 1992. Jap held off a SWAT team for five hours, while he pressed the edge of a prison razor knife to Bob's throat and negotiated for an end to the standoff. I don't even remember what set Jap off, but it was some slight he thought Westie Bob had committed. He didn't like the Irishman anyway. He was too mouthy.

Jap threatened to give Westie Bob a dose of his own medicine unless the feds handed over $300,000 in ransom money and provided him with a helicopter and a pilot. The other witnesses in Unit One were put on lockdown while the warden brought in a hotshot negotiator. The guy knew his job, and he was so good he could have charmed the sweat off a hog. Jap wound up settling for a tin of Copenhagen snuff.

In all the years I knew Jap, he never showed any more concern about killing a guy than he would over whether or not he got mustard on his baloney sandwich. That's just about what a life is worth in prison. A dab of mustard or a nicotine rush. Just imagine! The exchange of a tin of snuff can keep a live guy from becoming a dead guy. How about that?

Don't get me wrong. Ronnie Joe is my friend, and I wouldn't want to bad-mouth him, especially if he ever has a chance of walking out the doors of the joint a free man some day. I don't think that's ever going to happen, and anyway the truth is the truth. Jap Chriswell is a brutal, dangerous thug who you wouldn't want for a close neighbor, in or out of the joint. Huggard was no pansy, but Jap didn't hesitate to go up against anybody.

He acted like he was totally without fear. Judging by his behavior, he was also a man who was without mercy or remorse.

Just because inmates in the units lived much better than their brothers in general population, didn't mean that the same shit didn't go down. It just went down more often in general population, but the danger from fellow inmates was constant, regardless of whether or not you were a protected witness.

Protected witnesses didn't have to worry about being routinely gang-raped in showers, but that doesn't mean that rapes didn't occur in the units or that weaker prisoners weren't bullied by stronger inmates into giving blow jobs or occasionally allowing some tough, grizzled con to travel down the old dirt road. In the units, inmates still shook each other down, extorting money through threats and blackmail; beat and cut each other; and informed on the informers. Regardless of who you hung out with in the joint, if you had any sense at all, you knew enough to keep your eyes open for trouble. You couldn't trust your best friend. Everybody knew that we were in the units because we had ratted on our friends.

Violence can flare at any moment, and just about anything can set it off. Regardless of how hard the administration tried to keep the lid on, security lapses were bound to happen.

One of the most potentially serious breaches of security occurred while I was at Otisville, and one of New York City's finest walked into the visiting room to see his son while wearing his service revolver in a shoulder holster. No metal detectors were set up at the entrance at that time, and he was apparently so used to wearing his piece that he forgot all about it even though he was surrounded by some of the most vicious serial killers, mob executioners, and homicidal maniacs ever gathered together in any one place in the history of the world.

Nicky Barnes, a big-time New York City heroin
dealer, was one of the witnesses in the visiting room.
The cop finally remembered he was packing and said
something to one of the guards. The shit hit the fan, and
hacks showed up from all over. The cop turned over the
gun, of course. It was a dumb mistake, but the guy was
lucky. Nobody got hurt.

It was hard to imagine that metal detectors hadn't
been set up at the entrance to the visiting room, when
you consider the super-security status that was supposed
to be in effect throughout the witness units. Metal detectors were installed later, but they should have been in
place from the beginning. Security screw-ups occurred
in the units all too frequently. Protected witnesses can't
be totally protected all of the time.

Although this didn't happen on a unit, a guy who was
under special protection one time after testifying against
his father in a big case in Alabama came within inches
of being released to a bunch of his worst enemies. They
walked into the prison disguised as U.S. marshals and
started processing the poor sucker out. The paperwork
was completed and everything, when prison officials figured out just in time what was going on and put a stop
to it.

Administrators acted like it was a big mystery one day
at Sandstone when a black helicopter with no numbers
on it suddenly rumbled at low-level past the witness unit.
Guards hit the deck, while everybody in the cramped
little yard started scrambling for cover. I was one of
them, and because we were who we were, nobody had
to be ashamed about running. Almost nobody, anyway.

Floyd Carlton Canceres was finishing up his "minute" at Sandstone and he ran all the way to his cell and
scurried under the bed. He was still cowering there when
the strange helicopter cruised noisily out of sight behind
a line of trees and other witnesses filed back inside. It

wasn't Carlton's finest day, and he lost respect among his fellow inmates. When you're in the joint, respect is important. It can be a lifesaver, or merely a shield to protect an inmate from rape, extortion, and all kinds of other abuses by fellow cons. So far as I know, the mystery helicopter was never identified. It never came back. Tourists maybe, but I know they weren't from Japan. I didn't see any cameras.

Another time a bunch of people were hanging around in the main yard at Mesa Unit when a bullet from a high-powered rifle slammed into one of the seven-foot concrete walls. Nobody was hit, but a few inmates suddenly decided to see how fast they could eat dirt. The hacks shut the yard down for a couple of days, then opened it up again and told us the bullet apparently came from someone who was hunting or getting in a little target practice. It was just a stray bullet. Yeah, sure! Hunting accidents happen all the time. Maybe it was some kid who decided to drive out in the desert near the FCI to hunt rattlesnakes—or rats.

Inmates were a little nervous for a while after the shooting, but nerves are something you learn to live with when you've flipped. If the shot did come from a sniper, how in the hell could anyone figure out who the target was? Everybody in the units had deadly enemies, and some of the witnesses were known to have prices on their head. Gravano was said to be worth $2 million dead, and the assassin wouldn't even be expected to bring back his ears to prove his kill. Just do the job. That's all that was expected. Gravano and other witnesses knew there were hundreds of guys out there with the skills and motivation to track down a quarry and kill.

A security lapse of another type was illustrated by a couple of witnesses at Otisville who were computer nerds and who had hacked their way into the federal prison system's Sentry computer program. That was serious shit, because the database stores information about every prisoner in federal custody.

The hackers coerced or paid one of the guards to download the list into an IBM PC, then they manipulated it to cause release documents to come up for prisoners who weren't yet scheduled to be set free. Only one prisoner, an inmate at the FCI at Lewisburg, was released before corrections officials caught on and put a stop to the scam. They were just in time to prevent a couple of Mafia bosses from Buffalo who were serving life sentences from being cut loose. After the BOP learned about the scheme, the guard was suspended for six months, then fired. No one was ever charged with a criminal offense in the case, or so I was told.

That was also the case in June 1990 when the government accidently sold a pile of used computer equipment for forty-five dollars during an auction in Lexington, Kentucky. The hard drives held information listing all confidential federal informants and WITSEC participants.

The local yard-sale shopper who bought two truckloads of equipment knew nothing about the sensitive information that was stored on the hard drives until the feds contacted him. They were in a panic. They had discovered the mistake and wanted the equipment back. Seems that a government computer genius told to prepare the equipment for sale was supposed to scramble all the files, but he used a magnet or some other device that was too weak to do the job.

Tough shit. By the time the Gs discovered the screwup, the original buyer had resold everything. Apparently it was never recovered.

The Justice Department has been playing security catch-up with their computers ever since the electronic age was ushered in, and they've committed some horrible foul-ups. I haven't heard of anyone they've gotten killed yet, but they've come closer than they should.

Convicts have a lot of time on their hands, and they are constantly scheming, but sometimes prison administrators or higher-ups in the federal bureaucracy screw up all by themselves.

Fat Vinnie Teresa had his cover blown a few months after moving into phase two and being relocated with his family in Maple Valley, Washington. His earlier revelations led to the conviction or indictments of about fifty people who were either members of the Mob or were closely associated.

A grand jury indicted the snitch and several members of his family in December 1984 for allegedly smuggling exotic birds and reptiles into the United States. Suddenly anybody who was paying attention knew who Charles Cantino really was. He was a three-hundred-pound turncoat mobster from New England with a bad ticker and a $500,000 bounty on his head. During the first three years he and his family were in the relocation program, they were forced to move three times.

Michael Lloyd, an all-around criminal with a professional background much like mine, provides another good example of how playing good citizen and trying to help the feds can put you in harm's way. He grew up on Staten Island, where he was around mobsters from the time he was a teenager, but he was never a violent guy. Lloyd isn't some kind of desperate character who killed people, although he was locked up with a bunch of them. He stole things. Eventually he earned a thirty-year federal prison sentence for himself after rustling some cattle, breaking out of prison, and robbing a bank. He worked scores in different states, but was especially active in Pennsylvania, where he had good connections with other thieves and racketeers.

Lloyd just happened to get teamed up on a flight from "The Hut," the FCI in Terre Haute, Indiana, on his way

to the super max penitentiary at Marion with a powerful
New York Mafia boss named Carmine ''the Snake'' Persico. The flight Lloyd and Persico shared was part of a
BOP and U.S. Marshals Service activity established to
transport convicts being moved from one federal prison
to another.

A few years ago the marshals joined the transport operation with the Immigration and Naturalization Service,
and the two federal agencies now share a fleet of of thirteen white Boeing 727s that crisscross the country transporting convicts and carrying illegal aliens who are being
deported. The official name is the Justice Prisoner and
Alien Transportation System, JPATS. But cops and most
immigration people who are involved with it up close
call it Con Air, just like the name of the hit movie Hollywood released in mid-1997. Convicts have their own
nickname for the airplanes. They call them Big Bird.

Con Air jetliners shuttle between about forty American cities on a regular schedule, and transport approximately 6,000 prisoners every month. In 1996, JPATS
ferried 130,000 passengers. Most of the high-flying prisoners are bank robbers and people who were involved
in drug trafficking.

No first-class section and no stewardesses were aboard
to push drink carts or fluff up pillows for Lloyd and
Persico, who were dressed in tan federal prison uniforms
and blue canvas boat shoes. Instead most of the passengers flew handcuffed to their seats with their legs
chained and secured to eye bolts imbedded in the floor.
The wrists of prisoners considered to be especially high-
risk were secured with black boxes. Before boarding
Con Air 727s, whose only markings are logos of the
American flag on the wing, every prisoner is meticulously searched. U.S. marshals peer inside their mouths,
under their tongues, inside and behind their ears, behind
their collars, and under their arm pits, as well as inspect

the palms and backs of their hands. Arms and legs are carefully patted down. Each JPATS aircraft has two pilots in the cockpit, and crewmembers in blue jumpers help watch over and tend to the passengers. Cuffs and shackles remain on the prisoners even when they're fed box lunches or escorted to toilets; and two marshals armed with shotguns stand guard behind a protective wire-mesh screen at the rear.

At the conclusion of their flight, along with their fellow passengers, Lloyd and Persico were led shuffling in cuffs and shackles to waiting U.S. Marshals Service vans, while heavily armed officers manned a perimeter around the prisoners and the 727 until it lifted off the tarmac and roared safely out of range of potential snipers.

At Marion, the two men were assigned cells near each other and continued the friendship started while riding Con Air. Even though he was locked up in Americas' most secure prison, Lloyd's friend was still surrounded by an aura of power and authority.

Persico took over one of the smaller New York crime families after the former leader, Joe Colombo, was shot in the head and turned into a vegetable during an assassination attempt, and he was one of the people that Sammy the Bull credited for grooming him as a wiseguy. Sammy became a member of the Gambino family, but he was always friendly with the Colombos. He told me he especially liked Persico, because he was smart and fair.

The Snake may have been fair, but he wasn't smart enough not to unload his secrets to the new friend at Marion. Lloyd had his fill of prisons and was planning to clean up his act after serving his time. In 1988, he contacted Rudolph Giuliani in New York, and tipped him off that Persico was planning to have the prosecutors who sent him to prison whacked. Giuliani was U.S. attorney for the Southern District of New York, and he swung into action. A wall of security was erected around

Assistant U S. attorneys Aaron Marcu and Bruce Baird, the two prosecutors fingered for the hit. They survived the plot, and virtually owed their lives to the former hoodlum, who by a mysterious stroke of fortune was locked up with the New York Mob leader.

Lloyd agreed to keep authorities informed about everything he heard related to continuing criminal activities by Persico, including past hits and others that were reputedly in the planning stage. He was a good choice as a CI, because Persico was using him as a secretary. He wrote everything down for the Snake, typed his legal mail for him, and kept track of the important shit for the feds.

Inmates at Marion don't work out on a weight pile, sit around in a common area and play dominoes, or shoot pool. They're locked in their one-man cells for up to as long as twenty-three hours a day, even when they've been behaving themselves. Everything Lloyd managed to pick up from the chatterbox Mafia chieftain, he passed on to the feds. When he and Persico were transferred to the FCI at Lompoc, Lloyd continued to keep the Gs up to date on what was going on.

He helped the feds for eight years, and how was he rewarded? The same way I was: he served more time inside maximum-security prisons than he would have served if he had kept his mouth shut about the assassination plot and everything else he heard. He was feeding them so much information that they wanted him inside, with Persico, where he could be used.

At last, a series of blunders by prison officials and the feds made it too hot for him, and he was transferred out of Lompoc. He still had some time to do in Pennsylvania, but figured with credit for all the good work he did for the government and the extra time he served in the federal prison system that he would be paroled in a few months. No way! The Department of Corrections in the Commonwealth refused to give him credit for the full time he served.

Worse yet, he was back in the middle of his danger area, Pennsylvania, where he was well known to the local Mafia crime family and other racketeers. Lloyd figured that by that time his cover was blown and the word was out that he was a snitch. He wasn't even enrolled in WIT-SEC, but he asked for transfer to the Witness Protection Unit at Otisville until his parole was processed.

Instead he was locked up in general population, on the same cell block with members of Persico's organization. Then the government pulled the rug all the rest of the way from under the man who almost single-handedly prevented the possible assassination of two federal prosecutors. His name appeared on a list of federal witnesses stored in a government computer database that was available to other inmates and their attorneys. It was a horrible screwup, with the potential of becoming fatal.

Still, the feds weren't ready to admit Lloyd to the Witness Protection Units, and he was transferred to another prison. For his protection, he was locked up in the maximum-security detention area. Incredibly, despite all the foul-ups and double-crosses that kept Lloyd doing hard time and threatened his personal safety, the feds continued to call on him to testify as a witness at important trials.

Lloyd's story bothered the hell out of me, because I could see so many parallels with my own treatment. Lloyd wasn't in the witness program, but he spoke out in order to save the lives of a couple of people he didn't even know. Then he ended up with his own neck in the noose as his reward.

16

Toomba and the Black Prince

> A lie can travel halfway around the world
> while the truth is putting on it's shoes.
>
> *Mark Twain*

WITNESS-PROTECTION INMATES have fertile minds—and time on their hands for schemes involving everything from shortening their sentences by manipulating state and federal officers and the courts to dramatic escapes, new criminal enterprises, and wreaking revenge on their enemies inside and outside the walls.

Henry Leon Harris was a general with Chicago's feared street gang, the El Rukns, before he flipped and played a key role in bringing down more than fifty of his cohorts in a series of racketeering and conspiracy trials.

Then, while he was a federally protected witness, he helped shatter the career and ruin the good name of one of the Justice Department's best and brightest, William R. Hogan, Jr., a young assistant U.S. attorney for the

Northern District of Illinois who specialized in breaking up vicious street gangs like the El Rukns.

I didn't usually hang out with blacks. My friends inside the units were Aryan Brotherhood, bikers, and stand-up characters like Jap Chriswell. With the exception of Jap, who was a case all his own, they were uniformly and solidly white. The blacks preferred to hang out by themselves anyway, and they had their own things going down, their own rackets on the inside, their own plans for resuming their old criminal ways on the outside, their own food—and their boom boxes. They listened to gangsta rap, that hip-hop shit, and they had their own television shows. They watched basketball and Bill Cosby.

We didn't mix much, but my roomie at that time was a white guy who acted like he was an honorary black. Phillip Francis Walsh hung around with blacks on the inside and on the outside. He dated black women and that kind of thing, but he was okay and I got to know Toomba and a couple of his friends through Phil.

Toomba was a character, a friendly guy who loved to flap his mouth, and had a funny sense of humor. I sat in on some of his bull sessions while we were in Unit One together and listened to his war stories. Sometimes when he got wound up good, he wrapped a towel around his neck and absently messed around with the ends while he talked.

It was hard to tell when he was talking straight and when he was letting the bullshit fly, but he had good stories to tell. Toomba was fooling around trying to write a book, and he had some wild things to say, like trying to convince people that Abraham Lincoln was black.

He also knew everything about the El Rukns, their history, what they were into and who their leaders were, having been involved with them since he was thirteen.

A few decades ago, the El Rukns had other names for their gang. In the beginning it was called the Blackstone Rangers. Then it became the Black P-Stone Nation, before evolving into its final incarnation. The original names came from the street that was at the center of the gang's home turf, Blackstone Avenue, and from the black stone corner of a major Islamic shrine in Mecca called El Rukn.

Harris's El Rukn name was Toomba, and that's what people called him in the units where I met up with him. When I learned what his name translated into in Arabic, it broke me up. It means *The Faithful One*. Great name for a snitch!

Under whatever names they were using at all times, they spread fear, violence, and misery through the Windy City's Southside ghetto. They fought turf battles with other black gangs in the city like the Disciples or Gangster Disciples and with a ruthless drug-dealing gang just over the Indiana state line in Gary. Drive-by shootings, street-corner ambushes, bombings, cuttings, stomping—they did it all.

They were playing for big stakes: control of millions of dollars worth of heroin and coke sales, prostitution, armed robberies, burglary and extortion. Murder was nothing to them. Harris, other insiders, and some Chicago cops who specialized in investigating and breaking up street gangs, estimated the El Rukns and their predecessors may have murdered as many as 600 people during roughly a quarter of a century. During the 1960s, Chicago police estimated the peak membership at about 15,000, including kids as young as six years old and old farts of sixty.

That was about the time that President Lyndon B. Johnson and private liberal groups funneled a huge bundle of cash into the gang as part of a Great Society scheme to reform all those drug dealers, pimps, stick-up men, shakedown artists, extortionists and killers. LBJ, and liberal sympathizers who saw the P-Stoners as dedicated black political activists, figured they could rechannel the gang's energies into productive pursuits. Sure, they're going to give up their guns and drug money to learn how to flip hamburgers, pump gasoline, repair cars and clerk in haberdasheries.

The Washington crowd obviously didn't know much about big-city street gangs. Either that or they had some other agenda, and they didn't care what their supposedly well-intentioned transfusion of taxpayer and private money was really used for. It was like manna from heaven. The gang was put in charge of big-time social programs, then ripped off the government and foundation money as fast as it came in. They had a great racket going.

Some of the P-Stoners also used the money and knowledge gained through their new contacts with the government to spin off part of their old gang into a religious organization, the El Rukns. It was the same bunch of thugs, but now they claimed to be Sunni Muslims, and suddenly they had religion to hide behind. They set up a few soup kitchens around some of the projects and played the game—they were in the same business as before.

Although Chicago was the base of the El Rukn operations and the center of the gang's power, they spread out to other cities around the country. At various times, they were linked by police to contract killings, served as celebrity bodyguards, and hobnobbed with important cronies of Mu'ammar Gadhafi, the dictator of Libya. Gadhafi tangled with Ronald Reagan while he was president, and the United States bombed the shit out of Libya's capital city.

While I was sitting around with Phil, Toomba, and their friends, the former El Rukn general boasted that the gang had been planning to set up a crime syndicate that stretched all over the world. I believe it. They were on their way and they could have carried it out.

Toomba was like a lot of witnesses in the units who left all their old friendships and lifestyles behind forever when they rolled. Even though he knew that if he was ever recognized by one of his homeboys on the streets of South Chicago he would be a dead man, he still had a soft spot in his heart for the El Rukns. The gang had been his whole life, and he took a certain pride in his accomplishments as an El Rukn even though he wound up betraying them.

Toomba was recruited from his home in Milwaukee, where his folks owned a funeral parlor; and he was one of the brightest stars of the new enterprise. As other more senior hoodlums were eliminated from the scene through long jail terms, shootings, drug overdoses and such, he moved quickly up through the ranks. His rise was quite an accomplishment, because according to police estimates, while he was involved with the El Rukns, membership ranged from a few hundred to about 4,000. Then Toomba got caught in an embarrassing situation and rolled. So did some of his pals.

Toomba's troubles were directly tied to the misfortunes of Noah Ryan Robinson, the millionaire half-brother of the founder of the Rainbow/PUSH Coalition and two-time Democratic candidate for the presidential nomination, Jesse Jackson. Jesse and Noah have the same old man. Noah's story was fascinating, and Toomba knew all the good parts.

When Noah got in trouble, he was living high on the hog, shuttling between Greenville, N. C., and Chicago, where he was making fistfuls of money handling government contracts set aside for minority businesses. He was head of a federally funded project called the Breadbasket Commercial Association, Inc., an arm of Operation PUSH, which was organized by his brother, Jesse. The Breadbasket outfit was designed to give minority business owners a leg up in bidding for public contracts.

According to news reports at the time, much of the work Robinson obtained through the program was subcontracted to white-owned businesses who actually performed the construction. Robinson had other business interests as well, including real estate holdings and a string of fast-food joints. Noah had almost 1,000 people working for him in five states, and in 1987 *Ebony* magazine ranked him among the top 100 black businessmen in the country.

William R. Hogan, Jr., got on Noah's trail when some prosecutor contacts in New England confided that the big-time operator in Chicago and Greenville was believed to be using some of his fast-food joints to launder money for the El Rukns.

It was the kind of story that made Hogan prick up his ears and go to work. He got his opportunity when he learned about the ambush murder in Greenville of a boyhood friend of Robinson's who was a former employee. Leroy Cashmore Barber was assassinated after the two men had a violent falling out. Nobody called Barber by his first name. They used his nickname, Hambone.

Hambone Barber wasn't in Noah's class. He had a monster drug problem, dropped out of school, and did some serious time in the joint in South Carolina after a gun battle with police outside a Greenville bar way back in the 1960s. Apparently, all his life, he was a no-good and a bad ass.

Hambone eventually turned up in Chicago where he went to work for his old friend as a janitor. One day Hambone and a partner confronted Robinson and demanded $150. When Robinson refused, Hambone's buddy pulled a pistol and took a shot at him. There was only one bullet in the piece, and it missed.

The former boyhood friends ran into each other again a few years later in a Broad Street poolroom in downtown Greenville, when Hambone walked in carrying a drink and spouting a torrent of insults aimed at Robinson. That led to a fight and Robinson kicked the shit out of Hambone.

Robinson had his own nickname in the days before his brother Jesse became an important national figure with powerful Washington connections. People called him Po' Bean, and when he was a boy his father taught him to box. By the time the fistfight with Hambone came down, Po Bean's nickname had evolved into something more fitting for a grownup man of his stature. It was Mighty Po.

Worse things than a beating were in Hambone's future. On January 2, 1986, a few days after the fight, he was in the Bridge Lounge, a joint located in a shopping center owned by Robinson, when someone told him there was a call for him on an outside pay phone. Moments after Hambone stepped outside the building, a bushwhacker blew him away with one shot from a .38.

After a multistate investigation, the cops focused on Mighty Po and the El Rukns. They believed a crew of five hit men traveled from Chicago to carry out a contract on Barber. They also had a witness to back up their story. Hogan took the information and ran with it, figuring he had the opportunity he was looking for to bring down the El Rukns.

More than eighteen months after the shooting, a Greenville woman named Janice Denice Rosemond testified before a Chicago grand jury that was looking into the activities of the gang. Grand jury proceedings are secret, but the press speculated that she told the panel she saw Hambone shot in the head.

Someone else must have been impressed with the speculation in the news stories and rumors circulating on the street, because a few weeks after the woman testified, someone jumped her in her apartment and slashed and stabbed her five times. She survived the attack.

But the fat was still in the fire for Noah Robinson and the El Rukns, because Hogan was on their trail.

A handsome Irishman with a square jaw and neatly conservative buttoned-down appearance that mirrored his professional and personal life, Hogan could have been a model for the old radio show, "Jack Armstrong the All American Boy." He was a straight arrow, a doer, and workaholic, known as a fighter who accomplished whatever he set out to do. He had a reputation as a guy who always fought his battles on the side of good, against the forces of evil whether it was the Crips and the Bloods in Los Angeles or the Bandido biker gang in the Pacific Northwest. He went up against all of them.

Hogan specialized in digging up the dirt on vicious street gangs, and one of his most successful methods of accomplishing that was to find people in the top ranks whom he could turn. Once that happened, Hogan and his friends could tear the heart out of their organizations by sending their leaders and as many of rank-and-file soldiers as possible to the joint. The prosecutor was good at his job, and Toomba became one of his star rats.

Toomba flipped one sweltering hot summer day in July 1988 after Chicago cops picked him up in a Southside rooming house and told him he was in big trouble. They knew he was in on the murder of Hambone Barber in South Carolina, and had the paperwork all ready to file charges. Toomba was an experienced criminal, but he was young and figured he still had a lot of living to do. Later, talking about it in the units, he said he didn't want to fry in what he described as "the hot chair."

The general spilled his guts during the ride to the station house. He said Hambone's hit was ordered by Jeff Fort, who was the leader of the P-Stone Rangers, then

of the El Rukns. Other members of the gang called Fort
the Imam. That's a description for a Muslim prayer
leader and religious teacher. No one was allowed to call
Fort by his given name, but he had other titles his fol-
lowers sometimes used to show respect. The End was
one of them. The End had served time on various convictions ranging from narcotics trafficking to embezzling
money from a federal job-training program. He was
locked up in the FCIs at Terre Haute and Leavenworth
before he was finally transferred to the FCI at Bastrop,
Texas.

Fort continued to run the gang after he was impris-
oned. He's been at Bastrop for at least ten years now,
but nothing changed after he was transferred there from
the hut. He was still said to be the man in charge, com-
municating with his gang on the outside through coded
messages during collect telephone calls to his private
line at the Chicago headquarters. The generals listened
to his orders on a telephone intercom system.

Toomba was married to Fort's younger sister and was
head of the Rukn's drug network, but that didn't prevent
him from flipping when he got into serious trouble. He
ratted on his brother-in-law, and he ratted on Robinson.

The domino theory that got so much attention when
Americans were fighting in the war in Southeast Asia
also works when local cops and the Gs are mining information from the leaders of criminal organizations.
One guy flips near the top, and other guys begin flipping
down the line. One of the most important new stool pigeons was Tramell Davis. Sam Buford, Eugene Hunter,
Harry Evans, and Jackie Clay were others who turned
as the investigation progressed.

Tramell Davis was a gang big-shot who functioned as
security chief, and his El Rukn name was Emir Tacu.
Don't ask me what that shit means. They had their own
names and their own unique language worked out so

they could talk and keep secrets even if they were wired.

Buford wasn't an El Rukn. He was a freelance dope dealer in the South Side Chicago ghetto, whose profession brought him in close contact with the gang before he was charged with attempted murder and unlawful possession of weapons and drugs. Hunter called himself Saleem, and Evans was another general. The Rukns must have had more generals than soldiers.

Hogan and a staff of colleagues and assistants working for the Justice Department, along with some local Chicago cops, had their hands full. They were tied into a far-ranging, complex investigation that eventually extended for three or four years and ate up hundreds of man-hours.

Eventually it led to a series of federal grand jury indictments, including one that was more than three hundred pages long. Sixty-four El Rukns and hangers-on or other associates—along with Mighty Po Robinson were named in the indictments. Charges included conspiracy, fraud, bribery, kidnapping, weapons and narcotics offenses, along with twenty murders and seven attempted homicides. One of the murders was the ambush slaying of Hambone Barber. And one of the attempted murders was the knife attack on Janice Rosemond.

A grand jury in South Carolina returned criminal indictments against Robinson and another of his former employees. Robinson turned himself in on local charges tied to Hambone Barber's murder and was locked in the Greenville County Detention Center. A preacher friend accompanied him to the jail.

The big-shot businessman insisted he didn't have anything to do with the killing, although he admitted he had ties to the El Rukns. The ties would have been hard to deny, because he was one of a dozen or so community and business leaders from Chicago's South Side who had petitioned a federal parole board trying to get Fort an early release from prison on a Mississippi drug-conspiracy conviction.

Identifying himself in a letter to the board as the National Director of the Breadbasket Commercial Association, Robinson wrote that Fort had a track record of standing up for the little man who is too weak to stand up for himself. "I know of two other men in history who got in big trouble and eventually lost their lives for the same reason," he declared. The men were Jesus Christ and Martin Luther King.

I'm not a religious man, but tieing in the leader of one of America's deadliest and most sophisticated criminal gangs with Jesus Christ is stretching things a little too much for me. The federal parole-board suits may have had a similar attitude. Despite Mighty Po's glowing endorsement, Fort didn't get an early parole.

In Greenville, Robinson continued to claim his links to the gang were all business-related, and said he had hired El Rukns to work as guards in some of his restaurants that were in high-crime areas. The baddest cats in the neighborhood could come into his restaurants, and when they saw El Rukns in uniform, they behaved themselves. Made sense!

Robinson also spouted off about racial politics. He claimed he was being harassed because people wanted to embarrass his famous brother and shoot down Jesse's presidential campaign. I don't know about that. Jesse wasn't running all that strong anyway, and I don't think his half-brother's troubles with the law had anything to do with it. I mean, look at Jimmy Carter and his brother, Billy, the drunk. Billy had so many fans, a beer was named after him. Then there's Roger Clinton, who was a dope dealer and cokehead. His big brother was elected president twice.

Toomba, Davis, and some other generals or high muckety-mucks were flown to South Carolina for Robinson's murder conspiracy trial, and the testimony of the two high-ranking snitches about the hit was dynamite. Toomba testified that during a meeting in Chicago, Robinson "told us he needed hit duty." Robinson "mentioned $10,000," the witness added. Toomba passed the information to Fort, and the gang leader told him and several other El Rukns to "take care of it."

At a later meeting at Robinson's home in Chicago, the businessman gave him and his cohorts $2,000 to cover travel expenses to Greenville, Toomba said. He didn't mention if the rest of the money was paid.

During arguments over a defense move to exclude his testimony, Davis said outside the presence of the jury that he heard General Gangs, another El Rukn whose real name was Alan Knox, tell the imam: "Local wants this character on the tangerine scene changed, like yesterday."

Other witnesses explained that the word *local* was El Rukn lingo for Robinson, and Davis told the jury that "tangerine scene," meant the Carolinas.

"What does 'changed' mean?" the prosecutor asked.

"Change means killed," Davis said.

I would have loved to sit in on the trial and watch the faces on the jurors while this stream of shit was coming down. I would need help figuring it out, too. Hell, I couldn't even speak Pig Latin when I was a kid. One lawyer said the words reminded him of Lewis Carroll, and that the words didn't mean what they seemed to mean. They meant what Fort said they meant.

El Rukn-speak came up constantly throughout all the trials, and prosecutors always had to have translations of key words for the juries. The talk was colorful. For example, "Love, truth, and righteous" strung together in that order meant $2,000.

The number system was explained at the trial by Davis, and Toomba went over it again in Unit One while he was boasting about his old "family." There was method in the madness. The word "love" stood for one, 100, or 1,000. "Love, truth" meant two, 200 or 2,000." He went through the whole routine, but who wanted to listen to all that shit except Phil Walsh and his chums. I got the idea, but I wasn't going to waste time trying to learn the so-called language. Who would I talk to?

Neverthless, I remembered some of the words and their translations. Judges were described as "robes," and "souls" were cops, local police as well as the Gs. "Perfect" was marijuana. Their word for Nation of Islam leader Louis Farrakhan was "Pecan." Gadhafi was "young friend," and the United States was "the monster." They called Washington, D. C., "The Big Actor." Reagan was still president then.

The FBI and the BATF secretly taped 3,500 hours of El Rukn jabber during collect calls that Fort placed from Bastrop to his generals in Chicago and in other locations. He telephoned as often as fifteen times a week, and talked an average of two and a half hours each time. That was a lot of palaver, but Fort was running a big international business and he had a private army to direct.

Remarks by Melvin Edward Mayes during one of the conversations provides another good example of El Rukn talk. "They'll hear like they be in manifest in the science of up and the last words," he said. Davis translated the apparent street gibberish as meaning the gang was planning to blow up an airplane, and make sure that Gadhafi knew they were the people who carried out the terrorism. The whole vocabulary was like that; completely indecipherable without the help of an insider, a rat.

Fort worked it all out while he was doing time in the joint. Only generals were allowed to be in on the code. It made sense if you had secrets to keep, but it didn't work because it didn't account for the possibility of some of the imam's generals ratting out and giving the code away to the Gs.

The South Carolina jury convicted Robinson of being an accessory after the fact in the Rosemond woman's stabbing. One of Robinson's former employees told a jury that the hotshot businessman offered him $5,000 to kill the woman because she testified to the grand jury in Chicago about Hambone's execution. But Robinson's troubles with the law weren't over. They were just beginning.

In Chicago, Hogan was working his ass off on a pile of cases dealing with everything from terrorism, racketeering, drug dealing, conspiracy, and murder. He directed six El Rukn-related trials in eighteen months. Sometimes he and his staff of fellow prosecutors had two trials going on in the Dirksen Federal Building at the same time, but he was getting convictions. Toomba was one hell of a witness. He admitted he was a former high-ranking member of the street gang and that he was a former dopehead. That was in his past, he insisted however. He wasn't a Rukn anymore, and he didn't do heroin anymore.

He sounded believable, and the way he came across to the juries from the witness stand helped make up for a shortage of physical evidence in some of the cases. He and the other former El Rukns who turned testified about some meetings and crimes that happened twenty or twenty-five years in the past, and they convinced jurors they knew what they were talking about.

I wasn't there, but I know it wasn't always easy for Toomba and his fellow mouths. I did my time in the trenches, and learned how defense attorneys can tear the asses off snitches who testify. And when I testified, I didn't have a couple dozen El Rukns sitting in the spectator section scowling and shooting daggers at me with their eyes.

The trials were big news in Chicago. Fort and five of his pals were accused in a fifty-count indictment of scheming to carry out acts of terrorism in the United States in return for what they hoped would be a $2.5 million reward from Gadhafi in the form of a loan. For starters, they were said to have planned to bomb an airplane, murder a Milwaukee county supervisor, and to set up pro-Libya demonstrations in front of federal buildings.

Some of Fort's top people traveled to Panama, New York, Morocco, and Libya to negotiate the deal with Gadhafi's people, but it never went through. I don't believe it was ever proven in court that they managed to meet with Gadhafi himself. If they did, the Chicago gangsters would have outranked the North African dictator. Most of them were generals. He's only a colonel.

The only El Rukn on the Libyan trip who didn't outrank Gadhafi was called an Officer Mufti. That's just below the generals, who dealt personally with Fort. The mufti was considered to be too low-ranking to be allowed to talk to the Libyans. It was his job to keep his eyes and ears open and his mouth shut. Other lesser ranks are ambassadors, and at the bottom—EIs or soldiers—who deal the gang's drugs on the street. Toomba laid all the organizational bullshit out for us on the units.

I was impressed. Fort had everything set up like he was running an army, or a country. He produced his own language and put his personal stamp on their religion. Even more impressive, he kept all those bad asses in line and continued to run the operation for twenty or thirty years, even though he spent half that time in the joint. How many people can do that kind of thing? Imagine what the dude could have accomplished if he was legitimate and had all his old friends in Washington and

New York behind him? Of course that's a question you could ask about Lehder and other people I met in the joint. Being a crook don't mean you don't have a brain.

All of the El Rukn defendants were in the courtroom for the main trial tied to the terrorism and conspiracy counts except one. Mayes, whom the FBI said was "believed to be an integral part of the weapon purchases and terrorism plans" of the reputed conspirators, went on the lam. FBI spokesmen said they thought he was in Libya. He'd been there before. Mayes was Fort's executive secretary, the guy responsible for seeing that The End's orders were carried out and was one of the generals dispatched to talk with Gadhafi's people.

Surprising information was developed during the investigation and trial, linking famous entertainers and world leaders like Gadhafi to various gang schemes. Sammy Davis, Jr., once agreed to cosign a $250,000 loan for a building project on Chicago's South Side that the gang was backing. Supposedly they were going to renovate their Grand Mosque on South Drexel Avenue and open an ice-cream and flower shop.

The deal fell through, and that's probably a shame. An ice-cream shop would have been better than an armory. That was apparently one of the functions of their combination mosque and headquarters, because in the summer of 1986, the cops cut through locks and doors with acetylene torches there and at a nearby apartment, and hauled away truckloads of weapons. A rocket launcher, machine guns, hand grenades, an automatic pistol, other handguns and shotguns were confiscated. The gang had stockpiled enough weaponry to start a war, let alone carry out a little terrorism.

The Chicago trials were circuses. The jury in one of the main trials was sequestered and some jurors were dismissed after they reported frightening anonymous telephone calls to their homes by people who cautioned that they were being watched. Two sisters-in-law of Davis were wounded in a mysterious shooting in the hallway of a South Side public-housing project a week before his testimony. And Fort's fourteen-year-old son scuffled with security officers after he was evicted from the courtroom for trying to sit in the section reserved for the press.

The federal trials were marked with dramatic testimony. Some of the most disturbing revelations stemmed from Sam Buford. Buford said that he introduced an undercover FBI agent named Willie Hulon to Allen Knox (General Gangs). A few days later the FBI agent allegedly sold an M-72 light antitank rocket to Knox and Melvin Mayes during a meeting in a Holiday Inn in south suburban Lansing. The launcher, which was the same one police later carted out of the El Rukn headquarters, was deactivated before it was turned over to the gangsters.

Then, shortly after an assistant U. S. attorney and her colleagues won a big conspiracy and terrorism trial in another courtroom against Fort and some other senior gang leaders, the campaign to dismantle the El Rukns began to turn sour. Hogan and others began to learn firsthand just how dangerous informants and government witnesses can be to the professional and political health of prosecutors and cops who depend on them.

Buford claimed during his testimony that the government paid him $10,000 for his work as an informant, and said he continued to deal narcotics with the gang after he rolled. Davis got $10,000, and his wife and family also got some money, according to one of the assistant U. S. attorneys involved in the prosecutions. He didn't pin down exactly how much Emir Tacu's family walked away with.

There's nothing illegal about paying informers and helping their families if its done according to the rules, but when witnesses for the federal government begin talking on the witness stand about how much they were given to testify against their friends, it tends to leave a bad taste in the mouths of most jurors.

The government doesn't hesitate to spread taxpayer money around pretty liberally when they need a rat to nail big-timers like Robinson and Fort, but when I knew Toomba in the units he didn't talk like a man who had collected a king's ransom in return for information and testimony. Davis didn't come away from the courtroom with a fortune either, but he collected something more valuable than the cash. He plea-bargained a deal for a maximum thirty-five-year sentence. That's no minute, but he was involved in some heavy shit. He confessed to extremely serious felonies, including attempted bribery of a Cook County circuit court judge, running dope, and involvement in a couple of murders. One was Hambone's killing and the other was a hit on a South Side drug dealer named Willie "Dollar Bill" Bibbs.

Like other people who roll on big cases and become protected witnesses, Davis didn't have to worry about going into general population someplace where he would be whacked before the lights were turned off. He was looking forward to doing sweet time in a witness unit, and there's no way he was going to really do thirty-five years.

The End wound up with a brand-new seventy-five-year prison sentence after conviction for playing a major role in the loony scheme to squeeze money from the Libyan government by carrying out terrorist attacks in the United States. He was lucky. The prosecution wanted to hit him with the maximum 260 years. The judge also socked him with a $255,000 fine and said his property could be seized to pay the bill. A few years after the trial, the El Rukn headquarters was torn down.

Fort, Knox, and their pals were convicted on forty-nine of the original fifty counts in the indictment. The other charge was dismissed early in the trial. Robinson was also convicted in federal court of several charges, including conspiring to kill a business associate and a witness against the El Rukns, and of putting Fort in touch with East Coast drug dealers and sharing in the profits from the deal. In a later trial in Chicago, Robinson was convicted of defrauding the IRS, the State of Illinois and Wendy's International, Inc., by skimming more than half a million dollars from six hamburger joints he held franchises on.

The prosecutions shattered the El Rukns, but other gangs like the GDs, the Black Disciples, and the Black P-Stone Nation were waiting to take over their drug-dealing turf and move into other rackets left untended by the crippling of Fort and his bunch. One bows out, and another steps in. There's always someone waiting to move into the vacuum and take over a lucrative territory when something like that happens. The South Side gangs were already collecting hundreds of thousands of dollars in street taxes while the Rukns were still on trial. Crack, speed, heroin, pussy; everything was on sale, just like before.

But the first hints of the trouble ahead for some of the police and prosecutors involved in the long crusade to dismantle the El Rukns had surfaced during testimony by the government's paid witnesses. Toomba and some of his prison pals saw their opening, and they went for it.

When the scheme began to go down, I got a close-up look at exactly how it was put together and who was involved. Despite his help wearing a wire, working undercover, and testifying in open court against his violent friends, Toomba pulled a sentence of twenty-years-to-life. According to the terms of the plea bargain and other sentencing guidelines, he could realistically look forward to going up for parole after ten years, in 1998.

Serving ten years in the units was better than being sent to general population in some prison to be executed by other inmates, but Toomba wasn't at Sandstone long before he figured out—right or wrong—that he should have, and might have, cut a better deal for himself. For a hoodlum who had admitted helping carry out gang executions, dealing dope, and committing various other major crimes, the deal wasn't bad—until he began comparing it with some of the cushy arrangements made by people like Gravano.

Walsh and some other witnesses, including a Pakistani named Mushtaq Malik, agreed with him, and they all got together to figure out a plan to right what they had decided was a terrible wrong.

Walsh was a unique character, a California drug dealer and second-generation witness who wound up in the program after ratting out his old man. His daddy became the first family member to turn when he snitched on a bunch of criminal friends in Detroit and was rewarded with a spot in the witness-protection program for him and his family. Some people figured Walsh's old man merely got what was coming to him when his son ratted him out.

When I first knew Phil, both of us were relative newcomers to Sandstone, but he was on his second tour with WITSEC. He was a protected witness earlier before he was released, then he got into trouble again and snitched out some more people. Phil Walsh was already a career snitch.

Malik was a character of a different sort, whose criminal background paralleled Lehder's in some important respects. He became known as the Black Prince after setting up one of the world's biggest heroin-smuggling operations. It was based in his home country, Pakistan.

Malik was a notorious liar who tried to cut deals for

himself by concocting yarns about almost anyone from international drug smugglers to international terrorists. He brewed up one story trying to link the Palestine Liberation Organization to the bombing of the U.S. Marine barracks in Beirut. It didn't seem to bother him much when he was caught in lies, which often occurred when he was testifying. He once told a judge in Chicago that about 30 percent of his testimony as a protected witness was lies.

Most of the Black Prince's tall tale-telling, like the PLO bombing yarn, didn't get him anywhere. He had a rotten reputation as a witness, but it didn't prevent the government from continuing to call on him for testimony in different cases. He even admitted lying about the Massachusetts drug-smuggling case he testified in that initially got him into the witness-protection program.

Considering the maximum penalty of life in prison for the original charges he could have been hit with in Massachusetts, he was doing okay for himself. He plea bargained a thirty-five-year sentence, but was already looking forward to getting out in less than half that time. When I knew him at Sandstone, he had been in the units for about five years, and he was still concocting new stories to try and whittle away at the time he had remaining.

Toomba, the Black Prince, and Walsh sat around together for six months, plotting how they were going to blackmail the government into giving them Rule 35s (sentence reductions) by pinning accusations of prosecutorial misconduct on Hogan and some other members of his team. They were switching sides, and they told me I was welcome to get in on the action if I wanted to win a Rule 35 for myself. I didn't see how I could do myself any good joining in the scheme, so I passed. I didn't want anything to do with it.

Jackie Clay, another former El Rukn general, occa-

sionally added information or some of his own ideas but
didn't become deeply involved. For the most part it was
Toomba's, Walsh's, and the Black Prince's show, and
they put together a brilliant performance. Hogan was
pinpointed as the patsy, and setting him up was the key
to the entire scam. The scheming was common knowledge on the unit.

Little gatherings like theirs were going on all over, all
the time. A clique here, a clique there, all putting their
heads together to try and figure out ways to get early
release, or assembling plans for new criminal enterprises
once they became civilians again. Everybody had a
scheme; usually they had several. And there was always
plenty of time for skull sessions and listening to inmates
with fertile minds and the street experience to put their
schemes into action. It was like that with Toomba and
his pals.

They knew as well as anyone how easy it was to get
drugs inside the units. Security was lax, and anybody
with any experience at all knew how to smuggle them
inside. There was almost never any drug screening done
on the unit. Despite Toomba's testimony that he was a
reformed doper, he still had a taste for heroin, and while
he was traveling between Sandstone and the Metropolitan Correctional Center in downtown Chicago to testify
against his old friends in the El Rukns, he managed to
score all the dope he wanted. He had his own works,
including a custom-made syringe to inject himself, and
he had the outside connections he needed to get high
whenever he wanted.

During the trips to Chicago before the indictments
were returned, he and Evans had each tested positive on
urine tests. The tests turned up the presence of minute
traces of morphine, indicating possible heroin use. That
was in the back of Toomba's mind when he and his
witness chums began putting together their scam.

Walsh set the wheels in motion with a telephone call to his control agent, William Shockley, who was an assistant U. S. attorney in San Jose tied into a federal drug task force. Following Shockley's advice, Walsh wrote a couple of letters outlining some of the violations of the rules that reputedly occurred with witnesses during the El Rukn trials. Shockley turned the letter over to the Justice Department's Office of Professional Responsibility, in Washington.

Walsh told me they also met in Chicago, but the experienced con refused to come across with any more information unless the feds agreed to give him an immediate sentence reduction to time served. They were interested, so Walsh spilled the rest of the story the schemers had concocted in Sandstone.

He claimed he overheard Toomba and the Black Prince talking about how Hogan provided heroin to some of the El Rukns who ratted and also hid a pile of documents and other exculpatory information from fellow prosecutors and from defense attorneys. There was still more; juicy stories about witnesses held at the Metro CC being treated to dirty movies and private horizontal visits with wives or girlfriends while the men were waiting to testify. Prosecutors and other handlers supposedly looked the other way.

Soon after Walsh contacted Shockley in California, I talked to the unit manager at Sandstone and warned him that the federal prosecutor in Chicago was being set up. Hogan was a straight shooter, like Doug Abram, and deserved better. Basically I was told to mind my own business. I talked to a couple of other people about it but couldn't find anyone in authority who was interested. So I dropped the subject and settled back to watch the scam play itself out. Hogan was a big boy, and I wasn't his mother. I had problems of my own to deal with.

Other witnesses heard what was going on and began

piling on, in hopes of winning reduced sentences or other favors. They offered their own stories of reputed misdeeds by Hogan and other government employes involved with the El Rukn trial or in the care and feeding of witnesses at the Metropolitan Correctional Center.

Lawrence Rosenthal, a former assistant U. S. attorney who had moved into private law practice in the Washington, D. C. area, surfaced with a damaging story that fit in beautifully with the tale being peddled by the Sandstone Three. Rosenthal testified at a hearing that he informed Hogan about the drug tests before the indictments were returned, and the information was shunted aside. Hogan responded that the confrontation with Rosenthal never occurred. Misery, nevertheless, was coming at the Justice Department's Chicago golden boy from both sides.

Toomba, Walsh, Evans, and other protected witnesses, as well as BATF officers, U.S. marshals, and members of Hogan's former staff testified at the hearings about the supposed irregularities and lax, cozy treatment of the snitches. The Black Prince also added his two-cents' worth from the witness stand. Hogan strongly denied that he knew about the drug tests before the indictments. The results of the urine tests were disclosed to defense lawyers during the main trial.

The information was dynamite; there was a little something for everyone to chew on. Defense attorneys and others interested in reversing the El Rukn convictions had a feast of stories about alleged prosecutorial misconduct on the highest levels; and titillating dollops of sex continued to attract and maintain the interest of the press and public.

Drugs and dirty movies were easily available in all of the units, and there was no need for a U.S. attorney, a U.S. marshal, or any other federal flunky tied into the U.S. justice system to provide them to the snitches they were using in investigations or as witnesses. More significantly yet, it's impossible to imagine someone with Hogan's moxie and his reputation doing something as stupid as he was accused of doing. It wasn't his style.

A few years earlier before the scam came down, I may have been surprised that anybody in the Justice Department or the federal court system would buy into the bullshit story concocted by such upstanding witnesses as Toomba, the Black Prince and Phil Walsh. But they bought it, and by that time I wasn't surprised.

Walsh got his sentence reduction and walked out of the joint with a shit-eating grin on his face. Freedom was his reward for helping shoot Hogan's good name and his career down in flames. It didn't matter that there were holes in his testimony big enough to drive a truck through. One of his statements during the hearings that was pure bullshit was a claim that Toomba clued him in on some of the supposed illegal handling by Hogan while the two witnesses were typing letters in the law library at Sandstone.

The job of my friend Duke Basile was to take care of the law library at Sandstone, and he and I both know there weren't any typewriters in the room that worked at that time. Walsh was also bullshitting when he claimed on the witness stand that he overheard some of Toomba's accusations while the Chicago hoodlum was using the telephone.

That couldn't be true. The security of telephone calls by protected witnesses is closely guarded, just like their court documents or conversations with lawyers and the Gs they confer with at the units. The system at Sandstone was set up so that inmates weren't even in the same room during telephone conversations. They couldn't eavesdrop on each other.

Walsh was free only a few months before he got in trouble again and was tossed back in prison in California on a drug conviction. By the late 1990s, he was out again, and I heard he was in California hanging around with some of his old friends from the units.

Toomba filed to have his guilty plea tossed out on grounds that Hogan didn't keep his promise to see to it that he got less than the minimum twenty-year sentence. Hogan stuck by his guns, insisting no promise was broken and that Toomba knew he was plea-bargaining for twenty years. Toomba's sentence was juggled around slightly, but he remained in the witness unit. The date he would first become eligible for parole was still 1998. Then after word of the scheme got around in the units, some of the other El Rukns who turned jumped on the bandwagon and also got reduced sentences.

Like Toomba, however, the Black Prince was another major player in the scheme who didn't climb out of the toilet smelling like a rose. He had tried scamming the feds before and failed. Among other things, he had trouble passing polygraph tests, and he still had his old reputation as a bullshitter and con man. When the feds talked to him about the El Rukn affair, there were too many suspicious chinks in his story. They refused to reduce his sentence.

Malik wasn't as big a loser as the people of Chicago were. A trio of federal judges overturned the El Rukn convictions during the series of trials that Toomba, Davis, Buford, and other turncoat gang members like him starred in. Some of the cases were retried. Plea bargains were worked out for other defendants, and some dangerous gangsters who would probably never have walked the streets again were given their freedom. Four known killers were among the El Rukns who were cut loose after agreeing to plea bargains for time served. At one point, after the shit hit the fan, new trials were ordered for eleven of fifty-three convicted El Rukns. The sentences of twenty-three others were trimmed, including one life sentence that was cut to eight years.

I wouldn't want to be one of the jurors in the original trial, or one of the innocent people who testified against the El Rukns. The gang vividly demonstrated the kind of violence it is capable of when Hambone Barber was ambushed and executed in South Carolina, when innocent witnesses to crimes were stabbed and shot, and when hundreds of other killings were carried out in Chicago and in other cities. The El Rukns are vicious and they play for keeps.

Ironically, whenever Toomba is finally paroled, he's one of the people who's going to have to be most careful to keep a close lookout for his former homeboys. When he got together with Walsh and the Black Prince at Sandstone to put together their scheme, plans didn't call for overturning the convictions of his former gangster friends. Toomba and his cronies were merely after early releases for themselves. They weren't even especially after Hogan's ass. He just had the bad luck to be standing in their way.

The scam didn't come down exactly as it was figured, however, and some of Toomba's blood enemies wound up back on the street because of his efforts. I wouldn't recommend that he take parole to Chicago, Milwaukee, or to Tripoli. You never know who might be waiting for him to rehash old times.

Hogan, of course, was the biggest loser of all. His life turned to shit. In the midst of a rush of stories in the newspapers and on television, he was forced out of his $98,500 a year job and portrayed in the public eye as a man who betrayed everything he professed to believe in. The All American Boy was under investigation by the Justice Department's Office of Professional Responsibility. Early in 1996, almost three years after he was put on paid leave, the Justice Department announced that he was fired.

In his letter of dismissal, Associate Deputy Attorney General David Margolis wrote that Hogan had used poor judgment handling cooperating witnesses while they were inmates, didn't properly supervise a paralegal, and didn't properly secure government documents. The Washington big-shot accused Hogan of conduct that ''weakened the public's trust in the fairness of it's system of justice.'' Hogan was accused of violating some of the very laws he spent all his professional life trying to uphold.

The former Chicago golden boy filed an appeal with the U. S. Merit Systems Protection Board, asking for reinstatement to his job and payment of his legal expenses. Three months after the firing, he was reinstated on paid leave and given back pay while the Justice Department took another look at the foul-up. Then, in November 1996, the Justice Department fired him again.

The matter was still being fought out at this writing, but whatever the outcome may be, the former assistant U.S. attorney's life will never be the same. The All American Boy was good, but he wasn't Daniel Webster. He should have known that when you deal with the Devil, you aren't going to win.

17

Conning the Feds

INMATES WIND UP in the witness units because they're willing to lie, cheat, and double-cross anyone, from best friends to family members. So why should anyone be surprised when they tell whoppers to police, prosecutors, and prison officials?

Like Pruett, Toomba, and his friends, William Koopman understood how easy it is to con the Gs. Dozens of other witnesses, perhaps hundreds, have profited by telling local cops or the feds what they want to hear, whether or not there is any truth to the stories. But Koopman was a special case.

Everyone in the units knew the hulking gangster as Buffalo Billy, because he was from Buffalo, New York and looked as big as a buffalo. He was a giant, who was built like an engine block. A big engine block. His weight constantly hovered around the 300-pound mark, always over, never below, and he was about six foot three or four.

He was big enough to have been a professional wrestler, and could have held his own against heavyweights like Hulk Hogan and Hacksaw Jim Duggan. But Koopman had other career plans when he was a young man. He wanted to become a wiseguy with the outfit in his hometown.

Buffalo Billy had a big problem that stood in the way, however. His father was of Irish background, and his mother was Puerto Rican. That didn't exactly qualify him for full-fledged membership in La Cosa Nostra. So Billy settled for a role as a close mob associate. He became an enforcer and hit man. That's in addition to other things like burglary, gambling, dealing drugs—and driving a refuse truck.

I knew Billy from the the unit at Otisville, where we were locked up together for a while before our paths crossed again in Mesa Unit. We never became friends, but we got along and I learned a lot about him and his career. When he was on the street, he acted like he thought he was King Shit. Maybe he was! He packed a .9-mm pistol and loaded himself down with jewelry. Big silver crucifixes hung around his neck and huge flashy gold rings were on his fingers—all that stuff Italians and Puerto Ricans like. He looked like a walking dime store, except that the jewelry wasn't cheap kid stuff. It was real.

Koopman rolled after he was picked up in Buffalo and told he was going to be put on trial for the murder of John Pinelli. Pinelli was the son-in-law of Koopman's sponsor with the mob, Luciano Spataro, but there had been a falling out. So Pinelli was hit.

When Koopman sat down to talk to the law about the affair, he denied that he whacked Pinelli, but admitted he had been there. Then, Buffalo Billy pointed the finger at Luciano Spataro's son, Carmine. It was he, Billy said, who pressed the barrel of a .380-semiautomatic pistol to Pinelli's head and blew him away.

Billy wound up promising to testify on Carmine, and on the people involved in four other mob hits. That was good enough to get the big fellow into the witness-protection program and a total sentence of five to fifteen years. Apparently no one bothered to give Koopman a lie detector test to back up his story pinning Pinelli's hit on Carmine. The word of the hulking mob executioner was good enough to get the job done.

Buffalo Billy was tough, mean, and totally ruthless, and that's why I was so surprised when I ran into him the day after I was processed into the unit just outside Phoenix. It was the middle of the morning on November 12, 1992, in the day room, and I was all ready to begin kicking around old times and swap war stories about different cons we knew and what was coming down in Mesa. But Billy was fidgety, and despite the air-conditioning that kept temperatures cool inside the unit, sweat was running down his face and staining the arm-pits of his shirt. The odor of stale cigarettes and sour sweat clung to him like a cloud. Big guys like Koopman sweat like hogs, even when they're not upset, but clearly something was bothering him. That's not good, when a guy has a reputation like him.

"What's the problem, Billy?" I asked. "You okay?" Billy was fiddling around at a table, spreading butter on a couple of slices of white toast and heating up a plate of food in one of the microwaves when he turned and scowled at me. His lids were pulled down halfway over his eyes, and he was giving me a look like I was a lizard or some cockroach that just crawled out from underneath the tabletop.

"Fuck you, man. Can't you see I'm making Sammy's breakfast? When I get his eggs and shit together we'll talk. All I need is to fuck up his cappuccino, and there goes my fucking day. He's gonna be pissed if I don't get his breakfast to him on time."

Late breakfast. It was eleven o'clock in the morning. What was surprising to me was that Koopman should give a rat's ass about what time Sammy was getting his swishy little tail out of bed, or that he should be fixing his breakfast. Koopman was the little guy's gopher. They were a Mutt and Jeff team, with Jeff calling all the shots. Other cons joked about the hulking killer from Buffalo being Sammy's butt boy. Maybe so; probably not.

But there was no question that Koopman was Sammy's lackey. The big fellow slavishly catered to the little New York mobster's every demand. He fixed Sammy's breakfast, washed his clothes, shined his shoes, and ran his errands. He probably would have wiped Sammy's ass if he was told to. Billy spent his life sucking up to Mob wiseguys, and it was a habit he couldn't break even after rolling.

Despite Koopman's bootlicking inside Mesa Unit, I knew he was a dangerous man. There was good reason to tread softly during our first meeting inside Mesa Unit, because before I was transferred there I had already joined in a scheme with another notorious hit man to double-cross the big killer.

When Mike Graziadei learned I was going to be transferred to Phoenix, he arranged to pay me $10,000 to wear a wire on Koopman. I was promised another $10,000 and a vintage Corvette after I got the goods. Mike, who also came from Buffalo where he was in the car-repair business, was convinced that Billy helped frame him for a murder he had nothing to do with. He wanted me to get Billy on tape, admitting he was the real killer.

Putting on a wire was nothing new to me. That's what snitches do. I had worn so much metal for the law that if I was sold for scrap I could have outfitted the battleship *Missouri*. Wearing a wire on Billy and snitching on another snitch was no big deal to me. Once a guy like me rolls over and becomes a mouth, there's no going back. You snitch on your friends outside, and on your friends inside the joint. You snitch on people you've committed crimes with; snitch on crooked cops, judges and public officials, anybody you've got anything on or can get anything on that might help you gain a favor here or there. So I agreed to the scheme.

A $10,000 certified check was delivered to a friend of mine in St. Louis, and thousands of dollars worth of high-tech equipment was smuggled into the unit. My old lady at that time picked the stuff up at one of those specialty shops in Manhattan. A civilian employee at the prison helped us sneak in the microcassette recorder and wireless microphones inside the works of an old computerized guitar. The recorder was equipped with voice-activated recording devices, and the little mikes were good for up to five or six blocks. It was the same kind of top-of-the-line, cutting-edge shit I used when I was working with the task force out of St. Louis.

Everything was all set for action. Then, the whole thing blew up in my face. Instead of nailing Buffalo Billy's ass, I went to the hole. Another convict named Squeegie found out about the caper and tried to shake me down for a piece of the contract fee. My woman had recently traveled all the way from her home in New York State to visit me and Squeegie also thought she smuggled some marijuana inside, so he figured he had me by the *cojones*. He was wrong about her and the marijuana, but he was right about the scheme to wear the wire on Koopman.

The would-be blackmailer was a hard character who earned his nickname by killing a black convict with a squeegie. He tore it apart and used the sharp end to spear the guy, and the name hung with him ever since. He was proud of it.

Squeegie was also one of the busier tattoo artists on the units, but his work wasn't any good. I saw the job he did on a Chicago hoodlum one time, and it was all messed up. He did the guy's whole left side. The main character was a naked bitch holding a dagger. She was supposed to be a warrior, but one tit was an inch or so bigger than the other, and she was cross-eyed. Now this dude's gonna carry that around with him for the rest of his life.

My friend, Bones, was a much better artist. He was head of the Texas Syndicate, and was with the Texas ABs. Inmates weren't supposed to do tattoos, but nobody paid any attention to the rules and the administration didn't really give a fuck. Jap is totally tattooed down, and almost all the work was done inside the joint by Bones.

Bones had a professional tattoo gun, and I've seen them in other prisons. You can buy a Spalding & Rogers, a Higgins, the best equipment, through art-supply stores. In the hands of a shitty artist like Squeegie, even a professional gun can't make up for the lack of ability, however. He was a piece of shit and I refused to let him muscle in and extort me.

"Fuck you," I told him. "If you want to rat me out, go ahead and rat me out." So he did. No big surprise.

Pretty soon the administration had confiscated the smuggled tape recorder, tapes, and other paraphernalia I had lined up. I was teetering on tiptoes up to my chin in serious shit, and the administration was coming my way with a big wave-maker.

A few hours after my talk with Billy, I was locked up alone in a dinky, six-by-eight-foot cell. It was a cement and steel slot in the basement, beside a row of similar slots set aside for troublemakers when the witness-protection unit was first constructed there. A single light-bulb covered with a metal grate and sticking out from the middle of the ceiling, provided the only light. The switch was controlled by a guard.

I had screwed up big time and broken the unwritten rule: it's only permissible to snitch and betray your friends when the government says it's okay and approves of the double-cross. Graziadei wasn't the government. He was simply another poor slob like me. Worse yet, the target of our planned treachery had a powerful friend.

The next day I met him for the first time. The doors opened and a funny-looking little man with a barrel chest, fat face, and beefy nose was standing between me and the corridor. He nodded his head and the hack who had unlocked the cell door moved several feet away so that we could talk privately.

"I'm Sammy the Bull," the little guy growled.

I was still blinking my eyes in the sudden rush of light after spending hours in the semidarkness of the cell, but I could see him clearly enough to recognize him from pictures in newspapers and images on television. However, there are certain rules of behavior that prison-wise convicts must observe when they're dealing with fellow inmates. Among them, it's vital to never show weakness or gullibility. If you allow yourself to be intimidated or stepped on even once, you're venturing out on a slippery slope to Hell. Toughness, or the image of toughness, counts for everything.

"Yeah! So what the fuck is a Sammy the Bull," I growled back at him.

"Hey, Taylor, don' fuck wid me," he snarled. "Also, what duh fuck you doin' wid my friend Koopman? We don' have any problems here, and Koopman's my partner. Don't act stupid, Taylor. I can cause you a lotta grief."

Sammy may look like a demented munchkin, and sound like one of the Dead End Kids, but he talks exactly like what he is. He's a hoodlum with a junior-high-school education and a massive ego, who's used to brow-beating just about everyone around him. Even though the little man wasn't a very impressive linguist, his message was clear. I realized I already had enough problems without making an enemy of somebody with his kind of clout, as well as getting on the bad side of a plug-ugly like Koopman. Besides, my cover was already blown.

"Look, Taylor, Graziadei is lookin' to fuck Billy by gettin' him on tape," he told me. 'We know you're involved. Keep out of it. You don't know what I can do in this joint. Trust me. I can be your best friend. I want Billy to stay here. And fuck Graziadei.''

I told Sammy that I didn't know anything about any scheme to screw Koopman, and I wasn't looking for trouble. I'd be grateful if he could use his juice to help me get out of the hole, in fact. Sammy wasn't fooled, but he was conciliatory. He admitted to me that Koopman was a snake, but reminded me that the big guy was his snake. All I had to do was leave Koopman alone, and he would see to it that I got out of the hole.

Then he sprung a big surprise. Graziadei had rolled on me. I shouldn't have been surprised, but I was.

I told Sammy again that I had no beef with Billy, and that I would rather have both of them for friends than for enemies. Sammy was pleased with himself. He had carried out the role of conciliator; he may have been looking back on the heady days when he roamed the Brooklyn streets fixing things as Gotti's powerful underboss. He had proven to himself again that inside or outside the joint, he was a man of power whose personal attention and advice was respected and followed.

Before he nodded to the hack and swaggered off down the corridor, Sammy handed me a tray of ham, turkey, beef, and hushpuppies, with a cup of lukewarm cappuccino. The food was delivered special from a Phoenix restaurant. It looked and smelled good. I hadn't even spent a full day in the hole, and I already had cabin fever. I needed a shave and smelled bad. More importantly, I was as hungry as a shark. Lukewarm cappuccino or not, the unexpected feast was a welcome demonstration of my visitor's clout. When the hack returned half a hour later to pick up the tray, there wasn't a speck of bread or meat left.

A couple of days later I was released from the hole and returned to the main unit. Sammy was waiting and greeted me with a big smile and a hug. Thank God he didn't try to kiss me. The Guineas do that with each other. They kiss, then they whack the guy they slobbered on.

Sammy figured that because I wasn't going to go ahead and try to nail Koopman, that made me his pal. He was grateful, and in order to seal what he apparently believed was going to be a beautiful friendship, he told me he had telephoned Laura Ward to tell her what a great guy I was.

He said the assistant U.S. attorney was his federal baby-sitter, and he instructed her that she should help me out if I needed anything. Later, as I got to know Sammy better, he had other things to say about the woman who worked so hard to see that the government gave him VIP treatment. One time when he was upset about something he started raving that she was dumb, stupid, and a bitch. "I wouldn't fuck her with Johnny Boy's cock," he ranted. "I play her like a fiddle." That was the kind of appreciation he showed toward people who were good to him.

"You're good people," Sammy told me that day when I was in the hole. "Better than that piece of shit," he said of Graziadei. "We're gonna be buddies." Yeah, like Sammy and Laura Ward.

I doubt if Buffalo Billy shared his idol's high opinion of me, but it didn't matter. The same day I was sprung from the hole, Koopman was suddenly ordered to pack a suitcase, then hustled aboard a jet plane and transferred to an undisclosed location. A few months later he was released from prison altogether and moved into phase two of the witness-protection program. He served just a few months more than four years of his five-to-fifteen-year sentence, and almost a year of that was spent in hotel rooms or local jails and courtrooms while he was testifying in different criminal cases involving the Buffalo mob.

Sammy may have gained a friend, or thought he did, but he lost his most loyal gopher. No sweat. Other flunkies were already eagerly awaiting an opportunity to ingratiate themselves with the big-time rat—and with his powerful friends at the Justice Department and with the BOP.

Koopman, meanwhile, saved his best testimony for last. After my last brush with him, he was called on to testify again about the Pinelli hit and some other old Mob business in Buffalo—and dropped a big surprise on everybody. He said he wasn't simply along for the ride when Pinelli was whacked. He admitted he was the shooter, and he lied when he testified that Carmine Spataro was the triggerman.

Koopman said he pinned the killing on Spataro because he didn't want to embarrass his family. Some court documents indicate he may have had an entirely different motivation, however: he lied and stuck to the story even after Spataro was convicted and given a twenty-five-year sentence because he didn't want to lose the cushy deal he worked out to become a protected witness.

The documents also show that police and prosecutors who used Koopman and his testimony suspected for years that he was really the triggerman in the Pinelli killing. But Koopman stuck to his story all that time, so they let the matter drop. Good deal for Buffalo Billy. He wasn't even charged with perjury after admitting he told all those whoppers when he was on the witness stand.

Koopman couldn't even tell a lie and stick to it, but that wasn't unusual among people in the units. Witnesses were always getting caught in lies, but as Buffalo Billy knew, that didn't mean you would be kicked out of the program. It didn't even always mean that some of the convictions you helped obtain would be tossed out by the courts.

I met witnesses like the Black Prince in all of the units, who could have rivaled Scheherazade for spinning fantasy-filled stories that enrapt their listeners—and perhaps gain them freedom or fortunes. Luis Del Cid was one such witness.

Del Cid, a former lieutenant-colonel with the Panama military and Noriega's bagman, was the general's co-defendant when he plea-bargained for a place in the witness-protection program and a short sentence, then delivered damaging testimony against his old boss.

The turncoat testified that he delivered drug payoff money to Noriega. He tied him to the construction and operation of a cocaine laboratory in the Panama boondocks. Del Cid said the remote laboratory wasn't raided until after Noriega left the country. Noriega then met in a hurry-up conference with Fidel Castro in Cuba to talk over how they were going to defuse the situation and make up the losses to the Medellín cartel bosses.

The colonel's story sounded good until he was cross-examined and forced to take back much of his earlier testimony. It turned out that Noriega was not only in Panama when the raid on the drug lab was carried out, but he ordered it in cooperation with the DEA. Defense lawyers also managed to show that Noriega's meeting in Cuba with Castro didn't occur until six weeks after the raid, and it was scheduled far in advance.

No sweat! Before testifying, Del Cid was looking at a possible sentence of seventy years, but despite all his lies, his reward included freedom after serving only three years; a spot in the witness-protection program; immunity from prosecution by foreign countries for himself and for his family; a guarantee none of them would be deported; relocation; and rent and living expenses. Del Cid was also allowed to keep the blood money and other assets he acquired as a key player in the international drug-smuggling operation.

And Del Cid was only one of more than a dozen big-time operators whose drug-dealing activities were at least as bad, or worse, than Noriega's. Drug runners, money launderers, assorted multimillionaire riffraff—Panamanians, Colombians, and homegrown gringos from North America—all bought sweet deals for themselves with testimony against Noriega, much of it lies.

Even a political science professor called as an expert witness on the Panama military had so much trouble fielding simple questions about the country that his testimony was cut short.

Take Joe Lehder. While he was being held at the FCI in Atlanta, and prosecutors and defense attorneys were still tilting over his trial date, he mailed a letter to George Bush offering to become a rat. At first it seemed that nothing would come of Joe's hopes to cut a deal for himself by turning. Then he poked his head out of the rat hole and emerged as a promising key player in Noriega's prosecution—or so it seemed at the time. Joe was a bad boy and an international narco-trafficking kingpin, but the Panamanian dictator was even more high-profile. He was also higher on the shit list of the DEA, Justice, and other Washington powers, especially after drawing worldwide attention to his comic-opera standoff against American troops inside the Vatican Embassy.

The government had high hopes Joe would be a blockbuster witness, but despite his impressive ability to deliver dope, he couldn't deliver on the witness stand. He was forced to admit that he never met Noriega. He said he just figured that money he gave to some of his cohorts would be passed on to the general. He also spun a wild yarn about making a secret deal with the U.S. government that gave him the go-ahead to quietly smuggle cocaine into the country in return for helping the CIA or some other Washington agency move arms to the anti-Communist guerrillas in Nicaragua. It was the kind of story the media liked, but he didn't have the backup to make it the kind of conclusive testimony acceptable in a courtroom.

Did these lies make any difference? No way. The U.S. government stuck to its deal with Del Cid and with Lehder.

Noriega has been serving time ever since then, watching "The Wild Horse Saloon" on TNN. But early in 1997, he pulled a little surprise of his own. He claimed in a prison interview aired on a CBS Spanish-language TV network that federal prosecutors offered him a reduced sentence if he would tie Castro to the drug smuggling. Prosecutors said the claim was a lie, but one of Noriega's former lawyers backed up his version of the story.

"If you can get us Fidel Castro, we will reduce your sentence," Frank Rubino said his client was told. Noriega reportedly replied, "I don't know anything about him regarding drug dealing, so I can't help."

I'm convinced that most of the time, the feds know that they're being conned, but they don't care. Some things are more important than getting the right guy, or the guy at the top. Things like building up your conviction rate and attracting national publicity as a gang-buster. Building a reputation as a gangbuster worked political miracles for Giuliani, just as it did a couple of generations earlier for Thomas Dewey. Bill Hogan got different results. But federal prosecutors and local DAs are still out there pitching the ball, continuing to use RICO, the CCE, and every important criminal insider they can roll while grabbing for the golden ring.

During cross-examination at Noah Robinson's trial in South Carolina, Toomba told the jury he was promised as much as $100,000 from the feds for information about the crooked businessman and his former homeboy, Hambone. Toomba added that prosecutors promised not to ask for the death penalty against him for the role he played as a member of the hit team, if he cooperated.

Buford and Davis, and who knows how many more people involved in the cases that brought the El Rukns and Robinson down, also collected big cash payoffs for their work. Maybe it was worth it. The Rukns had to be stopped, and the only way to do it was to work through people who were on the inside. That meant man-hours and money.

The feds have an unlimited source of money available to them when they want to grease the skids under a big-time racketeer or some other high-profile crook. But they're a lot like the snitches they work with. They have a way of twisting facts, reneging on promises, and leaving little guys flapping in the wind once they're through squeezing all the blood and information out of them.

Not everyone fares as well as the Gravanos, Leonettis, Mermelsteins and Del Cids. The government carefully picks and chooses which witnesses it will keep its word to. It helps to be a big-time operator who's sentenced for federal offenses. Little guys like me who are doing time on state charges can easily be forgotten and lost in the shuffle.

18

Renegades

THERE ARE CERTAIN guidelines that govern the witness-protection program that must never be violated, even by men and women who have never played by the rules in their lives. Disobedience can lead to exile, a return to general population in a prison where everybody knows you're a rat. And it can cost you your life.

The main rule is never rat on the program. I began planning to do just that from the first night I walked into G-Unit at Sandstone.

I was already aware that WITSEC was deeply flawed, and that under the guise of necessary secrecy, terrible injustices and inequities were being carried out and permitted. I was determined to turn over the rocks and expose all the maggots, sandfleas, ticks, and stinkbugs underneath in order to create enough public pressure within the media and Congress to achieve much needed reforms. If the program was already so damaged and corrupt that it couldn't be repaired, then I wanted to see it eliminated. I figured that my own experiences with WITSEC were a good example of what was wrong.

With a couple of glaring exceptions, the law-enforcement professionals who brought me into the program hadn't kept their word, and I figured I deserved better than that. I wasn't shocked that someone would lie to me and make promises they never intended, or weren't able to keep. All my adult life I had inhabited a world where honesty was equated with weakness and vulnerability, and I expected the drug dealers, stickup men, racketeers, and bikers I hung with to lie, cheat, and steal whenever they had the chance.

But I wasn't prepared for assistant U.S. attorneys, DEA investigators, the Secret Service and U.S. Justice Department honchos to behave like a bunch of river pirates sailing down the Big Muddy. Even lifetime criminals, and that's what I was at that time, have a right to believe in something and in somebody.

Given my history and background, it may be difficult to accept, but I believed in the criminal justice system and in the concepts of right and wrong. Then I had the misfortune to allow myself to be sold a bill of goods by some fast-talking Justice Department and local law-enforcement hucksters who lured me into the federal witness-protection program before making sure I had all the bases covered.

Henry Harris may have been correct in suspecting he didn't get as good a deal as he should have when he flipped and testified against his El Rukn pals. Or he may have gotten exactly what he deserved. He was a killer, a junkie, and a vicious street hoodlum, so perhaps he got the best deal he had any right to expect.

There is no question in my mind, however, that when I was sucked into the program, some of my task-force handlers were already dealing out the first jokers from the bottom of the deck.

Gerald Shur, the father of WITSEC, was an altogether different type of character from my task-force pals. He set the program up, and he ran it from his offices in

Arlington, Virginia, until 1995, when I was already long gone and doing my best to make a new life for myself as a civilian. That's when he finally stepped down, a move that I personally believe was long overdue. I considered him to be a little dictator, and most of the witnesses I knew agreed with me.

Professionally he was the most dominant force in the lives of WITSEC prisoners, and the worst possible person to get on the wrong side of. Inside the units, he was a virtual God with the power of life or death. He could become the physical savior of an inmate, or he could be a vengeful enemy. He became my enemy from the time we first saw each other. He knew that except for a few glamor witnesses, the men in the units had given up everything. And he was ruthless about the way he used that knowledge.

As soon as I settled into Sandstone, I started collecting information about the program. I talked with every witness who would talk to me—on the record if they were willing, and off the record if they were afraid. I read the plea agreements of witnesses who were willing to share them with me, and many did. Like me, some of them were pissed off about the dirty deal they felt they had gotten from the program. Others, like Gravano, were show-offs who wanted to prove how smart they were and how slickly they had manipulated and used the Gs to their advantage.

Sometimes I took notes while we talked or while I was going through the thick stacks of legal documents an inmate chum had collected and was sharing with me. At other times, I tried to remember as much as I could, then hurried back to my own room and wrote everything down that I thought was important.

I also stubbornly pursued efforts to talk with the press. I mailed letters and I placed telephone calls to newspaper reporters in St. Louis. I wrote to editors at the popular men's magazines *Penthouse* and *Playboy*. The Upper New York State woman I met through my sister, had become a formidable advocate on my behalf, and she continued her efforts. I talked with people at all levels in the Justice Department, six or seven different department heads and other top bananas until I finally got a couple of minutes on the horn with Janet Reno. She told me the same thing everybody else did all down the line. Keep my mouth shut.

When WITSEC and the BOP began leaning on me and ordering me to stay away from the press, I appealed to the ACLU for help and besieged private law firm lawyers I thought might be likely to take on pro bono, free work, for someone in my situation.

Some people at the Missouri state branch of the ACLU put me in touch with lawyers at the national headquarters. After some consideration they decided against representing me. But they referred me to a huge private law firm in Washington that has about 200 attorneys, and one of their junior partners accepted my case, pro bono. Joel Townsend, of Moss, Dixon & Mossback, which has offices within easy walking distance of the Justice Department and the OEO, worked hard for me until we finally had a friendly parting of the ways. We seemed to have different motivations and goals. They were trying to force hearings on the program, and also wanted to set a legal precedent over First Amendment rights of witnesses. They were interested in a civil rights thing. I just wanted WITSEC to keep its word.

My contacts also helped me get in touch with Jerry Seper, the hard hitting investigative reporter who broke many of the stories about the Whitewater mess and other Clinton Administration scandals for the *Washington Times*. Seper was good, and he was experienced at plowing through the many levels of bureaucracy that shroud the activities of the high muckety-mucks who run things in our nation's capital, but he never managed to open a major crack in the secrecy of the witness-protection program. He tried to get hold of my old client list, but it was still locked up tight. All we managed to obtain through our joint efforts were a few papers with practically everything blacked out with felt-tip markers. Even my own signature was obliterated.

WITSEC officials had a death grip on information and documentation about the program, and they wouldn't let go—not even when the Federal Freedom of Information act was used. Adopted in 1966 and signed into law by President Lyndon B. Johnson, the act is designed to open up records of governmental activity to the public. WITSEC lawyers have their own interpretation of what the act requires, however, and no one can read much through the black smears made by felt-tip markers. Other methods of deleting information were also used. The few pages reporters probing the activities of the witness-protection program managed to obtain were delivered with almost all of the data deleted as ''classified information.''

At the same time Seper and I were trying to get together for a long talk, another investigative reporter with the *Pittsburgh Post-Gazette* was pushing his own probe of the program. Bill Moushey had developed special background and expertise on prisons during his journalism career and was looking into the operation of WITSEC. I was one of the people he wanted to talk to, but he was running into many of the same kind of problems that Seper was faced with.

Moushey, Seper, and other reporters couldn't simply telephone or write directly to me at the prison, like they might do with inmates who were not protected witnesses. They were required to send their letters to a special mail drop the Justice Department maintained in Washington. Then the letters moved into the system, and in most cases stopped right there. Forwarding the letters would amount to implicit confirmation that individuals were indeed inside the program, and that would compromise their security, according to the official reasoning.

That was a joke. I had testified in trials or gone undercover in five states, and anyone with even the slightest interest in my activities knew I was in the program. Members of organized criminal gangs, bikers, dope smugglers, and police and politicians back in Missouri and Southern Illinois knew I was a federally protected witness.

A representative of the OEO who met with me to discuss a possible interview with a reporter told me I couldn't even discuss the weather. People involved with maintaining inmate security had decided that weather conditions could be used as a tip-off to a witness's location. The OEO guy outlined very explicit parameters of exactly what I would be permitted to discuss, and warned that if I stepped outside the boundaries I could be tossed in the hole. The functionary's detailed explanation of what I would be allowed to discuss amounted to wasted time. I was never permitted to go ahead with the interview—while I was inside, anyway.

WITSEC administrators didn't want their inmates, or phase-two witnesses, talking with any outsiders about the program, especially not to the press; and they constantly cited the need for secrecy in order to protect the people under their control. I knew that according to the MOU I signed when I was first recruited into the program, I had a right to communicate with the press, so long as I didn't do anything to breach security. Being able to talk with reporters was part of my First Amendment rights under the U.S. Constitution.

Legally I had every right to talk to who I wanted to, according to my calculations. So I continued to rock the boat and make waves. That represented an unforgivable transgression and display of independence that the people who ran the program, especially Shur, weren't willing to tolerate.

The entire affair had me fed up, and I began shipping off letters to Congress and other federal movers-and-shakers, trying to convince them there was a need for hearings and a long hard look at the witness-protection program. My letters were forwarded to WITSEC officials. Inevitably, one day as I was standing in the common room talking with some of my friends, a puny little man with wispy gray hair and heavy, loose jowls approached. He knew who I was, and I knew who he was.

The little man wearing the seersucker polyester pants was aware of my activities, and he warned me he wouldn't allow me to "compromise the integrity of the program." He made it crystal clear that if I continued to insist on exercising my First Amendment rights to publicly tell the story of my life in the program, I would be stepping in shit.

Very deliberately, and with his eyes focused coldly on my own, Gerald Shur peered over his glasses and cupped his hands. "I have you right here," he said, firmly focusing his watery eyes on mine. "I am holding your life in my hands." Then he asked if I knew what would happen if he dumped me from the program and had me placed in general population in some federal penitentiary or sent back to the Missouri prison system.

"Yeah, I know," I said. "That would be a death sentence. I'll be dead."

Shur allowed the edges of his mouth to curl in a cold smile and hesitated for a moment in order to allow my own words to sink in. Then, after he was satisfied he had achieved the maximum effect, he told me to get away from him. We both turned and walked away. I guess neither one of us cared much for the company. He had made his point. Shur later denied the confrontation occurred, but the other inmates who were with me saw it go down. The witnesses included a friend of mine who was a high-line burglar and jewelry-store iceman.

The burglar was in a big shoot-out in a car in Pennsylvania one time, and three people got killed, so he was saddled with a life sentence there. When he finishes his federal time, Pennsylvania authorities are waiting for him and plan to stick him in general population. So I don't want to identify him. He's a good guy, intelligent, and he just got caught up in a bad situation over money.

There was no question in my mind that I was asking for serious trouble if I persisted in rocking the boat. But I continued rocking, even though I had heard stories about the way another troublemaker was taken care of. Everyone on the units knew the story of what happened to Ernest Danny Holliday.

Holliday was bad news, a vicious killer with a fierce drug habit and a hatred for blacks and Jews. He was doing life in the program after snitching on some rough West Coast–biker gangs on the outside, and the white supremicist Aryan Brotherhood on the inside. I made some bad enemies when I was helping the task force set up local hoodlums and politicians around St. Louis, and with drug dealers along the Mexican border. But I wouldn't have traded my enemies for Holliday's.

Holliday managed to stay drunk or high on drugs much of the time he was inside the units, and it brought out his meanness. He was admitted in the early days of the program before the special units were constructed, and he and a few other witnesses were locked up the MCC in Chicago. In those days, even more than today, some of the prison doctors gave inmates just about any kind of prescription drug they asked for. Holliday took advantage of that and constantly gobbled barbiturates combined with pruno.

After the Units were constructed and he was moved,

he continued to mix prison moon with barbies and stayed stumbling drunk most of the time. Drunk or sober, he was always mean, and he was always looking for a way to get under Shur's skin. He developed a special dislike for Shur, and whenever the WITSEC administrator showed up in one of the units where Holliday was held, the former biker yelled drunken antiSemitic insults at him. Sometimes he concocted excuses to talk with the program administrator by telephone, then used the call to plaster him with insults. No one would put up with that kind of crap if they didn't have to, and Shur didn't have to. According to the scuttlebutt among witnesses, Shur warned Holliday to lay off. If he wasn't happy in the unit, the administrator reportedly told him, he would see to it that he was transferred back to general population.

Holliday refused to behave, so he was transferred to the FCI at Bastrop, which was a notorious dumping ground for troublemakers from the program. He was barely processed into Bastrop before practically everyone there had identified him as a snitch, so the feds transferred him to the Montana State Penitentiary at Deer Lodge about sixty miles west of Helena. It was the same story. Some of his old homeboys recognized him and passed the word around that the new inmate was a snitch. Holliday did the only thing he could do. He asked the prison administration to put him in self-lockup. At his own request he was placed in the prison's special security unit where child molesters, sissies, and other weaklings who couldn't defend themselves—along with known snitches—were kept under constant lockdown to protect them from other prisoners.

The special-security units are nasty places to be. The cells are small and cramped, prisoners have no contact with each other, and they are allowed to shower only once a week under close surveillance. The only exercise available to them is whatever calisthenics they choose to do on their own such as push-ups, sit-ups and leg squats on the floor between the wall and their bunk. The cells have one advantage and one advantage only: an opportunity to stay alive.

Holliday lost even that chance on a Sunday morning, September 22, 1991, when prisoners at Deer Lodge rioted and a group of inmates stormed the protected unit. A little more than four hours later, when a small army of corrections officers and Montana State Police SWAT teams took the prison back, it was already too late for Holliday and four other special-security prisoners. They were all killed by their fellow inmates. Four of them including Holliday, were hanged, and all the dead were known snitches.

Holliday was marching toward a violent end all of his life, but no one should have to die the way he did. He was never sentenced by any court in the country to be executed for his crimes, and even if he had been, the manner of carrying out the sentence would have been far more humane than the way he actually died. Lethal injection, poison gas, even the electric chair are all quicker and carried out with less pain. Family members filed a lawsuit in Butte against the State of Montana for failing to protect him, and for the grisly manner in which he died. I never heard how the suit was settled.

Prison riots are nasty wherever they break out, and any time the inmates manage to take over even for a few hours, there's a good chance that known snitches will be tortured and killed. The prison riot that stands out as the most savage and grisly in U.S. history occurred at the New Mexico State Penitentiary near Santa Fe in 1980. As soon as the inmates took over the prison, a bloodthirsty mob of wild-eyed cons headed for the pharmacy to clean out the store of drugs. Then members of an execution squad armed themselves with tools from the plumbing shop and launched an assault on cell-block four, the special-protection unit.

Thirty-three screaming inmates were roasted alive inside their cells by flaming gasoline, or dragged out and charbroiled with acetylene torches, chopped to bits with axes, tortured with electric drills and sanders, and hanged by their fellow convicts. The rioters decapitated one inmate and paraded around with his bloody head displayed on a stick. When correctional officers, police, and the New Mexico National Guard retook the prison after thirty-six bloody hours, they found the mutilated corpse of an inmate known by his fellow cons as the King of the Snitches stabbed more than fifty times with a screwdriver. His eyes were gouged out.

Everyone in the witness-protection progam is aware of the danger from other convicts in general population, and the threat is constant. Any prison can go up at any time if the conditions are right. It happened in New Mexico, and in 1994 it happened at the FCI Phoenix.

A bunch of Muslims set off the Phoenix riot because the prison commissary didn't provide them with moon pies. It was Ramadan, the most sacred period on the Muslim calendar when the faithful go throughout the day without eating, then feast on special, favorite foods after sundown. The Muslims didn't get the moon pies they wanted, so they burned down the gymnasium, the library, and other areas of the prison.

My friends and I watched through the windows inside the unit while the Muslims were raising holy Hell. Heavily armed U.S. marshals surrounded Mesa Unit, snipers were stationed on a nearby hill, and helicopters were flying overhead. Firetrucks and special response teams of prison hacks were also armed with tear gas, so we figured we were safe. But I'm not ashamed to say I was relieved when after about a day of rioting, a squad of

U.S. marshals and Arizona National Guardsmen stormed the prison and put down the insurrection.

The Muslims didn't even put up a fight. They just laid down and gave up. All they wanted in the first place was their moon pies, but they were still mad as hell. The BOP transferred the troublemakers out to a new federal prison at Sheridan in northern Oregon, but as soon as they were released from the hole, they also burned that place. The BOP finally broke up the ringleaders and sent them to different prisons around the country.

It wasn't the state of Montana that killed Holliday, however. Along with many other WITSEC prisoners, I figured that one individual functioned as judge, jury, and executioner for Holliday. The former renegade biker became a walking dead man the day he was dumped from the units.

Curious things happen to protected witnesses who don't fit in; people like Crazy Dave. The dude's real name was David Harden, but everybody inside the joint called him Crazy Dave because he was a speed freak who was just blown out. He was in and out of almost all the units, and I liked him even though he was a hired killer.

Dave was the triggerman in the contract killing of a multimillionaire named Constantine "Dean" Milo who ran a big barber- and beauty-supply business out of the Akron, Ohio, area—and he was set up by his brother Fred. Dean was the family moneymaker, who built up the business and saw to it that none of his next of kin went wanting. But Fred was jealous and hatched the murder plot. Crazy Dave carried it out, shooting Dean in the back of the head execution-style. Then he got a pillow, pressed it over the poor guy's shattered skull, and shot him again.

Dave told me he turned on Fred and some other people involved in the killing after the check he got for the job bounced. Then he flew to Phoenix, where he did a

robbery and he got caught. A deal was cut, and the robbery charges were dropped in exchange for his guilty
plea and testimony in the murder case. He swapped his
confession and testimony for a life sentence, which
means about fifteen years or less. Ohio has the death
penalty, and murder-for-hire is the kind of crime it was
crafted for, so Dave cut a good deal.

Crazy Dave was such a wild character that he got himself thrown out of the units one time and sent back to the
joint in Ohio where he was locked up in the same tier with
the people he testified against. Would anybody believe
that was a coincidence? He didn't stay there long before
he was returned to the units, but the experience scared the
shit out of him. Dave tried working out with Sergey and I
for a while, but he couldn't handle it. We lifted too much
weight for him and did too many calisthenics.

He was a likeable guy whose friends on the outside
called him the Kid, and he was one of the few people
that Sergey tolerated working out on the weight pile with
us who weren't ABs or bikers. I knew Dave at Sandstone where Jap beat the shit out of him in the shower
one day. The administration transferred Dave out to protect him, and when we got together again at Mesa, he
hung around in my room a lot. One day Sergey asked
him when he was going to begin working out with us,
and Dave said "Tomorrow." That was it. As soon as
lockdown ended at about five o'clock the next morning,
Sergey was outside his room pounding on the door.

One thing good I can say about Crazy Dave is that
he tried to be a standup guy. But he was scared to death
of Shur and of the wrath of the OEO and other people
running the witness-protection program.

The WITSEC program was set up with only two
phases. Phase one, represented by the period when a
witness is incarcerated; and phase two, when he is
moved outside the walls and relocated with a new iden-

tity. Phase three is a term coined by some witnesses like myself, for what happens to people like Holliday who cross Shur or various other high-ranking bureaucrats who administered the program and are subsequently dumped from the program—either sent to general population in a federal or state prison or cut loose on the outside with no government support or help in establishing a new life as a law-abiding citizen and taxpayer.

When that happened, it made sense to have a grave picked out somewhere.

WITSEC officials make a big thing of boasting that no one has ever been killed while they were an active participant in the program. Don't you believe it. Protected witnesses aren't the only people who know how to tell lies. I've seen lists circulated by some of my fellow inmates indicating that as many as 100 witnesses have been murdered after leaving the protected units.

Shur and his toadies had a ready answer when the subject of murdered witnesses came up. The only people who were killed were witnesses who went to the media, otherwise breached their own security, or returned to their personal-danger zones, where the people or criminal gangs they snitched on were located. The only casualties were people who signed out of the program. Yeah! Sure! They all signed out of the program the day before they got themselves whacked.

You may also try telling the story about CIs and witnesses bringing their trouble on themselves to Adler Berriman "Barry" Seal or James Cardinali.

Seal was a bigger-than-life character, who was a veteran of the U.S. army's Special Forces and drifted into the drug-smuggling business. He operated out of a little airport in Mena, Arkansas, and flew airplane loads of dope for the Medellín Cartel and other narco-traffickers around South and Central America. After he was busted in 1983, he flipped on his friends and became a CI for the DEA and other government agencies. He quickly became one of the most valuable mouths American narcotics-control officers have ever managed to develop against international drug smugglers.

The DEA, customs, and other law-enforcement agencies got their first close-up look inside some of the world's biggest drug organizations, thanks to Seal. He brought back photographic evidence to the United States showing Pablo Escobar passing cocaine to a representative of the Communist Sandinista government in Nicaragua. President Reagan eventually displayed one of the pictures on national TV. Two of the people indicted in absentia as a result of Seal's photographic scoop were Escobar and Carlos Lehder. Eventually Seal helped convict seventeen defendants, including the former chief minister of the Turks and Caicos Islands with his undercover work and testimony.

After months of working together, Seal's relationship with the Gs soured, and he found himself in the middle between strike-force teams in South Florida and Louisiana and the judiciary in the two states. He was unhappy with the way he was being treated and he made one of the biggest mistakes of his checkered career. He joined up with a reporter for Channel 2 in Baton Rouge to make an hour-long documentary titled, "Uncle Sam Wants You," dealing with Seal's undercover exploits for the DEA and CIA, and his troubles with federal authorities in Louisiana. Federal authorities in Baton Rouge weren't pleased with the way they were depicted on the show by the beefy adventurer.

In a complicated deal, Seal eventually pleaded guilty to a couple of felonies in Louisiana for smuggling several hundred pounds of cocaine and money laundering; then, because of his cooperation with the DEA, he was given what amounted to a pass in another case prosecuted in Fort Lauderdale. The Florida judge let him off with time served, and because of the terms of the plea agreement worked out in Louisiana, the judge there couldn't order any punishment that was more severe than that.

So the federal judge in Louisiana ordered the most severe punishment allowable based on the agreement. He was permitted to set conditions of probation, and he ordered the three-hundred-pound former drug smuggler to spend six months at a Salvation Army halfway house in Baton Rouge without any protection.

"As far as I'm concerned, drug dealers like Mr. Seal are the lowest, despicable type of people I can think of," Judge Frank Polozola scolded the defendant. "In my opinion, people like you, Mr. Seal, ought to be in a federal penitentiary. You all ought to be there working at hard labor. Working in the hottest sun or the coldest day wouldn't be good enough for drug dealers like you."

The law-and-order judge was aware that Colombian drug lords had put a $1 million contract out on Seal if he was delivered alive; $500,000 if he was dead. But he refused the CI's plea to live at home where he could surround himself with bodyguards.

One chilly February morning, the man said to be the most valuable informant the DEA had ever recruited was ambushed by a team of Medellín cartel hit men outside the halfway house and blown to pieces with a MAC-1-machine pistol equipped with a silencer.

Even though Seal was expected to testify against Colombia drug chief Jorge Ochoa-Vasquez, the people at the Justice Department didn't shed many tears over their former star snitch. They immediately passed the word that any federal drug agent who traveled to Baton Rouge to attend the funeral would be fired.

James Cardinali is another witness who learned the hard way about the dangers of pissing off the wrong people involved in the federal criminal justice system. The former New York mobster vanished in 1991 shortly after he paraded in front of the U.S. District Courthouse in Albuquerque complaining that the government dumped him and marked him for death. The onetime wiseguy who testified against Gotti as a protected witness, dressed casually in sharkskin trousers, an open-necked white shirt, and a pair of dark sunglasses for the demonstration. He also selected a big sandwich board with a bull's-eye target painted in the middle and the words *Mob Star* and *Witness*.

Cardinali's imaginative protest attracted a brief flurry of attention from the press, and his photograph moved on the AP wire service, along with statements outlining the complaints that he was dumped from the program and virtually sentenced to death. He stepped over the line a few days later when he flew to Washington, D.C., to appear on the "Larry King" television talk show without first obtaining permission to leave his assigned state. Almost immediately after returning to New Mexico, he was picked up for parole violation and jailed. Then he vanished.

So, did the powers that be belatedly decide to take their unhappy rebel back into the program and relocate him all over again with a new identity? Don't bet on it! Cardinali's fate was the subject of frequent conversations in the units, and I never met a single witness who had the slightest inkling about where he was or what happened to him. If a witness did happen to run across Cardinali, his location wouldn't remain a secret for very long.

Wherever Cardinali may be, and whatever happened to him, I'm convinced he is another witness who learned the hard way that whoever decides to expose WITSEC to the light of public scrutiny is playing with their life.

19

Thank You, Mr. and Mrs. Taxpayer

> We've had enough of mortadella.
> We can't take it anymore.
>
> *Giuseppe Calascibetta, accused Mafioso*
> *who was sick of the monotonous*
> *jail menu in Turin, Italy*

WITSEC INMATES LIVE lives of privilege behind bars, especially wealthy hoodlums and drug smugglers and their cronies.

Professional hit men and former leaders of major criminal gangs involved in everything from narcotics and prostitution to extortion, gun-running and international terrorism enjoy luxuries behind bars that most of the Ozzie and Harriets on the outside can only dream about.

I've personally attended pig roasts where the meat is slowly barbecued over mesquite wood specially brought into the prison for the party, chatted at champagne and caviar bashes, and feasted at smaller, more private gatherings on King Crab claws from Alaska, lobster flown in from Maine, choice cuts of Nebraska beef, and fine chocolate imported from Switzerland.

No discriminating host of a proper party on the witness-protection units would consider not winding up the festivities with cups of freshly ground cappuccino, followed by snifters of a fine brandy. Then it's cigar time, or for the less traditional and more modern inmates, time to break out fat spliffs of potent sinsimilla or a few lines of high-grade coke.

Most of the big-shot witnesses had personal cappuccino machines in their cells. It was a sign of status, especially among the Mob guys from the East Coast. Lehder and some of the other Latins preferred the dark Cuban coffee that's strong enough to stand a spoon in, and they kept a ready supply in their cells. Every group had their own preferences.

One day at Sandstone, Malik and some of his cronies were sitting around talking about food when the conversation turned to bean pies. I had never heard of them, but learned later that they're popular with blacks and people from the Middle East. Most of the white guys didn't care for them. They were probably an acquired taste. But Malik placed an order with a Middle Eastern restaurant in Chicago, and thirty of the crusty, flat pies were flown to Sandstone the next day. There were enough to serve all the black inmates on his unit. The little Pakistani shelled out $177 and said the pies were worth every penny.

There was nothing shady about the Black Prince being able to place an order for delivery of bean pies from Chicago, or from just about anywhere else in the world he may have selected. He ordered them through the Sportsman's Club.

The organization exists on all the units and has the same name, except on Mesa Unit where it was known as the John Smith Society, but regardless of what it's called, the function is the same. It's a combination money-laundering and worldwide commissary network set up with regular accounts inmates use to make deposits in outside banks and write checks on. The funds are set up so that the identity of the person writing the checks is protected from outsiders. When I was inside Mesa Unit, inmates used a California-based bank. It's the same bank the BOP uses. When I was at Sandstone, they used a bank a few miles south in the little town of Hinckley.

The societies are another good example of an element of the witness-protection program that started off reasonably with a legitimate purpose, then got out of hand while OEO and BOP bureaucrats closed their eyes to what was going on. Originally the anonymous checking accounts were designed to permit prisoners to buy clothing, occasional grooming aides like electric razors, and other items related to normal everyday needs. Of course the inmates abused the system. They behaved like little kids whose mom and dad refused to put a foot down. They continued to take more and more, waiting for someone in authority to tell them no. No one ever did.

Not all the inmates had the kind of money to throw around that celebrity witnesses flashed, but most of them had enough to help them live well while they were on the units. A big portion of the money was payment from government law-enforcement agencies for their testimony; and some witnesses had additional millions of dollars they were allowed to keep from their drug smuggling or other criminal operations.

When Gravano was throwing a bash or had something to celebrate, he bought Dom Perignon through the society. If Lehder decided he had gone too long without fresh lobster, he had the seafood flown in and the money was deducted from his accounts. It was all perfectly legal.

The food prepared in the inmate kitchens was excellent, but almost every night someone would order from the outside. Southwestern food; tacos, tamales, burritos, pollo con arroz, and that kind of chow was especially popular on Mesa Unit. But the inmates ordered a little bit of everything—from Chinese food, like egg rolls and pork fried rice, to buffalo wings and pizza. Local restaurants delivered chow to the gate, where guards picked it up, then wheeled it into the unit on hot carts for the inmates. The hacks were given checks or cash to pay the delivery men with, along with generous tips.

Guards picked up larger deliveries of food every Friday, then delivered it on a little flatbed truck or on a dolly so the inmates could store it in their private iceboxes and freezers. The government also had freezers available, but most of the inmates preferred to use their own. The incongruity of correctional officers, honest citizens with spouses and families, and annual paychecks hovering around $30,000, acting as errand boys for some of the worst desperados, renegades, and human maggots in the country wasn't lost on me. And they knew they had better cooperate.

Most of the guards were pretty decent. When they had something to say to us, they usually called us by our initials or used the inmate's nickname. Unless there was trouble of some kind, they called me Bud, like everyone else on the unit. There were a few women guards on all the units, but most of them were dogs. More often than not, one of the inmates would get close to them, then use them to smuggle things, pass messages, and do other favors. Sometimes an inmate managed to get a blow job for himself, or closed the door to one of the offices and knocked off a quickie.

Guards in the units wore gray pants, white shirts, and spit-shined black shoes. They didn't carry guns, clubs, or anything like that. Weapons were available to them in case there was serious trouble, but they weren't kept close by. For the most part, we weren't those kinds of troublemakers. We weren't violent, like some of the hard-core cons on the general population side of the prison. We didn't have reason to be. We were being treated well.

Occasionally some hard-ass hack who figured he was better than the inmates and that it was his job to put them in their place, was assigned to the units. When that happened, the inmates saw to it that he was dumped in a hurry. At Otisville one time, witness inmates staged a sitdown. We went on a work strike because we refused to deal with the new unit manager, who transferred in from the super-maximum-security prison at Marion. He didn't like protected witnesses, but we weren't level-six prisoners like the people he lorded it over at Marion, so we simply stopped everything. We were put on lock-down for a while, and about thirty inmates were eventually transferred, but the troublemaking unit manager also left. He went back to Marion to be with his own kind.

Another prison administrator made the mistake one time of not allowing Sammy the Bull to order a dozen lobsters for a big Sunday dinner the little serial killer was planning. The big-shot hack was bounced out of the unit on his ass, and Sammy got his lobsters.

Any guard who wasn't properly accommodating to one of the celebrity witnesses was quickly returned to the main prison, or he and his family were suddenly transferred to an FCI somewhere hundreds of miles across the country. Meanwhile, some upstanding citizen like Joe Lehder or Sammy the Bull, whose complaints got him transferred there, were back in the unit living it up.

Rich witnesses kept their iceboxes stocked with favorite chow. Everything was the best, prime cuts of filet mignon, and other fine foods and drink. Financially, I wasn't in their class, and was barely able to keep enough credit in my commissary account to buy cigarettes, toilet articles and an occasional can of Classic Coke or a candy bar. But I shared in the good fortune of my fellow witnesses, anyway. Almost everyone did.

Celebrity witnesses bought so much food and drink that there were always piles of leftovers to go around, and inmate cooks knew how to prepare it as well as any fine chef in a top-flight restaurant on the outside. Several of the inmates were amateur cooks, and some of the Italians especially liked to show off their skills putting together a mouth-watering plate of linguini with clam sauce or some other personal specialty such as rigatoni with sweet peppers, chicken marsala, and steaming pots of fettucine, raviolis, and pastas. They knew what they were doing, and I learned a lot about cooking and good food while I was on the units.

A former amphetamine cook whipped up some of the best meals on Mesa Unit. He was a Greek guy who worked in food service, and everybody called him Tommy Beans. When he was on the outside, he lived for a while in Bullhead City, Arizona, in the Mojave Desert, where he had a reputation for getting whacked out on meth and walking around his trailer home buck-ass naked except for a pair of cowboy boots and a gun-belt around his waist holding a holster with a pistol. On one side of the tiny kitchen, he would be brewing up a batch of methamphetamine; and on the other side, a big pot of beans would be simmering on the stove.

Tommy was a standup guy who didn't take shit from anyone, including the parole board. Every time the board called him up for an interview to make parole, he would tell them: "Go fuck yourself. You gave me seven years, and I'm doing seven fucking years." Tommy didn't want some little-girl parole officer on the outside with a psychology degree telling him when he could take a shit or who he could hang out with. He wanted it to be over when it was over, and that's what he served: seven years.

Tommy worked out with Sergey and I, and he cooked steaks, baby-back ribs and that kind of stuff for us when we wanted something special. We hung out together, and I could have gotten fat and lazy on his food if I didn't watch my diet and work out regularly. He turned out your basic meat-and-potato meals. Or beans!

Another guy at Sandstone was even better than Tommy, but he wasn't merely a cook. He was a Swiss guy who spoke four or five languages and was a master chef and baker. I've never tasted food in my life, not even my mom's cooking, that was as good as his. He used to run a fancy restaurant in Miami before he got into trouble for dealing cocaine big-time, then flipped and testified against a U.S. customs agent. With his professional credentials and talent for cooking, he could have made it legit anytime.

He cooked some food for me, and it melted in my mouth. It was fine, classy cuisine, the kind of dishes I had never heard of before. He was like an artist creating a masterpiece while he fussed over specialties like grilled duck in black cherry sauce, racks of lamb with mint jelly, prime filet mignons, and desserts ranging from delicate soufflés to tasty cheesecakes and a south Florida favorite, key lime pie.

The professional chefs and amateur cooks had an excellent, well-equipped kitchen to work in. At Mesa and most of the other units, the government provided inmates with barbecue pits, charcoal, and lighters for outdoor cookouts. Every prison has inmate musicians, and every so often some of the guys would get together and play a few sets during the outdoor parties. Favored prison bureaucrats were feted along with the various kill-

ers, bikers, and drug smugglers at some of the gatherings.

Sometimes I went for months without ever tasting institutional food, except for the fresh veggies Sergey and
I helped ourselves to from the salad bar. I ate with Lehder and other guys whenever they had something special
brought in. Joe loved smoked oysters, and always had a
pile of them around. He boasted that they kept him
young and horny. Usually when he was talking about
smoked oysters, the conversation drifted to the beautiful
Cuban wife he left waiting on the outside.

Although I wasn't all that fond of Gravano, I enjoyed
his food. It was always meticulously prepared, but I
never got to sample Koopman's cooking. He was gone
by the time Sammy began inviting me to be his dinner
guest, but other guys who took Buffalo Billy's place
were as anxious as he had been to keep the little fellow
happy. The food was always excellent, and so were the
drinks.

20

Living High

IF A PROTECTED witness has the money, imagination, or the right friends, few pleasures are denied to him. This includes getting high on dope and booze.

In most prisons, cannabis is readily available as it is on the outside. An inmate, or a few inmates, will set up business as the local dealer and jealously guard the territory while handling all the action in a particular cell block or in some other area.

Guards can be bribed, coerced, or in the case of female COs (correctional officers)—romanced into breaking the rules by smuggling just about anything, ranging from pot, coke, and heroin to hacksaws, guns, and cash. Once a hack has taken that first step and is securely hooked, their convict handlers never allow them to look back. It's a bit like rolling and becoming a government snitch.

Obtaining prison contraband is even easier in the units than it is in general population. There is no limit to the ingenuity of a man behind bars who has time and determination to urge him on. Visitors, of course, are a major source of contraband. Dope is smuggled inside messy diapers and transferred during hugs, it's passed mouth-to-mouth between inmates and wives or sweethearts, and it's packed into any and all available orifices in the male or female body.

I sat in visiting rooms and watched while contraband was passed to inmates from family members or friends. But one of the most popular methods of bringing in contraband was tied to the Sportsman's or John Smith societies.

If a witness claimed to like a special brand of coffee that was generally available only in New Orleans, he could order a few pounds directly from the importer or wholesaler in Louisiana. It was no problem at all for contacts there to put together a package with a couple of cans of the coffee along with another sealed can that was filled with marijuana, cocaine, cash, or whatever other contraband the witness might really have his heart set on. It happened all the time.

A hack might open the package when it arrived at the prison, but the cans inside would be passed directly to the inmate. Who's going to be suspicious enough to cut open a can that's factory sealed?

There were times when the smuggling schemes misfired or broke down. That goes with the territory, and always has. Win some, lose some. But getting your fingers burned with a little contraband dope in the units didn't mean the end of the world was coming.

Inmates caught with a quarter-pound of coke and bundles of heroin paid for their carelessness with a couple of days in the hole. That was about as bad as it got in the units for that kind of infraction. And the hole in the units wasn't like the hole in general population; it was like comparing the Bates Motel from the movie *Psycho* with the Waldorf Astoria. Most of the inmates who were sent to the hole for possession of drugs stayed high the whole time they were locked up. They turned on day and night. It was a good way to pass the time until the hacks unlocked the door and sent them back to their regular cell.

I never heard of anyone who was prosecuted after being caught inside the units with dope. It simply didn't happen. As long as they did nothing to seriously rock the boat, witnesses were teachers' pets, and they were given breaks that would never have been available to general-population convicts. Protected witnesses knew exactly what they could get away with, but they were constantly trying to extend the limits.

Protected witnesses didn't even need to smuggle the dope. All they had to do was report to sick call, complain of some imaginary illness, and walk away with enough powerful uppers and downers to remain stoned for a week. It didn't cost them a penny, and there was the added advantage of safety because there was no smuggling involved and the drugs weren't contraband.

Percocet-5 is a non-narcotic analgesic available over the counter on the outside that was a big favorite while I was at Mesa. Sometimes it seemed like half the guys on the sick-call roster walked away with a supply of the drugs in their hands. They kept their stash in their cells but went through them in a hurry. It isn't a highly dangerous drug when taken in the doses it's designed for, but it can knock you for a loop when you swallow them by the handful or take them while you're boozing, and that's exactly what witness inmates did. Why not? The supply of pills was easy to replenish. All it took was a few minutes back in the medication line.

The only day there was no sick call was Thursday. The doctors were all over in the main prison on Thursdays; that was the day set aside as the major sick-call day for general-population inmates. On Thursdays, a physician's assistant filled in for the doctors on the units and handed out medication three times a day, in the early morning, at about one P.M., and finally at six or seven P.M.

Witness inmates who were genuinely sick enough to need hospitalization, or who needed other care that couldn't normally be provided by the prison's medical staff, were taken outside. Going to an outside sawbones or dentist was an experience that had to be lived to be believed.

One of my teeth went bad while I was in Sandstone, and I was driven sixty-five miles northwest to Duluth to get a root canal. I rode in a specially equipped van that was armored and had blacked-out windows. Three carloads of U.S. marshals and correctional officers drove ahead of the van, and three others trailed behind. It was a major security operation, but I thought it was ironic that the people who were supposed to be protecting me all wore bullet-proof vests and flak jackets, and I dressed in my normal clothing without any body armor.

I liked Duluth. It's a pretty city at the southern tip of Lake Superior, so there's a lot of water and it reminded me a bit of San Francisco. But I didn't see much of it. As soon as I stepped out of the van onto the sidewalk, my bodyguards rushed me down the middle of the street and into the building to the dentist's office.

The rush was partly my own fault. My bodyguards were behaving a bit too nonchalantly, so I told them about all the enemies I had who would like to have me whacked. Hell's Angels, Colombian narco-traffickers, the Mexican Mafia. I got their attention. They were looking up at rooftops and inside high-rise windows like they expected somebody to try popping me any minute. It pepped the operation up and got the adrenaline working. A little paranoia never hurts.

Inside the building, the hallways and elevators were cleared ahead of time and we marched right into the dentist's office. There was just him, his assistant, and my bodyguards. A few minutes before the dentist finished his work, one of the bodyguards went outside to alert the people waiting with the escort cars. Then we repeated the earlier process. I was hurried through the deserted hallway, crammed into a waiting elevator with my bodyguards, and rushed down the street to the van. I jumped in the van, and we all peeled away.

Another time in Mesa Unit when I had problems with an irregular heartbeat, really bad chest pains, and fierce headaches, the docs hooked me up to a monitor in the dispensary. Doctors in Sacramento, California, read the monitor while I was still hooked up and made the determination about whether or not I needed outside treatment. They sent me to a hospital in Phoenix.

Security was even heavier for my hospital trip than it was when I was treated by the dentist. I was transported in the same kind of van and was in the middle of a similar caravan, but cops were all over the place—and they were strapped with enough heavy artillery to start a war. Cops stalked through the hospital corridors carrying machine guns and packing pistols in their holsters. It was another Ninja event. About half a dozen of the bodyguards were dressed in black fatigues, and they were all business. There was no chatting up the pretties at the nurses' station or idle chitchat with passersby.

There were no passersby. The hallways were cleared, and even doctors, nurses, and other members of the hospital staff were kept out of our area while I was given an MRI and a CAT scan. I had heavily armed bodyguards with me every minute from the time I left Mesa Unit to the time I walked back inside the doors. The head witness-security marshal for the Phoenix area was on site and directed the operation. About a dozen guards were split pretty evenly between correctional officers and marshals. The hospital staff and citizens who were in the area must have thought that a John Dillinger or an Al Capone was being treated there.

Sick-call lists were printed to allow for twenty-five names, but it was normal to see forty-five names jammed into the spaces on the front and on the back of the sheets. That was drawn from an inmate population on the unit that averaged about sixty people. No one in authority seemed to question why about 75 percent of the population showed up on the sick lists every day. A phenomenal sickness rate like that would have crippled any army in the world, and even among civilians would have been recognized as a sign that some kind of epidemic had broken out. The only epidemic on the units was an epidemic of getting high.

Although I robbed pharmacies for a while and skin-popped or snorted an occasional hit of skag while I was on the outside, I never got hooked on anything until I was in Mesa Unit. Then I got hung up on Xanax, a powerful prescription drug that's prescribed as an antidepressant. On the outside of the walls, Xanax is popular with housewives and people with high-stress jobs, but they're so strong that they're not supposed to be taken for longer than two or three weeks at a stretch. On the units I swallowed Xanax every day for almost six years, starting off with a normal adult dose of 1.5 milligrams three times a day, and working my way up to three times that amount. Xanax is designed to calm nerves and help people sleep, but the heavy dosages kept me so zoned out that half the time I felt like I was sleepwalking. By the time I left Mesa and the care of medical professionals who knew how potentially addictive the antianxiety pills are, I had a fierce habit.

Shortly before leaving the witness program, I conned the old doctor into prescribing regular Friday-night injections of a powerful narcotic painkiller. I told him the administration was leaning on me because of my threats to expose the whole sordid witness-protection program mess, and my nerves were shot. I couldn't concentrate and I couldn't sleep. My complaint wasn't totally fiction, but the main thing I was looking for was a little respite from my problems. The shots provided that, and every Friday night after the sawbones approved my prescription, I floated out of the dispensary. Then I spent half the weekend hovering a few feet over the floor and feeling good.

Other inmates had similar experiences with a variety of drugs prescribed by sick-call physicians. And many of them are walking around on the outside today strung out because of the easy access to legal drugs while they were protected witnesses at Mesa or inside one of the other units. Many of the drugs are much stronger than Xanax or Percodan and can cause hallucinations or paranoia. Compared to some of my fellow witnesses, I was one of the lucky ones.

My friend Jap provided a big share of the booze that inmates on the unit used to wash down their prescription pills and capsules, as well as prison moonshine for general partying and hell-raising. He was a true Georgia boy, and could put together a portable still to brew wine from just about anything that will ferment, ranging from ketchup and tomato paste to grapefruit and strawberries—or prunes and raisins.

Anyone who has spent a little time in prison knows about "pruno." It's become a generic name for prison moon, and gets the name from prunes, which are one of the most common ingredients. Prison commissary chiefs love prunes. They're easy to store, keep forever, aid regularity, and they're even nutritious, so general population inmates can usually count on the daily menu to include prunes at least once or twice a week. No matter how vigilant the hacks may be, however, there are always a few prunes that wind up in the hands of a prison brewer.

It's the same with other fruits, especially when someone with Jap's unique skill is around. Other inmates in Mesa Unit called him the Wine King, and he deserved the title. Every unit had its own vintner, just like every general population prison has a few guys who are expert at turning out pruno, but Jap made the best shit I ever tasted. And I've drank some powerful pruno in my time.

Anyone can make a rough prison moonshine wine by dumping their breakfast cereal in the sink of their cell, adding water and waiting for it to curdle and ferment. Jap didn't mess with that kind of primitive shit. He concocted real wine that was as smooth and silky as a young whore's ass and carried a kick like a .44-caliber magnum. A couple of times he made saki, real Japanese wine, from rice. It took about two months, but when it was finally ready it was as clear and sweet as good Ozark mountain moonshine and could knock you for a real loop.

Jap said the saki was supposed to be sipped hot from little tiny cups, but we drank it from our coffee mugs. All it takes is a couple of swigs, and good night. After a saki drinking session, more than one righteous, stand-up dude spent the rest of the night face down on his bunk.

One dude who spent time with the navy on some little island in the middle of the Pacific Ocean was always rattling on about the fine, clear wine they made out there with coconuts. Just knock a hole in a nut, slip some rice and sugar inside, then bury it shallow under the coral sand for a few days to give it a chance to heat up. Fine, so where in the hell were we going to get coconuts on the units? Maybe Malik could order some.

Jap's saki was fine, but our favorite ingredient was strawberries. It was good, potent, and could be turned out in a fraction of the time it took to brew up a few gallons of rice wine. Whenever we were able to get our hands on five gallons or so of the berries from the commissary, he made fine strawberry wine. Sometimes he made the wine in big plastic buckets, but most of the time he used the five-gallon plastic bags that milk for milk dispensing machines come in. Jap would take one of them, rinse it off real good, and drop inside one pound of sugar per gallon of hot water. Then he would add a heaping tablespoon of yeast, and finally dump in the fruit or rice. When all the ingredients were in place, he tied the bags to a hot-water pipe and waited for it to ferment. It usually took about three or four days before it was ready to drink.

Even in the units, inmates couldn't simply tie a five gallon plastic bag of home brew to a hot-water pipe and leave it in plain sight. At Sandstone, we knocked a hole in the wall of my cell and used hot-water pipes behind the mirror. We located the pipes while we were drilling through the concrete to construct a shelf for some of my gear. After the shelf was in place, the hacks filled up the hole with four concrete blocks. As soon as they left, and before the cement dried, we pulled out one of the blocks that was directly behind my mirror. The mirror bolted to the wall, and all we had to do to get inside was unscrew two little bolts, lift out the blocks, and there were the pipes and a big empty space.

Jap usually tied four five-gallon bags of wine to the pipes at a time. Then we simply replaced the concrete block, screwed the bolts back in place on the mirror, and waited. I left the hot water running twenty-four hours a day, and we never had a single bad batch.

There was one big problem with brewing the wine in the wall at the rear of the cell. While wine is fermenting, it smells to high heaven, and the hacks couldn't miss the sweet, fruity odor that constantly hung over my cell.

So I began picking up big bunches of fruit at breakfast and dropping orange peels, grape skins, and chunks of pineapple and whatever else I could get hold of inside my wastebasket as cover. I also kept three or four apples and oranges laying around and slowly rotting on shelves or on top of my washstand. The hacks were still suspicious, and for a while they shook down my cell every other day, but not once in more than two and a half years did they ever tumble onto our secret stash.

A couple of years after I was transferred out of Sandstone, I heard that my former next-door neighbor told the administration where we made the wine. They closed the hole up for good by filling it with concrete, but by then it was too late. Jap and I were both in Otisville. After I left there, we got together again in Mesa Unit.

Jap hadn't changed. He was still doing a big-time wine business and concocting twenty or thirty gallons at a time in the ceramics room. It was a small room about twenty-five-by-twenty-five feet, and it was cluttered with clay, molds, kilns, and lockers. One time the hacks found a hundred gallons of wine behind the metal lockers and carted it away. Still they didn't get it all, and Jap simply went back to work. After a few days he had replaced the loss. Pruno was fast and easy to make. Again, the big problem was the odor. The ceramic room should have smelled like clay if anything, but while Jap was around, it always smelled like spoiled fruit. It was a dead giveaway.

Jap was transferred out of Mesa a few months before I left, and eventually wound up at the FCI Allenwood. He's a real tourist, and has been in every one of the witness units. I missed him when he was moved. So did a lot of other inmates. He was a righteous dude, and one helluva winemaker.

People lost entire weeks coasting on Jap's prison vino, or on a combination of his wine and the prescription pills they picked up on sick call. One month shortly before he left Mesa, he mixed up 100 barrels of the stuff. Then he announced a contest to see who could drink the most during a single month. I managed to do away with a few gallons, but I was never in the running. I had business to take care of and couldn't afford to stay constantly stoned on Jap's wine. He won his own contest anyway. It was a hands-down showing. No one came close to the personal prize-winning performance of the master vintner himself.

21

DIAL 1–900–SEX

THE FEDERAL TELEPHONE System (FTS), is one of the best friends a protected witness has.

Most of the men spend hours each day making telephone calls all over the world, and it doesn't cost them a penny. Would you like to guess who foots the bill? You do! The John Q. Public and Plain Jane Citizens.

A few inmates like Sergey and I got up early in order to be first outside in the exercise yard; but when the cell doors on the units were unlocked at five or six A.M. every morning, about half of the protected witnesses made a beeline for the telephone sign-up list. They kept the FTS lines humming until eleven at night, when inmates were locked in and the phones were shut down for a few hours. The next morning, it was the same story all over again.

On the units, the phone system was set up so that inmates could reserve twenty-minute slots, but if someone wanted to make a longer call, their friends could sign up for them. Then the inmate could talk for hours. It was merely a matter of getting himself and his friends to the head of the line.

An alternate method that worked even better was getting an assistant U.S. attorney or the FBI to send a memorandum to the prison telling the unit manager to provide an inmate with extra phone calls. Sammy Gravano used FTS phones to keep in touch with his chum Crazy Phil Leonetti after the Philadelphia mobster was released from Mesa and moved into phase two. An FBI agent set up conference calls for them.

According to regulations, individual inmates were supposed to be limited to six calls a month unless there was some reason for an exception to be made—like the requests from Justice or the FBI. I knew guys who were making twenty to thirty calls every week.

A guy I was with at Otisville and in Phoenix worked cases from the units with his DEA agent in Detroit, setting up his old friends. He was almost always the first man on the phones at both places, and usually talked for an hour or an hour and a half. It was the same in all the units. Certain inmates always did more than their share of the talking.

The witness-unit phones buzzed with conversation all day, every day, Sunday through Saturday, including holidays. Witnesses talked to lawyers, to wives, girlfriends, other family members, and to old business associates. No one at the prisons or with the OEO asked inmates who they were calling or why. Prison staff were prevented from monitoring our calls because we were on a protected-witness unit. It was against regulations. Sometimes a guard or someone from administration tried to convince us that recording devices were being used, but we knew that was bullshit.

Occasionally someone from management got on another telephone to eavesdrop on a conversation if they suspected an inmate was scheming to bring drugs or other contraband inside. But they had to have a good reason—some evidence of wrongdoing or doubledealing afoot before they could record or listen in.

On the general-population side, every telephone conversation except talks with personal attorneys is recorded. In addition to that, a correctional officer sits in the same room with the inmate making the call. A convict can be having what should be a private conversation with a girlfriend, his wife, or some other family member, and a hack is right there beside him with a phone pressed to his ear, listening to every word.

In recent years, technological advances in the prison-telephone business have made official eavesdropping and call monitoring even more convenient, with such developments as voice-print identification and other safeguards set up to combat inmate fraud and other abuses. The new VPI system is just getting off the ground, but the process is designed to begin when the prisoner is booked into the institution. His voice is recorded at that time, capturing the distinctive audio imprint. Later, when the prisoner places a telephone call he is required to speak his name, and repeat a personal identification number.

Phone companies and prison authorities are also working on a supercomputer system to monitor conversations and red-flag words or slang terms such as "escape," "split," "contract," "hit" and others that could indicate funny business might be going on. (So how will they deal with El Rukn-speak?)

Running prison telephones is big business. Direct-dial collect calls from prisons and jails brings in more than $1 billion in annual revenues for various telephone companies, equipment suppliers, and goverment agencies. Telephone companies compete fiercely for prison contracts.

The customers are locked up and aren't in a position to shop around for better deals, but they are constantly seeking new ways to beat the Man and figure out how to work telephone scams. Telephones may be no more than harmless diversions to many prisoners, but the wonders an inmate with desire and imagination is able to work over the wires would amaze most people.

Most lockups, with the exception of witness-protection units, set up the convict-calling systems so that a recorded voice announces at the beginning of the conversation that the call is originating at a prison. In some prisons, the calls are interrupted at intervals by repeat announcements of the recorded warnings. Many prisons also limit inmates to calling a few numbers on previously approved lists.

Some systems are designed as well so that inmate calls are automatically terminated the instant anyone on the receiving end tries to transfer them to a third party. It's a useful shield established to keep prisoners from trying to use a wife, a mother, or a crony on the street from passing on a phone call to someone who is being set up for threats, extortion, or fraud.

A few years ago a convicted child molester in a Florida lockup was accused of using the telephone to try and set up the contract killing of a five-year-old girl who claimed he had sexually abused her. The child molester lost his telephone privileges and wound up with a peck of new problems.

Convicts love telephone stories, and yarns about scams or hoaxes pulled off by imaginative inmates can become important elements of prison lore. While I was at Mesa, prisoners at a couple of jails in Burlington county, New Jersey, were playing an ingenious telephone-tag game that authorities figured cost local taxpayers at least $50,000 a year in lost revenues from pay phones. They also ran up staggering telephone bills for some private citizens of the county.

Inmates got hold of a secret New Jersey Bell code that allowed them to transfer or forward calls anywhere they wanted to in the world. They picked names at random from local phone books and stuck the poor unsuspecting saps on the outside with the bills. The two county jails had a total of thirty-seven pay phones available to inmates, and they were in use most of the day before authorities finally figured out what was going on and put a stop to it. It's the kind of story that other convicts pass around, trying to figure out new angles.

In Colorado, a prison inmate was accused of using a cellular phone to cheat a Japanese brokerage firm out of a small fortune. He opened accounts and placed orders, operating like any big-time trader and apparently no one at the brokerage company had any idea he was locked up in a penitentiary until it was too late. The big-time trader got around the recorded warnings that the call was coming from prison by going cellular.

Other prisoners use the telephone and the mails to woo naive or man-hungry women attracted through personal-contact advertisements or other means, and work them for money and favors. The telephone can be a wonderful thing, but in the hands of a convict with time, imagination and nothing to lose it can become a devastating tool for fraud, extortion, and a host of other crimes.

Our calls were private, and we talked to whoever we wanted to talk to, wherever we wanted to call. We could phone next door to Phoenix if we wished, or we could place international calls to Karachi, Tripoli, or Cali and Medellín. It made no difference. The cost to the inmate was the same: zero! And there were no interruptions by periodic recording identifiers. A large number of the calls were made to exotic locations around the world because we had so many international drug smugglers, arms dealers and other big-time operators. People like Malik, Lehder—and Jimmy Chagra.

Jimmy was my next-door neighbor in Mesa Unit for a couple of years, and he was a wiry piece-of-work with a round face, thick, heavy lips and a fast, cunning mind. All you had to do was toss some kind of question at him involving numbers, and he came up with the answer right away. He had a mind like a calculator.

We got along okay, and shared a mop and a bucket. Jimmy always started out by swabbing his cell, then passed the mop and bucket to me so I could do the honors in my own living spaces. He was a good guy to know because he ran the commissary. Most inmates had a job on the units, but nobody ever died from overwork. Sammy the Bull's job was taking the cover off the pool table every morning and folding it up.

Chagra's real name wasn't Jimmy, although that was what everybody called him, even the law back in El Paso. His name was Jamiel Alexander Chagra. He looked like a Mexican, but he's of Lebanese descent.

He was a high-stakes gambler and big-time narcotics trafficker in El Paso and Las Vegas when he was convicted and sent to prison for being a drug kingpin, then became the target of what at that time was, and may still be, the longest and most expensive investigation in the history of the FBI.

The Bureau spent four years and more than $11 million unsuccessfully trying to prove that he paid a Dallas hit man to assassinate U.S. District Judge John Howland Wood, Jr. Then Jimmy cut a deal with the feds and promised to testify against a Boston man who accepted a contract from him to whack Assistant U.S. Attorney James Kerr. In return, Jimmy was given a spot in the federal witness-protection program.

He negotiated the agreement with a couple of prosecutors in El Paso, and with the chief of litigation in the criminal division at the Justice Department in Washington. The deal was approved by the trial judge who moved up to take the murdered jurist's place on the district court. Ironically, Jimmy didn't even have to testify against the Boston hit man, a guy named James R. Kearns. Kearns agreed to accept a sentence of life in prison in return for a promise by Justice not to prosecute his wife.

Jimmy Chagra was at Marion doing thirty years without parole on the drug conviction in 1984 when he was moved into the program, a little more than a year after he was acquitted at his trial for allegedly hiring Charles V. Harrelson to kill the judge. If the name Harrelson sounds familiar, that shouldn't be surprising. The hit man is the father of Woody Harrelson, who later became a star of the television series, "Cheers."

Charles Harrelson was convicted of the judge's murder and sentenced to life in prison without parole. After serving several years at Marion, he was transferred to the new super-maximum penitentiary in Florence, Arizona. Ironically, Harrelson had previous personal experience as a snitch. Back in 1959, he played a role in a sensational case in Orange County California, involving three dudes charged with killing a man and shooting the hands and ears off his wife. Harrelson was locked up in the Orange County jail on robbery charges with one of the accused shooters and wore a wire and transmitter. He got the guy to admit involvement in the shootings by claiming he needed to have someone killed. Then Harrelson testified against him at the trial. Honor among thieves? Sure, and the Heavens Gate suicides really were picked up by a UFO trailing the Hale-Bopp Comet!

Harrelson was a more proficient killer than Kearns. Kearns ambushed the assistant U.S. attorney while he was on his way to work in El Paso, but the prosecutor escaped being killed by sliding to the floorboard of his Lincoln Continental when two gunmen leaped out of a van and opened fire with a shotgun and an automatic rifle. The luxury car was riddled with bullet holes, but the driver was uninjured. Kerr was lucky to survive, and he knew it. He changed jobs and left town. Harrelson, on the other hand, blew Wood away with a single shot in the back from a sniper rifle outside the judge's Chateau Dijon townhouse a few days before he was to preside over Jimmy's drug conspiracy trial.

The former U.S. attorney who initially assigned Kerr to break up the Chagra operation wasn't happy with the decision to move Jimmy into the witness-protection program. Jamie Boyd reminded reporters that Jimmy had already tried to break out of Leavenworth. "Frankly I think he ought to be in a hard-time joint," he told the *Houston Chronicle.*

Prosecutors had put together a tough case with some pretty impressive evidence that included more than one thousand hours of recordings captured through electronic surveillance, telephone taps, and wires worn by undercover operatives and snitches. One of the tapes included an incrimininating conversation recorded by an inmate snitch at Leavenworth. Prosecutors blamed the refusal of Jimmy's lawyer brother, Joe, to testify against him for spoiling the murder conspiracy case.

"Harrelson wasn't supposed to do it until after the trial, when the appeal was coming up," Jimmy can be heard saying on the tape. "That way I could get a different judge." Judge Wood had a reputation as a no-nonsense jurist who handed out frontier-type justice and was known as Maximum John.

The investigation was big-time, the biggest FBI operation since the sniper slaying in Dallas of President Kennedy. That's no surprise, considering that Wood was the first federal judge to be assassinated in the United States in more than a century.

Although prosecutors weren't able to convict Jimmy of ordering the murder, he pleaded guilty of conspiring to kill Kerr and pulled a life sentence. He was already down for thirty on the drug conviction, so the pool hustler and card shark wasn't likely to be lining up bank shots or combinations on some pool table in El Paso or showing up at the poker tables in Vegas for a long time.

Prosecutors also convicted Jimmy's wife, Liz, of delivering the payoff money, $250,000, as part of the conspiracy to kill the judge. Jimmy was a softie when it came to his wife and insisted that his plea bargain include a ten-year reduction in her thirty-year sentence. But the reduction deal was wiped out after she appealed her sentence for conspiracy, tax fraud, and obstruction of justice and won a new trial. She was convicted again, and the judge socked her with another thirty-year sentence, the same as before.

According to the deal, the sentence reduction would apply only if she lost her appeal, so Jimmy didn't have anything left to bargain for her with. He felt bad for her, but what could he do? He had his own troubles.

Liz was at the minimum-security federal prison in Lexington, Kentucky, while we were at Mesa, and Jimmy was all shaken up when he learned that she had cancer. The FCI Lexington, which years ago was the U.S. government's main dumping ground for druggies, is the last federal penitentiary that houses both male and female inmates. Jimmy wasn't worried about that. He was heartbroken by his wife's illness, and he became a regular caller on the FTS phones whenever she was conscious and well enough to talk.

Despite Jimmy's obvious affection for his wife, he was a treacherous little dude who liked to smoke a joint or blow a line of coke now and then, and he didn't hang with anybody. He was pretty much on the level of Sammy and Joe Lehder, and lived high with his own espresso machine in his room. He had everything you could imagine, stuff like short-wave radios, stereo radios, Bose speakers like Paul Harvey advertises, gourmet coffees, all the best foods you can think of. You name it, and Jimmy had it. If he wanted anything, the administration made sure he got it.

He liked to shoot nine-ball on our pool table with a guy who owned an electric-supply company in Chicago and had something to do with the Mob. The guy was always boasting that he was going to be the next Albert Tocco. Tocco was the boss of the rackets in the suburban southside, extending down around Calumet City before he got whacked. Jimmy and the big-talker from Chicago played for $1,000 a ball, and sometimes they kept the table busy four or five hours while other inmates stood around placing bets on who was going to sink the nine-ball.

After we got to know each other awhile, he told me that the Wood assassination was a drug hit. He didn't say he set it up, just what it was. People on the witness units know the dangers of flapping their mouths, so they tend to be guarded about what they say to their neighbors. But there's a lot of time to kill, and after awhile you tend to start talking about things.

Jimmy didn't want to come up before Wood on the drug conspiracy charge because he knew that the judge would be tough, and if he got convicted Maximum John would throw the book at him. Judge Wood hated dope, and he had even less regard for anyone who was tied to the narcotics business. He was a premier ass-kicker.

According to Jimmy, he made millions smuggling drugs, but he gambled a lot of it away. Lebanese like to gamble, he said. Jimmy didn't come right out and tell me that he still had a few million dollars stashed away, but based on his lavish lifestyle at Mesa I think he managed to find a way to put a few bucks aside for a rainy day. He liked to live good, ate well, and still gambled, shooting pool with the Chicagoan, shooting craps, playing cards, whatever was happening. He didn't waste his time with penny-ante bets. He had some money salted away somewhere.

In 1991 a tax court in El Paso gave him a welcome shot in the arm with a ruling that the IRS owed him and his wife a $600,000 refund because the agency collected too much in taxes from their gambling earnings. All the thieves aren't in the joint, but dudes like Jimmy Chagra and me wouldn't have all the awesome power of the federal government behind us if we decided to try dipping our hands in somebody else's pocket.

The free phones were also handy toys, which inmates used to fight boredom. They placed bets with their bookies on horse races, football games, and other sporting events, and they spent thousands of taxpayer dollars on 900-sex lines, listening to women with sensuous voices describe in intimate detail the various kinds of lewd activities they would allegedly enjoy sharing with the inmate. For $3.95 a minute, which was the going rate while I was in Mesa Unit, sex-line sirens provided breathless descriptions of kinky sexual activities, punctuated by moans, groans, and squeals of feigned passion. Some inmates became addicted to the calls, and swore the 900-line calls were the best sex they ever had.

Prison authorities finally stepped in and called a halt to the sex-line operation after they got an eye-popping look at the bills inmates were piling up. Citizens paid a big buck for the calls, however, before the administration figured out what was going on.

The phone-sex fiasco wasn't the only way witnesses found to abuse their FTS privileges. They used the phones to carry off all kinds of scams that cost businesses and private citizens millions of dollars. Enterprising witnesses had the perfect opportunity to set up con games and fleece the public.

Each witness entering the program is required to provide a list of at least ten aliases to authorities, to be used at various times in correspondence with the outside world. So inmates used some of the ready-made aliases to place telephone orders for merchandise that was never paid for, making the Gs unwitting accomplices to massive ongoing fraud. Witnesses have successfully ordered a little bit of everything through the mail from new microwave ovens and designer clothes to computer programs.

Credit-card scams provide another lucrative avenue for inside the walls that are hatched and carried out by protective witnesses using FTS and the mails. Stolen or phony credit-card numbers, and new cards issued in the names of witness aliases were used to obtain everything from merchandise to cash advances. When the BOP uncovered one credit card scam, witnesses would respond with another that had a new and different twist.

Creditors who attempt to collect for their goods or seek recompense for other losses, are faced with a brick wall when they appeal to federal authorities for help. Because of the non-disclosure rules regarding civil litigants, the government is put in the position of routinely violating its own policies. As a result, the Department of Justice, the nation's chief law enforcement agency, winds up acting as a barrier to law enforcement. All the resources and power of the government are lined up and working to protect the guys on the other side of the dispute.

In 1983, one of the rare audits of WITSEC by the U.S. General Accounting Office (GAO) showed that in a single six-month period in 1980, creditors were busting their balls trying to collect $7.3 million from thirty-two witnesses.

Even though the BOP finally managed to put a lid on the phone-sex operation in the units, it was no big deal to most of the witnesses. The real thing was available

from girlfriends and wives, as well as from hookers who
showed up at the prison on visiting days pretending to
be close relatives or sweethearts.

For a while when I was at Sandstone, wives and girlfriends could visit right in the rooms of inmates. They
cooked their own meals and ate in the rooms, and when
they wanted more privacy they simply hung big sheets
of cardboard or blankets up over the door. One of the
rules of prison etiquette is you don't walk into another
inmate's cell unless you're invited. You don't even look
inside, because whatever might be going on in there is
none of your business even if the inmate isn't doing
anything more suspicious than curling up on his bunk
and sleeping.

Even later after I was moved to other units and visitors weren't allowed inside cells, witnesses were permitted to kiss, hug, and hold hands in visiting rooms
with their wives, other family members, and girlfriends.
Officially witnesses weren't supposed to be allowed con-
jugal visits like they have in some prisons in California
and a few other states. But there are ways to get around
the restriction.

Male-female sex isn't as unusual an occurrance in
many American prisons as most people believe it to be,
and at least one death-row inmate fathered a baby while
he was behind bars. Serial-killer Ted Bundy got his old
lady pregnant with a daughter while he was on death
row at the Florida State Penitentiary in Starke. Inmates
and their lady friends reportedly went at it under the
tables and behind the water cooler in the visiting room
there.

After Lloyd was transferred to Lompac with Persico,
he tipped off the feds that the Mafia kingpin was getting
it on with one of his attorneys in the lawyer's visiting
room, according to a news report. The feds reportedly
set up a video camera in the ceiling of the visiting room

and caught one of the torrid makeout scenes on tape. After that, the Snake spent some time in disciplinary custody, and the attorney was required to conduct their subsequent meetings in the public visiting room.

Bundy and "The Snake" Persico would have loved the visiting room on the witness units, because sex there was an everyday occurrance. So was boozing, with good, professionally distilled liquor brought in from the outside. Girlfriends smuggled pints and half-pints of Jack Daniels or Chivas inside, then bought soft drinks from the machine. I watched other inmates at Otisville gulp down the soda pop, then furtively refill the can with good booze and sit there getting ripped. The women carried out the empty bottles when they left.

Visiting rooms in most of the units doubled as the TV rooms, and chairs and comfortable couches were scattered around with little coffee tables in front of them. A guard was always on duty, but he didn't hassle anybody. He usually sat off in a chair by himself either reading a newspaper or fighting to keep from falling asleep. The inmates took advantage of the situation by pushing a couple of couches together, back-to-back at the far end of the room, where the guard's vision was blocked. Then they took turns on the back couch.

Female visitors who planned to get it on with their men prepared for the festivities ahead of time by wearing dresses with full skirts and nothing underneath. Then when it was their turn they simply climbed on their man's lap and went to town. It happened every day, and a lot of babies were made on the witness units.

22

Acting Class

LIFE ON THE units isn't all fun, feasts, and partying. Witnesses must attend acting class, and to the feds who depend on the performance of inmates in courtrooms all over the country it is the most important activity of the day. Much of the activity directed by the feds also violates the very laws they are sworn to protect, to say nothing of legal system ethics.

Every morning in Unit One, Mesa, Allenwood and in every other prison-within-a-prison set aside for protected witnesses, FBI agents, DEA, and other law-enforcement officers show up bright and early to prepare inmates to testify. They interview the witnesses, feed them new information, and leave boxes of case files to read and study.

Sometimes the feds come in for three or four weeks straight, whatever it takes until they're sure the witness knows how to handle himself and exactly what to say. A witness can sit in a room for seven or eight hours a day with four or five FBI agents, assistant U.S. attorneys, or a state prosecutor, while the law officers repeatedly go over what they want from him. It's exhausting work, and I'd rather haul hot asphalt or dig ditches anytime.

If a witness messes up in acting class and blurts out the wrong thing, they won't tell him, "Oh, I don't think you should say that." No way! They tell him, "Say it this way." Then they run through the answer they want, word for word. If the witness has to practice the answer, he practices it until he has it down pat. Answers to what may appear to be the most inconsequential questions can be crucial inside a courtroom, and that includes the manner of delivery as well as the content. The information has to be right, and delivered perfectly. Snitches involved in the same case are routinely housed together so they can compare stories and keep them straight.

Behavioral psychologists and jury consultants tell them how to talk, how to sit, and how to respond to the tactics and specific questions of defense attorneys while they're giving depositions or are on the witness stand. Bikers are ordered to shave their beards, and ABs to cover up their tats. Hairy faces, ponytails, and swastika or skull and dagger tattoos with blood drops don't make good impressions on jurors, or on judges.

Appearance and communication are keys to favorably, or unfavorably, impressing jurors. Courtrooms are foreign environments to most people, as strange, awesome, and threatening as the interior of a South American rain forest, and witnesses are taught to become more comfortable there and to fit in. The advisors and consultants construct the character they wish to project for the witness and to make him as convincing as possible when he testifies.

Witnesses are told how to project themselves, when to look at the jurors, whether they should smile or show an impassive face. The U.S. attorneys, or assistants, have hand signals worked out so they can pass messages to witnesses while they're on the stand about how to act.

They're like baseball managers. In the courtroom they do everything but spit and scratch their butt.

They're always looking ahead to the courtroom where the judge and the jury are going to be the only audience that counts. They explain how you can wriggle off the hook if a defense attorney is really boring in and starting to get to you. Just stop and ask for a drink of water, or say you don't understand the question and make the lawyer repeat it several times. It throws the defense lawyer off balance, and gives the witness time to compose himself. It's basic courtroom strategy if you're a lawyer, but not everybody knows about it when they need it. Protected witnesses know about it, because they're schooled and run through their paces before they ever step inside a courtroom to testify in a big trial.

The shrinks and feds even tell witnesses how to cut their hair, and they pick their courtroom clothes. Celebrity witnesses owned their own fine suits, tailor-made. Dudes like me were loaned suits, even shoes, or whatever we needed, because we couldn't afford to dress the way the Sammy Gravanos and the Crazy Phil Leonettis did. We didn't wear Armani suits and Bruno Magli shoes in real life, why should we want to do it in the units?

Sammy the Bull was coached by some of the best Mob prosecutors in New York, and he got such a swelled head and inflated sense of his knowledge and importance that he passed on expertise and advice to other witnesses. People got Sammy's advice whether they wanted it or not. For a snitch who could qualify for developmental-disability payments if he wasn't already living like a king, Sammy became a real Steven Spielberg of the Bighouse. He became a self-appointed director who knew just what to do to make even the most ruthless serial killers look sympathetic, or at least believable, to a jury.

I watched him on television while he was standing
with his hand raised and taking the witnesse's oath before testifying in one of Gotti's trials, and the little hoodlum looked like a CPA. He was spiffed out in a gray
seersucker double-breasted suit, with white shirt, fine
silk tie, black shoes and socks, and looked like anything
but the vicious gangster and hit man that he really was.
Everything was carefully coordinated and perfectly
matched. The defense lawyers were dressed flashier than
he was. It wasn't until Sammy began to talk that the
illusion was destroyed.

Even the advice of a roomful of shrinks and Justice
Department hotshots can only change so much. Sammy
was Sammy, and eventually the jury saw the real gangster for what he was. The prosecutors were ready for
that, of course, and they admitted up front that he was
one of the bad guys. That's why he knew what he knew.

Sammy never testified until he was thoroughly
coached and prepared. One burst of Gravano temper accompanied by a torrent of threats and curses in response
to the needling and browbeating of a squad of defense
attorneys, and he could have blown the entire case. But
Sammy behaved. He was a good witness, because he
knew what he was talking about. He was like a Hollywood actor playing a big scene. And he was on target
because he understood that he was involved in a game
of acting tricks—high theater.

Not every witness performs as well, and despite the
intense preparation and coaching sometimes they lose it
when a defense attorney is pounding at them, pointing
out their considerable flaws and tracing their sordid
criminal pasts. Impeaching just one prosecution witness
in front of a jury can be devastating and sink even the
most carefully crafted government case. A woman defense attorney summed it up nicely at one of the El Rukn
trials when she quoted an old proverb to one of the gang

turncoats who was on the witness stand by declaring:
''Who you are speaks so loud I can't hear what you
say.''

Just about any job I can think of beats being a professional snitch and protected witness. It's especially
hairy when you're undercover, helping set up one of
your friends or testifying in an open courtroom. A good
defense attorney doesn't allow a protected witness to
keep many secrets that could be helpful to his or her
client.

Witnesses aren't through with acting classes when
they leave the units. They're also put through their paces
after they are transported from prisons to hotel rooms or
cramped offices in federal buildings in cities where they
are scheduled to testify. Once the feds have their claws
into someone, they demand everything, the whole kit-
and-kaboodle.

While I attended acting class and listened to other
inmates who were schooled for hours about how to work
the system and manipulate the opinion of judges and
juries, the facts about this beast we call the criminal
justice system began to sink in. It isn't at all like the
famous movie *Twelve Angry Men,* where a courtroom is
a place to go to see that justice is served. The courts
aren't about guilt or innocence, or right and wrong.
They're about which lawyer is the slickest at fibbing,
fudging, and picking out legal loopholes that will get his
or her client off or, if it's a prosecutor, that will get the
defendant convicted. Successful criminal lawyers and
prosecutors know how to keep evidence that is injurious
to their case out of trial, and how to keep helpful evidence in.

And they know how to manipulate witnesses. There
are more than one million lawyers in this country, and
some of them are very good indeed at picking out legal

technicalities or playing up emotional issues that will work in their favor.

Another activity for veterans of federal witness-protection acting classes is performing before shadow juries. Minitrials are set up ahead of the real thing, and jurors are selected to deliberate guilt or innocence. Shadow jury decisions and the reasoning behind them are then used by lawyers to critique strengths and weaknesses, and to develop strategy for the big show. The jurors are debriefed by lawyers and other experts, who quiz them to determine what effect various evidence and testimony had on their decisions.

Sometimes two or three mock trials, each with a different jury, are held by lawyers for one side or the other. Of course the mock jurors have to be fed and accommodated in motel rooms. Video equipment is usually used, and sometimes special rooms with two-way mirrors that the guinea-pig jurors are unaware of but lawyers and psychologists can watch through during deliberations are used. It's an expensive process, but the government has plenty of money. That's what taxpayers are for.

Reactions of individual jurors are also valuable in the process of selecting the real panel finally designated to sit at a trial and deliberate guilt or innocence. Attorneys try to get jurors with similar backgrounds and attitudes to guinea-pig jurors who have come down on their side after the mock trials. Every possible trick or tactic that might work to tilt the balance of justice is brought into play in big-time trials. It's a chess game, and the best players win.

The shadow-jury game is played by other officers of the court, as well as by people who are expected to testify. Prosecutor Marcia Clark made a drastic change in her wardrobe and hairstyle shortly before the beginning of the O. J. Simpson trial, after members of a shadow jury in Phoenix indicated they were critical of her appearance. She made herself look softer and more feminine, in an obvious move to tone down what some people considered to be her normally tough courtroom demeanor. She even began occasionally smiling at Judge Lance Ito.

Shadow juries, of course, also pick out other flaws in planned presentations by the prosecution and defense. Testimony that is weak, or especially strong, can be pinpointed and built on. At other times testimony by a witness at a shadow trial may open up dangerous areas helpful to the other side; and when the faults are spotted and pointed out, alterations can be made before the real courtroom proceeding begins. It's a high-stakes game that, depending on the particular case, can make the difference between life and death, freedom or personal ruin, and a lifetime behind bars.

The only difference to me between testifying before a mock jury and the real thing was that I knew that when the trial was actually underway, I was nearing the end. Mock-jury trials were warmups and the pressure continued to build. When a real trial ended, I could take a deep breath, kick back, slip on the headphones, and listen to some shit-kickin' music for a while, and return to the weight pile with my friend Sergey. I didn't like being gone too long, because it was too easy to get out of shape.

23

Pond Sludge

AMONG THE TOXIC mix of hit men, narco-traffickers, Mafia kingpins, and street-gang hoodlums assembled in the witness-protection units, John Harvey Adamson stood out like a raw chancre on top of a boil.

The psychotic killer frightened and disgusted even some of the most hardened criminals in the units. His crime, blowing up a crusading newspaper reporter with a car bomb, was nasty enough, but other inmates had committed offenses that were as bad or worse.

His general attitude inside the walls turned almost everybody off. It was the simmering sense of menace, and the glee he showed at violence and suffering experienced by other people. During the six years I was locked up in witness protection units at Sandstone, Otisville, and Phoenix, I never met an inmate I felt more hatred and disgust for than Adamson. He was pond scum, the closest thing to pure evil I have ever experienced in any human being.

He looked like Ronald Reagan's old co-star in the smash hit, *Bedtime for Bonzo*. The one with all the hair. At Mesa, Adamson was on his home turf, and he was so used to the Arizona heat that he lolled around outside with his shirt off to show his fat belly while the sun turned him brown as a toad. He had thick, black hair that he combed straight back, and he had a habit of running his fingers through it. Nobody else would ever want to touch it. He kept enough grease on it to fry eggs.

If there had been any doubts in my mind or in the minds of other inmates in Mesa Unit that Adamson was irredeemably evil, they were dissipated on April 19, 1995, the day that the Alfred P. Murrah Federal Building in Oklahoma City was blown up by a truck bomb and 168 people were killed. It was the deadliest terrorist attack on U.S. soil in the history of the United States, and hundreds of people who survived the devasting blast lost arms and legs or were otherwise scarred for life. One survivor's eye was ripped out of the socket.

Adamson was thrilled, and he didn't show a glimmer of human compassion for the victims of the outrage. As soon as the first news stories were broadcast on CNN, he began jumping up and down. "Oh man, that could have been me," he crowed. "That could have been me that blew away all those assholes."

Adamson hated anyone who had anything to do with the government. But people with the government weren't all that unique in holding down a spot on his enemies list. I didn't know hardly anyone the ape really liked. He loved seeing people get hurt, and he was especially turned on by bombs.

He watched news reports of the Oklahoma City bombing over and over, taking occasional breaks to lumber through the common area and outside into the yard where he collared any inmate he could find to talk about the tragedy. He was getting his jollies off, and his eyes glowed with excitement. They were bright and weird, like he had just taken a big hit of crystal meth. But it wasn't meth that had him hyped up. It was the bombing.

Watching and listening to Adamson made the goose flesh pop out on my skin. Evil and hate oozed out of his pores.

Before any details were publicly disclosed about the composition of the bomb, he was telling people what it was made of and how it was put together: fertilizer and fuel oil. Bombs and bombings were his area of expertise, and he wanted everybody to know that. He didn't give a shit that a bunch of babies and other people were killed. That made the whole story more exciting. Adamson loved bombs.

He was a tow-truck driver and a wanna-be mobster on June 2, 1976, when he attached six sticks of dynamite to the undercarriage of a new little white Datsun owned by *Arizona Republic* reporter Dan Bolles. He had lured the Phoenix newshound to the hotel Clarendon in the middle of the downtown area with promises of information about reputed Mafia links to some big-time local politicians and a shady land deal.

While Bolles was inside the Clarendon waiting for his contact, Adamson was outside putting the bomb in place. When everything was in order, Adamson telephoned Bolles in the hotel lobby and said he couldn't keep the appointment. Bolles, a lanky man who was six foot three, loped out to his car, slid into the bucket seat, turned on the ignition, and began to back out of his parking place. That was when Adamson, who was watching from a vantage point a few hundred feet away, activated a remote-control device, transmitting a signal to a receiver attached to the explosives, according to police.

The dynamite exploded beneath the reporter's legs, ripping away his new powder-blue leisure suit, blackening his face, and horribly damaging his body. Bolles, who was the father of seven children, lived for ten agonizing days before finally breathing his last on June 13.

By that time, doctors had amputated both his legs and an arm.

Incredibly, Bolles was conscious and able to talk lucidly to police investigators from the time they arrived at the blast scene to just before he died. When the first civilians reached his side on the hot asphalt of the parking lot, he told them: "They finally got me. John Adamson was the man. Find him." He never deviated from that story, and continued to blame Adamson for the bombing.

Adamson did an incredibly professional job for a truck driver who was known as a barfly and a big-time bullshitter—and who constantly boasted about all the Mafia bosses and other powerful racketeers he knew. He was the kind of character who sat around in darkened barrooms wearing his ever-present black sunglasses, acting important and talking tough.

Somehow he learned to put together a devastatingly effective bomb, how to place it for maximum effect, and how to detonate it. Almost all the force of the explosion was exactly where the killer wanted it to be, directly underneath the reporter. Except for the area around the driver-side door, at first glance from the outside the car appeared to be hardly damaged. Adamson was proud of his handiwork.

When police moved in and charged him with murder, he quickly named a couple of other local men as being involved in the killing. He pointed the finger at James Robison, a husky plumber from nearby Chandler who reputedly had Mob ties as the character who actually triggered the bomb. He accused a Phoenix contractor named Max Dunlap of paying him to carry out the contract killing.

Dunlap was a close friend of a powerful local mover-and-shaker named Kemper Marley, who was one of the biggest liquor distributors in Arizona and had just taken a journalistic ass-kicking from Bolles that ultimately cost him a position he held on the state racing commission. Adamson testified in court that Marley was behind the killing, but the prominent Arizona landowner and businessman continued to vigorously deny having anything to do with it until his death in 1990 from cancer. He was never charged in the case.

Meanwhile, Robison was convicted of setting off the bomb, and Dunlap was found guilty of participating in the plot. Both men were sentenced to death. Adamson, who pleaded the Fifth Amendment to beg off answering some questions from their defense attorneys in court, cut a deal with the prosecution and got away with a sentence of twenty years and two months.

The case wouldn't die, however, and after Robison and Dunlap spent two years behind bars, the Arizona Supreme Court tossed out their convictions. Adamson refused to help retry his cohorts in the killing because he thought he deserved a better deal, and he was again put on trial. This time he was convicted of murder and got the death penalty, but he escaped Arizona's gas chamber when the state's capital-punishment law was declared unconstitutional.

Dunlap was convicted again of murder and sentenced to life without the possibility of parole for twenty-five years. Robison was acquitted in a separate trial, but later pulled a five-year sentence after admitting to trying to hire a hit man to kill Adamson in prison.

Adamson moved into the witness-protection program in 1990. For twenty years he lived a charmed life, but it's not because he makes friends so easily. About the only friend he had at Mesa was his cell mate—Sammy the Bull. They got along like two peas in a pod during the eighteen months they spent double-celling together. At lockdown, the shades were pulled in front of the door and whatever went on there was their business. I don't

want to know about it, but it was impossible not to hear
Sammy screaming sometimes about what a punk and
backstabbing baby raper Johnny Boy Gotti was. Sammy
never stopped mouthing off, and went on all day and all
night until he dropped off to sleep. Maybe the cellies
got along because Adamson was such a good listener.

He wasn't the only person who listened to Sammy.
The New York gangster was the eyes and ears of the
administration, and everybody knew he was telling the
hacks everything he knew about whatever his fellow inmates were up to. But he was no worse than Adamson
or at least one other snitch who was once the Arizona
bomber's cell mate. Everybody ratted on everybody.

In the late 1970s while Adamson was being held at
the Metropolitan Correctional Center in San Diego, he
shared a cell with a bank robber and scumbag mob hit
man named Gerald Denono. Among others people, Denono admitted killing a Las Vegas showgirl and chopping up a Fort Lauderdale area real estate agent with a
butcher knife. The knife had a big, thick blade, and he
used it to pin the Florida real estate gal to the bloody
mattress her body was lying on.

Denono was a former Newark cop and a slick character who figured he could make more money working
the other side of the fence, and eased into the federal-
witness protection program by ratting out a Florida cell
mate who was accused in a sensational Palm Beach murder case. Then he flipped in San Diego and told the feds
Adamson confessed the Boles bombing to him. That led
to Adamson rolling. He deserved a cell mate like Denono.

Adamson was a nasty piece of work, and a general
pain in the ass who openly spied on other inmates and
generally pushed his weight around. He spied on me,
and went to special pains to make sure that I knew exactly what he was doing and that everyone else on the

unit knew. It was an open secret that I was working to expose the ills and foul-ups connected with the program.

Early in 1995 while I was preparing for my release from confinement in a few weeks, Adamson made a point of following me to the telephone. Before I even began to talk, he settled onto a nearby chair with his neck craned forward, staring at me like some buzzard to make sure I knew he was watching my every move. He couldn't listen in but he wrote down the exact time I dialed my number, and recorded the amount of time I talked on a sheet of paper.

I figure he turned the information over to prison officials, so they could retrieve the tapes that were automatically made of my calls and check to see if I was violating the prohibitions against unauthorized media contacts. The law prevented the administration from doing the initial eavesdropping on me unless they had a pretty solid reason to believe I was violating the rules or otherwise up to no good. Adamson was a different story. He played by his own rules.

What could I do? Pop the guy? Start a fight? I was all ready to wave goodbye, and if I allowed him to provoke me into doing something violent, I would find myself in the hole or doing additional time somewhere in general population. I gritted my teeth and put up with it.

Other people had gotten a taste of the same shit from Adamson. About the only thing that seemed to make him happy while he was on the units, except for celebrating the bombing of the federal building, was stirring up trouble for other inmates. He thrived on it. There was no way I would allow him to create new problems for me, now that my time was so short.

Shur wasn't fooling when he warned me that renegade witnesses who threatened to blow the whistle on the program would pay in spades for their troublemaking. My handlers and program functionaries hadn't been around to do the usual interviews to prepare me for relocation and a new life as a protected witness on the outside. There was good reason for that; strong sentiment had developed, indicating that I probably didn't qualify because of my media contacts.

Everybody knew I was talking with the press. I had a couple of conversations with a senior editor at *Penthouse* about the article we were planning to work on. He also had some other friends in New York in the newspaper business that he said he would introduce me to when I got out.

Moushey was another journalist I was still keeping in touch with, courtesy of the FTS. We agreed to meet as soon as possible after I was released. Adamson perched on his stool, staring at me during all those conversations and witnesses on the unit were keeping their eye on things, waiting to see what happened. Nothing did!

It didn't help matters that I continued to refuse to back down. So far, the administration had blocked my efforts for a sit-down inside the units with reporters to discuss the blemishes, shortcomings, and weaknesses of the program and my treatment by WITSEC, the OEO, and other agencies involved with protected witnesses. Once I was on the outside and cut loose on my own as administrators were threatening to do, it would be a different story. Even as a parolee, I could talk to whomever I wanted to talk to, and when I wanted to talk.

As far as the administration was concerned at that time, I was probably the most unpopular man on Mesa Unit, and was being given some of the same kind of shit that was eventually thrown at my friend, Dave Harden. The BOP said it wouldn't offer any support programs to me that were available through my sending-state, Missouri, where I was originally sentenced. If I wanted that kind of support, I had to sign out of WITSEC and return to Missouri.

About the only person involved with the program who was still trying to help and get me moved into phase two was my case manager. She was a good woman and she appeared to be sincerely concerned about my safety and future if I was dumped from the program without any of the support promised to me when I was recruited as a protected witness.

There was no one else to go to bat for me, and it seemed that every time I stepped up to the plate on my own I struck out. When my father was dying of cancer, I pleaded, promised, and cajoled authorities to allow me to return home under guard to see him one last time. They refused the request. Cooperation and favors, I had learned long ago, was a one-way street for protected witnesses like myself. Administrators were going by the book, and apparently they saw no special reason why they should do me any favors.

A threat-assessment study conducted by WITSEC professionals as part of the prerelease process strongly indicated that my life would be in serious danger if I returned to Missouri after leaving Mesa Unit. I wasn't surprised. Shortly after I was transferred to the FCI, I received a troubling letter from Vicki's mom. Vicki got the shit stomped out of her at a biker picnic, and her mom wanted to know if there was anything I could do to keep it from happening again.

According to Vicki's mom, and to other people I talked to later, she was at a benefit the Hell's Angels staged in south St. Louis when somebody pointed the finger at her as a snitch. Some of the old ladies started working her over, then a bunch of big, fat, greasy Hell's Angels jumped in and joined the stomping. Luckily some friends of ours were there and pulled her out of the mess. One of the guys threw her over his shoulder, and they got her into a car and drove away. She was banged up pretty bad and stayed in the hospital for three or four days.

Vicki's mom thought maybe I could talk to somebody and prevent it from happening again. Hell's bells, if I tried talking to any of the Hell's Angels about our problems, it would probably just make things worse. My enemies back in St. Louis had long memories, and although I never ratted on any of my old biker friends, they're pissed off at me anyway. They hate snitches. Somebody once said that time doesn't make the hurt go away. How true that is.

Similar findings in the threat-assessment report ruled out California, Arizona, Illinois, and Florida. They were all states where criminal elements existed with reason to hold deadly grudges against me for working against them with the law. Huge areas of the country were off-limits for me, and virtually wiped out any territory I was familiar with and had family and other support.

Considering all my problems, Adamson was about as troublesome as a flea on an elephant's ass. It wasn't anything I couldn't deal with. It was just a question of biding my time, and the problem would go away. It would have been appreciated more if my other problems were so easily solved.

In August 1995, a bare four months after Adamson reacted with such glee to the bombing of the federal building in Oklahoma City, he was escorted out of Mesa Unit and moved into phase two. He was fifty-two years old, and had spent almost exactly twenty years behind bars. The man who so brutally murdered a newspaper reporter, then rejoiced at the mass murder of nearly 200 innocents, beat the death penalty, beat prison, and he beat the system.

When Adamson finally walked out and climbed into a waiting car on his way to a secret destination selected for him by WITSEC handlers to begin a new life, I wasn't there to wave goodbye. I left the unit a couple of months ahead of him. Nevertheless, nobody on Mesa Unit that I know of was sorry to see him go. He wasn't their problem anymore. It was up to the poor unsuspecting schmucks on the outside world to deal with Phoenix's mad bomber. They can thank WITSEC.

24

Phase Three

FEDERAL BUREAUCRATS IN charge of WITSEC had already proven they knew how to deal with renegade witnesses long before my release date approached.

When I left Mesa Unit for the last time on June 23, 1995, my first scheduled day of freedom after ten years behind bars, including six years in the federal witness-protection program, I got the first taste of my personal payback.

Instead of a quick, covert trip to a new home, a new identity, and job promised to me when I first entered the program, I was given the bum's rush. At two o'clock that morning, I was suddenly roused from my bed by a pair of jail guards armed with machine guns and roughly ordered to get dressed.

My case manager, who had sincerely tried to get me moved into phase two where I belonged, stood helplessly at the side, wearing a bullet-proof vest and mumbling apologies. I couldn't believe the guns and the vest. What did these people think I was going to do—turn into some raving, homicidal monster just because I was being tossed out on my ass?

While I stood uncertainly in my boxer shorts and T-shirt, rubbing my eyes, it took me a few minutes to figure out what was going on. Gradually my case manager's embarrassed apologies began to sink in.

The big shots at the OEO, the BOP, and Justice had ignored her efforts to arrange for me to move into phase two. They overruled her recommendation, and they brushed off the findings of the threat-assessment report, which determined that a small army of desperate characters were anxious to murder me. My enemies would be practically lining up outside for a chance to whack me the first time I showed my head.

Tough shit! That's what happens to square pegs who won't fit into round holes. They get hit on the head, over and over again until they're so messed up they finally slide into place. I remembered Danny Holliday and James Cardinali. Now a new name was being added to the list of witness-protection program losers: George Emmett Taylor, Jr.

It was my welcome to the notorious phase three of the federal witness-protection program. After putting my life on the line to defend apple pie and the American way against the forces of evil, I was being dumped out on my ass. Goodbye, thanks for the good memories, and don't hurry back.

I barely had time to climb into my pants, button up my shirt, and tie my shoes before the hacks shoved a small prepacked bag of my personal items into my arms and began hurrying me down the dimly lighted hallway. There were no goodbyes, and the last words I heard before stepping outside into the predawn darkness of the desert were the cautions of my case manager. She warned me not to return to Missouri if I valued my life.

A couple of hacks in the car drove me about half a mile down a dark road to the main gate and ordered me to get out. They handed me thirty dollars in cash and a one-way airplane ticket to Portsmouth, Virginia, where I had a job lined up with my brother-in-law and was expected to report to a probation officer as soon as I arrived. My immediate future included about three years of parole status. Except for that, I was a free man and on my own.

A taxicab was already waiting at the gate to drive me to the Phoenix Sky Harbor International Airport, but I wasn't going to get very far with thirty dollars. It's a long drive from the FCI to the airport, and thirty dollars wasn't even enough for the fifty five dollar fare.

We drove across the desert while I watched the sky begin to lighten up over the eastern horizon, and I pondered the shitty deal I was getting compared to the VIP treatment contract killers like Gravano and drug-smuggling kingpins like Mermelstein, Carlton, and other major criminals were given by their WITSEC handlers. When they walked outside the protected units for the last time, they had millions of dollars, new lives, and new homes waiting for them.

WITSEC administrators even kept their word to serious scumbags like Pruett, Adamson, and that ilk. Serial killers, Mafiosi, crazed bombers; they were all good enough to qualify for kid-glove treatment and movement into phase two. I wondered if perhaps my problem was I simply wasn't vicious enough, or a big enough crook to warrant their kind of treatment.

I also worried about the glum possibility of getting dumped out of the cab when my money ran out, then standing alongside the road with my thumb out while the sun heated up the desert. I was thinking about something I read that said in the average summer desert heat there of around 109 or 110 degrees, the body loses about three pints of liquid an hour. I don't know how many pints of liquid a normal human body has inside it, but if I had to get out of that taxi, I was ready to do some praying that a soft-hearted motorist would be kind enough to stop and give a poor ex-convict a ride. Fat chance! I was a big, solid guy with hair down to my shoulders, a beard, and anybody who might be driving in the area had to know that a federal penitentiary with guard towers and razor wire on top of the walls was only a few miles down the road. I knew I could stand alongside the highway until I keeled over and died, and nobody would have given a shit.

Finally, I simply told the driver that I was almost broke. "When you run up thirty dollars on the meter let me out, because that's all I can pay," I said. I was lucky. He was an ex-con and sympathetic. He agreed to take me all the way to the airport for my thirty dollars, and he waved goodbye when I climbed out and walked into the terminal. It was a bit of human kindness that was timely and appreciated.

It was an incredible experience simply looking around in the crowded airport and seeing all those people—women, kids, old farts with canes. There was nobody I could pick out as a serial killer, big-time drug smuggler, Mafia hit man, or international terrorist. There wasn't even an FBI guy in a dark suit and a buzz cut. There were just regular people. It was a different world; one that I was determined to become a part of and inhabit from then on. I had my fill of prisons, of hacks, and of petty bureaucrats who expected you to sign a paper before you took a shit.

My Good Samaritan cabbie had left me a couple of dollars, and the first thing I did when I walked into the terminal at Phoenix Sky Harbor was drop a quarter into a pay phone and make a collect call to my sister in Virginia. I told her I was broke and where I was at. She promised to immediately wire me some money. It was good news and I knew I could count on her. After saying goodbye, I turned and walked into a bar where I ordered my first frosty cold draft beer in more than ten years. Then I had another while I retraced memories of the decade—and tried not to think about everyone who was waiting for me out there.

25

A Marked Man

MY DECISION TO buck the organization and become a renegade witness by exposing the wasteful practices, shameful inequities, and dangerous flaws in the witness-protection program carried a high price tag.

All my old stomping grounds, the places I knew best, and locations where my personal-support system of family and friends were the strongest were virtually off-limits to me. St. Louis was the worst possible place I could go. I was on everybody's shit list, from outlaw bikers to organized-crime families, hillbilly gangs, and corrupt politicians. If I returned there, my life wouldn't be worth as much as a Justice Department promise.

Janet Barton, who worked in Jefferson City, was my parole coordinator, and she helped save my ass when I left the units. She worked hard to see that I was treated right and arranged to get me paroled to my brother-in-law in Virginia. I went to work in his construction business. I couldn't get parole in New York State where my lady-friend lived because I couldn't find a job in that area. Plans to join her and her kids were put on the back burner.

Obtaining and hanging on to a legitimate job posed

special problems, not only because some employers might be turned off by the fact I was an ex-convict, but also because it could compromise my security. Protected witnesses who move into phase two are provided with new Social Security cards and other identification that enables them to work under assumed names. If I used my own Social Security number when I was filling out an application and other paperwork for a job, I would be pinning a target to my chest just as surely as Cardinali did when he paraded in front of the federal courthouse in Albuquerque.

My enemies in the criminal world, and in the criminal justice system, could use my Social Security number and other identification to track me down anywhere in the United States. I was a marked man. I knew it, and the people I associated with knew it. So for the first few weeks I was out, I stayed close to the Portsmouth and Norfolk area, working in construction. But my reputation preceded me.

My parole officer told me not to bother coming to his office in downtown Portsmouth. He said I could check in by telephone, unless unusual circumstances required a personal visit. His receptionist's desk was clearly visible through a huge window and he didn't want to take any chances that she might be shot. That was his story, but he made it pretty clear that it was his own ass he was worried about.

Many federal workers, especially those involved in the legal-justice system or with tax collections, were still nervous over the Oklahoma City bombing. No one wanted to be in the wrong place or with the wrong person at the wrong time. And whoever I was with and wherever I was at, I was that wrong person.

My parole officer asked me to meet him at restaurants a few times, but he never showed up. So I telephoned him at his office to ask what was going on. He came right out and told me: there was so much heat on me that he was afraid if somebody came after George Taylor he could get whacked just because he was keeping the wrong company.

There was heat on me, all right, but it wasn't mobsters who were doing the hassling. It was FBI, U.S. marshals, and who knows what other agencies were involved? One time I was with my nephew and had a nasty confrontation with some feds because one of them was taking pictures of me with a video camera while we were riding the ferry boat from Portsmouth to Norfolk. Another time I was in Norfolk when a bunch of feds moved in on me, and I ran into the offices of the *Virginian-Pilot* to get away.

One of the reporters wanted to write a story about the affair, but I passed. The reason the feds were hassling me was because I had contacted reporters, and they wanted to know what I was talking about. Three days after I was practically thrown out of the witness program, I had a long sit-down meeting with Bill Moushey at a hotel in Virginia Beach. He flew there to do the interview. I was also working with my editor at *Penthouse* on the article about my experiences in the witness-protection program.

Now that I was out of the program, there wasn't a fucking thing that Gerald Shur or any of his friends could do to prevent me from talking with anybody from the press that I wanted to. They couldn't run my life anymore, but that didn't mean that everybody had given up trying to suppress the story. For a while, Janet Barton, who was also my witness security-parole coordinator, got weekly calls from the OEO and people with Inmate Monitoring, asking if she knew of anything I was doing that could give them an excuse to violate my parole. They wanted me sent back to the joint. No more witness units! They were talking about general population, which for me meant the death penalty.

Janet didn't play their game. It wasn't her job to lean on people who were trying to restructure their lives so they could live normally and stay out of prison. She always gave me the impression that she believed in trying to rehabilitate people instead of pushing them over the edge so they would reoffend.

The pressure in Virginia finally got to me, so I split for New York State and moved in with Jean, whom I married, and her kids. One of the first things I did after knocking on her door was telephone Janet in Jefferson City. I had her 800-number and instructions to call if I had any unusual problems that she should know about. Splitting for New York without notifying my probation officer in Virginia was the kind of problem she was talking about.

Janet listened to my explanation of what was going on, then said she would send me a travel permit. She added that she was marking it for next-day delivery because she didn't want me getting in trouble for violating parole. When the parole officer in Portsmouth heard what was going on, he freaked out because I hadn't done things exactly according to the book. He should have been happy. He didn't have to worry anymore about some mad-dog biker or crazed Mexican drug smuggler blowing him and everybody else in the parole office away while they were trying to get at me.

The parole problems were worked out without any serious hassle, but the minions with the Justice Department didn't let up the pressure. They began hanging around again, and a few days after I moved in with my wife, intruders kicked in the door at the house while I was away and stole a bunch of stuff. It was a curious burglary. All the thieves took were my daily planner, tape recorder, several audiotapes, and a boxful of documents containing information about federal witnesses and the WITSEC program. A stereo, jewelry, cash, and other valuables that would normally be the first things carried away by burglars were left behind.

The house was in an isolated rural area upstate, but after the burglary, I bought a couple of Rottweilers to beef up security. The dogs were fiercely loyal to me, and I named one of them Sergey, after my longtime friend from the Hell's Angels. The other was named Bogey, after my grandfather Bogey Van Boven. The Rottweilers didn't give a shit who they were named after, though. They just did their job.

Although I was fed up with government investigations and testifying at the trials of a mixed-bag of criminals, the Gs hadn't had their fill of me. In June 1996, Duke and I testified at the U.S. Senate Judiciary Committee hearing in Washington, where I had a verbal shootout with Senator Biden. We were the only two people who had been in the program who were called to testify.

Most of the people called at the hearing were bureaucrats: people from Justice, the OEO, BOP and agencies tied to administering the program. The hearing got off to a bad start for me when a letter written to Biden by Mike Reap was read into the record by the Delaware senator saying that I was not to be trusted. At least the letter mentioned my cooperation with the federal government in Missouri, Florida, Arizona, California and Illinois. The hearings went downhill from there, and they were a joke.

Thanks to my testimony at the hearings, I was suddenly considered to be an expert on WITSEC, and that gave my testimony in certain big criminal cases around the country potential value for defense attorneys. Suddenly I was getting more grief, and finding out that I could be subpoenaed to testify in any mob trial in the country that might have a federally protected witness involved.

F. Lee Bailey contacted me and asked if I would testify at the trial in a federal courtroom in Brooklyn of one of his clients, a racketeer named Joe Watts. He wanted me to tell the jury a few things about protected witnesses, how superstars were rewarded, and how the program worked. At that time I didn't know Bailey, and I didn't know much about Watts except that he was connected to the Gambinos, Sammy's old mob family, and that he couldn't become an official wiseguy because only his mother was Italian. His old man was Welsh, so for some crazy reason mobsters who had dealings with his son called him Joe the German. Maybe they flunked geography when they were kids.

Turned out when I learned a little more about him, that Joe the German dropped a few bodies off in dumps for his mobster pals. Sammy once told me that Watts was involved in the plot that led to assassinating Big Paulie Castellano so that Gotti could move into his job. But the trial Joe the German was facing in Brooklyn was tied to the murder of a lesser light in the mob, some street soldier who got on the wrong side of the Dapper Don. Whatever!

I agreed to appear because Sammy the Bull was expected to come out of semiretirement and testify against him. That's why Bailey wanted me on the other side. I was looking forward to seeing Bailey and Gravano go head to head in the courtroom. My former nemesis from the Fleer case, John Appelbaum, flew into New York from St. Louis to advise me, and I drove to Manhattan from my home. We were put up in a nice New York hotel, all expenses paid by Watts' defense team.

When we met with Bailey at his luxury townhouse in Manhattan, he was fresh from the O. J. Simpson trial, where he crossed swords with prosecutor Marcia Clark, then tangled with his fellow defense-team lawyer, Robert K. Shapiro. Bailey's not a hard guy to pick a quarrel with, but he's a defense lawyer. Picking on people is his job. We talked awhile and had a few drinks. Bailey was tossing down martinis, and they didn't appear to make any difference in his mood or ability to explain the finer points of his business. When John and I left, we climbed into the shiny white limousine that was waiting outside at the curb. Then we had to get out because it was Bailey's. Our limousine was black.

Just before the second day of Watts' trial, he agreed to a sweetheart plea bargain: instead of life in prison, which the prosecution previously demanded, he copped out to a six-year sentence that, because of time served, would make him eligible for parole in six months. Sammy didn't testify, and I didn't testify. Watts's immediate problems were over, but it was another story for Bailey and for me.

Bailey was a fascinating character, who was as interesting as anyone I met in the joint. He landed in the joint himself a few days after we parted company. While Watts' trial was shaping up, his hotshot lawyer was already up to his ears in a serious jam over $6 million worth of stock he got from a French-American narco-trafficker named Claude Duboc, who was filthy rich. The drug smuggler and money launderer had agreed to forfeit the stock, but Bailey used some of it to cover expenses and his fee. The shit really hit the fan after the court learned that while Bailey was holding on to the stock, it skyrocketed in value to $27 million, which the high-flying lawyer planned to keep for himself. Bailey admitted using a chunk of the stock as collateral for a loan from a Swiss bank to put a down payment on a house near Palm Beach, and eventually the judge, the prosecutor, and the IRS were all busting his ass.

Bailey wound up being arrested for contempt of court, and he was printed, posed for mug shots, then put in leg irons and transported to the Federal Detention Center in

Tallahassee. He remained in custody for more than five weeks. During that time, while the value of the shares dropped—he was $5 million poorer when he was able to pay off the bank and get the stock released to the court. Then he was sprung.

Two days after I met with Bailey at his townhouse in Manhattan, I was grabbed by a pair of deputy U.S. marshals and whisked off to a federal courthouse seventy miles from my home. They questioned me there for hours about my contacts with journalists before I was at last permitted to leave.

A couple of months later I was driving along State Highway 17 a few miles southeast of Binghamton after a trip to Manhattan to work with my editor at *Penthouse* when another car passed me, then pulled off to the side of the road about half a mile ahead near a steep dropoff. It was a four-door Chevy and looked like a cop car. It had followed me all the way from Middletown, and I was driving about 65 miles per hour with my radar detector on. As I approached, the driver suddenly darted directly across the highway into my path. I swerved and my 1991 Pontiac Firebird nosed into the heavy-wire railing along the edge of the road. It was a piece of luck that the front end of the Firebird is low and very aerodynamic, so it was trapped under the wires and didn't tumble over the cliff. But the front tires were ripped off and the car was totaled. I was shaken up, and my chest was slammed into the steering wheel by the impact, but I wasn't seriously injured.

The other car backed up, and the driver who was wearing a peaked hat that looked suspiciously like those that New York State troopers wear, glanced in my direction, then pulled away. Less than five minutes later, three New York State Police patrol cars pulled up by my wrecked Firebird.

The investigating troopers made out an accident report, issued me arrest notices for a slew of misdemeanors, and took me to the nearest highway-patrol barracks. I was charged with failure to yield, driving while intoxicated, driving under the influence, and accused of illegal possession of prescription drugs. They found a bottle of Xanax in the car. I had a legitimate prescription and was tapering off from the habit I developed while I was inside Mesa Unit. All the charges were eventually dropped, except failure to yield, which I paid a forty-five dollars fine for. I realized I had been put firmly on notice. I was still a very unpopular guy, and I'm convinced someone was trying to assassinate me.

Shortly after that, the series of stories about the WIT-SEC program was published in the *Post-Gazette,* and *Penthouse* ran my article. The sudden rush of media attention led to the U.S. Senate Judiciary Committee hearing headed by Orrin Hatch, at which Duke and I testified. Did the hearings make any difference? I haven't heard of any massive shakeups of WITSEC coming down the pike since the hearings were concluded. Big talk often leads to little action. So what else is new?

While I was getting my first look at Washington, D.C. since delivering some of my escorts to the congressman there, and meeting with writers and publishers, I was also losing an ongoing battle against forced transfer of my parole back to Missouri.

The irony of the situation wasn't lost on me. When my old man was dying of cancer, the threat assessment was too high, and the liability factor was too high to permit me to slip back into town for a couple of days to see him—or to attend his funeral. Suddenly everything was turned upside down. I didn't want to go back to Missouri, but I was being forced back into my most immediate danger zone by the very people who wouldn't allow me to even visit before. What happened to the high threat assessment and the liability factor? No one seemed to be very interested in that anymore, except me. And what I believed or what I wanted didn't mean diddly shit.

I reluctantly returned with my dogs and my pickup truck to the St. Louis area. The pressures on my marriage were simply too great, and my wife and I agreed to a divorce, then I settled down in a rural lakeside retreat that my old man left to me when he died. I spent about $1,000 installing a security system. The entire house was surrounded by lights tied into separate lines so that if one was cut the others would still work. A buzzer was rigged to ring in the house anytime one of the lights went off, even if a bulb burned out. Two special sensor lights were also set up on each corner of the house.

Sergey and Bogey accounted for another important element of my self-defense system, and I installed a microphone next to the doghouse so I could hear them if they growled or barked. Since I'm on probation and not allowed to have a gun in my possession, the dogs accounted for my only offensive weapons.

My so-called friends in Washington didn't have me back in prison, but they had accomplished the next best thing. I was back in southern Missouri, where I was surrounded by my enemies.

Afterword

CAN THE FEDERAL witness program be rewired, somehow tightened up and salvaged? Should anyone even try to save it?

Some critics are convinced WITSEC was too flawed and had too many built-in self-destruct elements from the beginning. Even proponents who support continuation of the program must admit that it is out of control and in need of serious restructuring.

It makes sense to protect non-criminal witnesses, and I have no complaints about arranging to shield people who have merely had the bad luck to become victims of ruthless racketeers and killers from retribution for their cooperation with the law-enforcement establishment. No citizen should have to worry that he or a member of his family will be raped, murdered, or otherwise brutalized because he performed his civic duty and testified in court about knowledge of a criminal or a criminal act.

People like Joe Salerno, a hardworking plumber, who was placed at the top of the Philadelphia Mafia family's hit list after he was maneuvered into becoming a reluctant witness to the murder of a mobster, is an example of people who must be protected. Leonetti was the triggerman in that hit, and admitted it years later after he was acquitted at a trial, then flipped. Salerno testified against the Scarfo Mob and ultimately helped bring it down, but he paid a high price. He was forced to hide out in the witness-protection program, where he led a Gypsy life, traipsing around the country from one place to another. He lost his home, and Mob hit men shot his father—who survived the hit. Salerno decided to be a good citizen, a decent man, and helped the feds nail a bunch of mobsters. It blighted his life.

There are other Joe Salernos out there, but this isn't their story. Innocent civilians who have never been part of the criminal underworld, or who have had minimal involvement aren't the problem participants in the witness-protection program. Government audits show that criminals account for more than 37 percent of the people in the program. That's far too many.

Hit men like Gravano, multiple killers like Pruett and Red Dog, and murderous narco-traffickers like Lehder aren't innocent civilians. There's a point of diminishing return. What was accomplished by giving Gravano a free pass for informing on and testifying against his former mob boss, John Gotti? What possible crimes could anyone commit that would be any worse than the nineteen murders Sammy the Bull has admitted to?

The media didn't care. Sammy became an important player on the television talk-show circuit after voluntarily leaving the program in 1996. The preening little hoodlum did TV interviews with people like Larry King and appeared on the cover of *Parade* magazine while promoting a book. According to news reports, Sammy left WITSEC about the time his wife Debra voluntarily left him. Don't believe every cover story you hear. It's simply not true that they're split up, and it's my understanding the marriage is still intact.

My former cellie Duke Basile didn't last as long in phase two as Sammy did. But Duke didn't leave of his own free will. He was playing golf one time after relocation when he had the misfortune of running into an old Chicago acquaintance. When he contacted a deputy U.S. marshal to report his cover was blown and he needed to move, he was ordered to stay right where he was or be kicked out of the program. Duke had no choice and told the marshal he was moving on, regardless of whether or not he was given help. The marshals showed up on his doorstep with papers to sign, resigning from the program. Duke probably saved his life when he signed, but it cost him the support and protection promised to him when he entered WITSEC. His experience wasn't unique.

Dave Harden let the Gs convince him he was no longer in danger from other convicts over his testimony in the Milo murder scheme and agreed to check out of the program. As soon as he showed up at the new prison where he was to complete his time, other inmates took one look at his federal marshal escort and fingered him for a rat. He was threatened, and at his own request was locked in solitary. Then when he tried to get back into the program, there wasn't a place for him. Dave's luck was still running true to form.

The unique pressures and abrupt change of lifestyle for many witnesses moving into phase two, or on into phase three, are brutal and can be fatal. And the fatalities are more likely to be suicides than paybacks from deadly enemies. A rare Justice Department study a few years ago showed an alarmingly high suicide rate among protected witnesses after moving into phase two and beyond. Most of them, even the survivors, don't react well to pressure.

Henry Hill, who became one of the best-known protected witnesses in the country after his story was told in the book *Wise Guys,* and movie *Goodfellas*, has been in and out of trouble since he moved into phase two in the mid-1980s and relocated in the Seattle area. He was rearrested on a drug charge and in 1987 was tossed out of the program for using coke. He did some prison time for whacking his ex-wife around, and by early 1997, cops picked him up in a New York airport hotel room after he left California to do radio and TV interviews without getting permission from his parole officer. Hill told reporters he screwed up and got drunk after seventeen months of sobriety, causing him to miss his flight.

That may not seem like a big deal for an operator who was in on the $5.8 million Lufthansa heist at JFK airport in New York in 1978, then ratted out his partners, but it's illustrative of the lives of the criminals who move in and out of WITSEC. No matter what the stakes are, it's incredibly difficult for them to play by the rules. Big rules or little rules, inside the joint or out in the neighborhoods, it's all the same.

Almost everyone has complaints, regardless of how they've been treated. In early 1996, Carlos Lehder appeared at a hearing for Noriega, who was jockeying for a new trial, and bitched that the government double-crossed him by reneging on a secret deal to reduce his sentence.

A few months later, Crazy Phil Leonetti was on ABC's *Prime Time Live,* complaining to Forrest Sawyer that the government hadn't kept its word to him. He whined that the FBI didn't give him the full protection or the help finding a job that was promised. Crazy Phil was duded up with a wig and enough heavy makeup to pass for Rudolph Giuliani at a drag ball, and was backed up on the show by his pal Tommy DelGiorno. But the message was clear; after the feds squeezed out everything they could and exhausted his usefulness, they threw the screws to him. Welcome to the club, Phil!

One of the most disturbing aspects of the program is the government's failure to adequately monitor the activities of witnesses after they move into phase two. People like Sonny Pearson and James Dyson Kristian, Ph.D (a title he affected but did not earn) are simply dumped next door to unsuspecting neighbors and left on their own, and it's basically their call as to whether or not they decide to return to their old ways. If they decide to resume their criminal life, then they have the same advantages of new identities and official cover that Pruett used so effectively. Nobody has a clue, not neighbors and not local police, until they explode into a sudden rage of violence.

A 1992 audit that focused on witnesses admitted to the program in 1989 disclosed that one of every five committed crimes while they were in protected status. That's way too much, and shows that someone isn't doing their job. Which should be the most important concern of the people inside the law-enforcement and legal-justice system—protecting criminals who roll and become witnesses or protecting the innocent public?

The answer should be obvious, but some of the people at the Justice Department and the OEO apparently have yet to figure that out because they are behaving as if they came to a different conclusion. A couple of years after the audit, Attorney General Janet Reno and Vice President Al Gore announced plans by the Administration in Washington to make greater use of witness-protection programs to fight crime by persuading gang members to testify. The new Justice plan was probably worked out about as carefully as the assaults on the Branch Davidian compound at Waco and on the Weaver family at Ruby Ridge. Maybe they can get Bill Hogan to give them an introduction to Toomba or the Black Prince.

Careful monitoring of phase-two witnesses must be placed near the top of the list of required reforms if the program is continued.

Major changes must also be made in the process for enlisting and weighing the relative value of protected-witness testimony against the targets of investigations. In my humble estimation, the severity and heinous nature of the crimes committed by a Sammy the Bull Gravano and a Carlos Lehder Rivas cancel out the value of their testimony against a John Gotti or a Manuel Noriega.

I understand and appreciate the difficulty of meeting the demands on prosecutors and investigative teams dealing with sophisticated, well-organized, and highly secretive criminal groups for information that will lead to indictments and hold up in court through convictions and appeals. Based on my experience, I'm convinced that most people in law enforcement couldn't find their ass if it was tattooed on their forehead.

But I disagree with the so-called conventional wisdom so often cited to justify the program—that the only means of gathering the intelligence and evidence necessary to break up those criminal enterprises is to get a higher- or lower-level member of the organization to roll.

Today's law enforcement agencies have a rapidly growing arsenal of sophisticated, twenty-first-century investigative techniques available to them that a fictional Sherlock Holmes or a real-life J. Edgar Hoover would never have dreamed of. Of course there are wiretaps, which are being approved by the courts and used with increasing frequency by investigative agencies, but other more imaginative developments are also available to modern lawmen. They range from incredibly small transmitting bugs, tiny radium-powered dots that pick up sound within a twenty-five-foot radius and can be de-

tected for twenty miles, ''bug guns'' that fire radio transmitting darts into the sides of houses or windowsills, and
devices for tracking cordless phones and intercepting
faxes to infrared detectors and ground-penetrating radar
capable of exposing drug tunnels or locating bodies.

This is not to say that witnesses who sit down and
spin an insider's story aren't convincing to a jury. They
can be, and regardless of whatever happens to the federal
witness-protection program, turncoat hoodlums will continue to be an important factor in broad-ranging investigations of the activities of sophisticated criminal gangs.
Just don't try to tell me that they are the only answer.
They're not. And they shouldn't be, especially when the
price of their testimony is freeing someone like Marion
Albert Pruett, James Allen Red Dog, or Carlos Lehder
to continue their criminal ways.

Even highly educated people schooled in the intricacies of law, who are extremely sophisticated and aware
of the perils of dealing with known criminals have been
hurt by their associations. The last inmate I talked to on
what turned out to be my final night inside Mesa Unit
was Jackie Clay, and the former El Rukn general was
bragging that he was a star. He said he knew from the
beginning that Malik and Toomba and the others were
lying through their teeth in the Hogan affair, and it was
only his performance as a star witness setting the record
straight at a hearing that got the federal prosecutor his
old job back. Of course Hogan lost his job again, and
he is still fighting to clear his name.

The point is, if someone as sophisticated and knowledgeable as Hogan was in the ways of professional criminals who turn snitch can be ambushed and bloodied,
what chance does the average citizen—or another
crook—have to defend himself against the fantastic
schemes created by these people? Snitches can build
magnificent castles from even the most flimsy chimeras,

and they tell convincing stories. That's what they do. That's what they're rewarded for.

In the meantime, what happens to the George Taylors, the James "Duke" Basiles, and the Dave Hardens who have been brought into the program with promises that police and prosecutors either cannot, or are not willing to, keep? I believed in the promises that were made to me, and partly through my fault and in larger part through the fault of others, I was double-crossed and hung out to dry.

When I was young and committing all those crimes, I thought the whole thing was a big joke. I was no punk, but I also wasn't some hard-ass guy who went around murdering people. There was money made, and I met a lot of unforgettable people. I sold a lot of pot and a lot of coke and heroin, just making it day by day, and it was fun and a joke until the feds and all those task-force dudes got involved. So all that shit is over now, and I'm not sorry for that. I'm just sorry about the way it happened. If I had it to do all over again, I would just take my medicine, do my time, and tell the people offering me witness protection to fuck off.

That's my advice to any other criminal who is thinking of rolling so he can clear the books and get a fresh, new start in life through the federal Witness Security (Protection) Program. Don't do it, because the people you're dealing with can't be trusted.

I've been accused of harboring a vendetta against the government, and that's not true. The only problem I have with the government is that when they tell something to somebody who is cooperating with them, they should keep their promises. It doesn't matter if it's a handshake, a nod of the head, or if it's written down. They should keep their word, but they don't. They lie to people, they screw them over, and then they call their own witnesses rats, snitches, and canaries, whatever comes to mind.

They should remember that they are using those snitches to point out things to them because they're so stupid and naive that they would never solve any crimes on their own unless they fell over the answers. And they can't get the answers they want from people like Mother Teresa or Billy Graham. They have to deal with people like me, Sergey, Duke, Jackie Clay, Crazy Dave, and Crazy Phil because we know where the bodies are. We know the secrets. America's prisons are full of criminals who were convicted and sent there on the testimony of other criminals.

I'm not so naive that I expect the federal witness-protection program to be abolished, but I will be greatly disappointed if it isn't revised to ensure far closer oversight, tightened up, and significantly trimmed to restrict it to a few special cases a year, as Rudolph Giuliani promised to do a long time ago. But I don't plan to hold my breath. Government programs tend to expand rather than decrease.

And WITSEC is no longer the only game in town. Many states now have their own witness-protection programs, as do some of America's major cities. Other nations have also established witness-protection programs, sometimes to include cooperation with authorities in the United States when both countries share involvement in the same cases. I've heard reports that criminal witnesses and members of their families from Colombia have been quietly transported to the United States and relocated with new names to get them out of harm's way in the drug-wracked country.

In Florida, a nasty poltical flap erupted early in 1997 when it was publicly revealed that Puerto Rico was quietly relocating protected witnesses there and to eleven other states. Some of the witnesses had already gotten in trouble with the law again, usually over drugs. And according to Puerto Rico's Special Investigations Bureau, which runs the program and is the island's top investigative agency, they had temporarily lost track of some of the men.

I've smuggled and sold drugs, and I've helped put other traffickers away, and I'm exhausted and fed up with the life. I'm anxious to put all that behind me. A new woman has entered my life, and she knows about my past, yet she is loving and supportive. She's a blonde, blue-eyed Aryan beauty, and we've already been through much together. For starters, she has experienced the trauma of being chased out of her home when mysterious gunmen cruised by my old man's place on the lake and shot it up with machine guns. No one was hurt, but the message was clear. My enemies knew where I was at, and they were letting me know it was payback time.

My criminal enemies aren't our only problem. Missouri has a law now that is being used to classify me as a dangerous offender, because of my past crimes. So I'm required to go to court once a week and piss in a bottle. I don't do crime anymore and I don't do drugs, but I have to submit to weekly urinalysis.

My past repeatedly comes back to haunt me in other kinds of ways. A couple of days after my woman and I moved to our new location, police back in the area we just left telephoned my parole officer to ask for a mug shot of me. They were checking out a bank robbery and wanted to talk to George Taylor. I never was a bank robber, but back in the old days I was a crook, and they're not letting me forget that.

My girlfriend and I are both hoping someday to put the fear and the hassle behind us. I worry constantly that somebody is going to walk up behind me and shoot me in the head. Except for that, I'm really happy.

Fierce, hateful enemies are also waiting for me inside the walls of various prisons around the country, and I'm determined to continue turning my life around so that I will never have to spend another day inside. There's no choice. Prison for me would mean a death sentence. Sure, they could lock me in protective custody. I know how safe I would be there, about as safe as Danny Holliday.

Burying me in protective custody would just mean that my enemies would chain my cell door, lock it, and throw gasoline or kerosene in there and strike a match. Instant barbecue. They do that kind of thing all the time at lockups like Jeff City. That's the way it is in real prisons, and if I am ever forced to go back, I would prefer general population. That way I can at least put up a fight for my life—and not die like a dog.

But I don't plan to go back. That's why I'm minding my *P*s and *Q*s, and doing everything I can to stay out of trouble. My parole is scheduled to expire in 1998, and the first thing I plan to do when that happens is pick up a passport. Then I'm leaving the United States forever, moving to Amsterdam and renouncing my American citizenship. I have family in the Netherlands and plan to stay there. I've had enough of crime, criminals, the FBI, U.S. Marshals Service, the BOP, and being subpoenaed to testify in trials whenever the Gs decide that they have one more little job for me. Been there, done that!

Yes, I'm still bitter and still disappointed in the lop-sidedness of the treatment given to federal witness-protection superstars—and then the run-of-the-mill types like me. While my girlfriend and I were being chased out of our home, Sammy the Bull Gravano was coming out. He was appearing on television and talking about his decision to leave the federal witness-protection program that treated him so well.

It took awhile. Sammy was a phase-two protected witness for more than two years before he decided it was time to leave. That's a long time for someone like Sammy the Bull to take orders and play by the rules. Keep your eyes peeled for the next installment.

George Emmett "Bud" Taylor, Jr.